Island in the Sky

THE STORY OF GRAND MESA

Island in the Sky

THE STORY OF GRAND MESA

By

Muriel Marshall

WESTERN REFLECTIONS PUBLISHING COMPANY®

Montrose, CO

ISBN 1-890437-07-7

Library of Congress Catalog Number: 99-60188

Second Edition

Cover design: Laurie Goralka Design
Cover photo: Muriel Marshall, inset courtesy Delta County Historical
Society
Text design: Kellie Day, SJS Design (Susan Smilanic)

Western Reflections Publishing Company®
219 Main Street
Montrose, CO 81401
www.westernreflectionspub.com

In memory of the Carpenter, Walter Marshall

Contents

Illustrations

All photos by the author unless otherwise attributed.

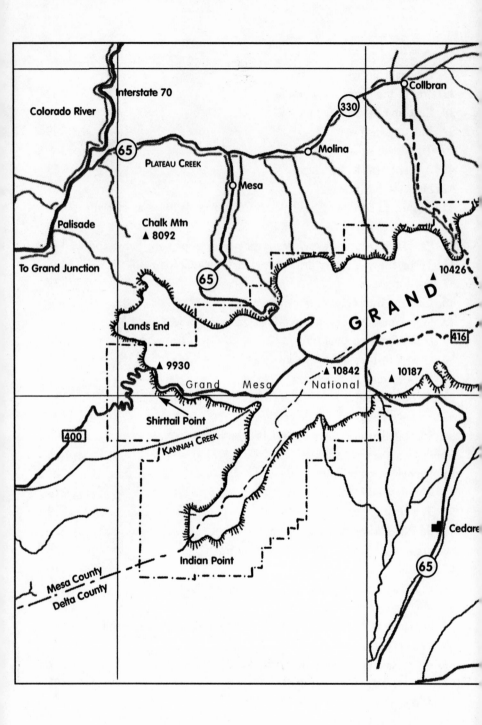

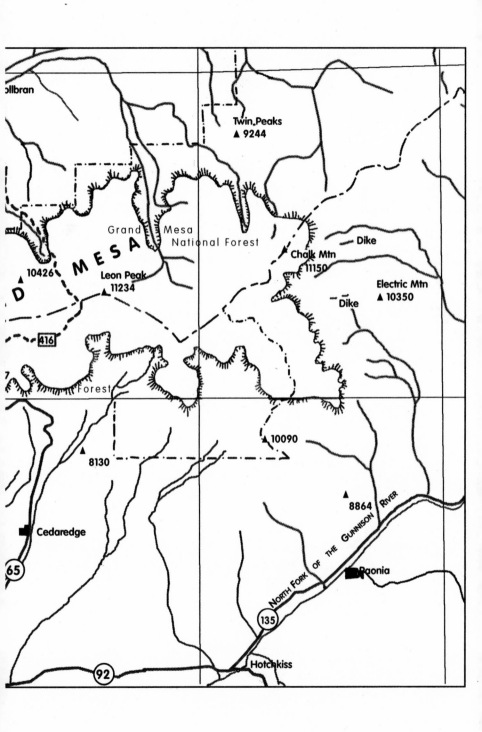

Island, Table, Layercake...What Is It?

It is big and tall, magnificently beautiful — and weird.

A vast flat top, dropping off in sheer black cliffs, reflecting the sky from three hundred lakes, it sits two miles above sea level and one mile above the valleys and towns encircling its feet.

You never heard of the sky island called Grand Mesa? The Rocky Mountains keep it up their sleeve. If it stood over in Kansas it would be the best known mountain in the world — not quite as tall as Mt. Everest, but more mysterious.

Home of Departed Spirits, the Utes called it; *Thigunawat*, their word for Heaven.

Indians, soldiers, cattlemen, miners, and one English bigwig have homed on, fought over, and pulled shenanigans on this flower and forest covered sheet of lava in the sky. There was the rich tenderfoot from New York City who stocked his Grand Mesa range exclusively with cattle of the male persuasion, then complained of the poor calf crop. In straight-faced memory of him, it is said, the Grand Mesa map is full of bull — Bull Creek, Bull Basin, Bull Flats, Bull Reservoir....

The Forest Service — genteeling Grand Mesa maps — left the bulls in place but took the holy out of Holy Terror Creek, the fork out of Forked Tongue Creek, the hell out of Hell and Brimstone Corner, the dirty out of Dirty George Creek (sanitizing its name when it became a source of city water), and the "n" word from the stream where a black homesteader built his stone cabin.

There was Old Man Moore who discovered gas and oil in the mountain when he lit his pipe near a leak and got his beard singed off... There were all those poachers who killed elk by the score, not for steak or antlers but for their two front teeth.

But the mountain itself upstages its history.

Looked down upon from high enough in the air the flat of Grand Mesa resembles a gigantic prehistoric beast with open jaws, a wriggling tongue that is Kannah Creek, bony spine that is Crag Crest, and a fat, tree-furred body rolling down to bare-belly adobe badlands above the incredibly recent towns and farms that ring it round. One of the beast's hind legs angles off toward Paonia, its tail tilts up Chalk Mountain and the iron-rich core of Electric Mountain that got its name by drawing dragon fire from thunder storms.

Grand Mesa is immensely bigger than its flat top, measuring more than 2,000 square miles within the five rivers that cut it away from the rest of the Rocky Mountains. Two major highways slither along two sides of it, intersecting at its western base — Interstate 70 and U.S. 50. Now do you know where you are?

People who live with Grand Mesa cite its brag name: "Largest Flat-top Mountain in the World," then try to bring it down to size by comparing it with something they can get a handle on....

Grand Mesa, they say, is like a huge ship heading into the prevailing westerlies, riding high above turbulent seas of gray-spume 'dobie badlands.

It is like a fortress castle with rock battlements rising sheer, hundreds of feet high. As a matter of fact it did share the name "Battlement" with its little sister mesa to the north in early Forest Service annals.

In its flatness it is so like a vast table that an early cartographer gave it the Spanish name for table — mesa. The table is always set for company, covered with snowy damask in winter, graced in summer with a cloth of all-over flower embroidery and set with hundreds of crystal-blue lakes. This profligate floweriness has won it another metaphorical nickname: "Roof Garden of the World."

The Mesa, they say, is like an immense layer cake topped with icing of chocolate-dark lava spread on stacked layers of strata, the whole resting on a fluted pewter cake plate of 'dobie-bordered river bottom. In this popular comparison it would be a very crumbly layer cake, held together only by the icing.

Grand Mesa is "like" so many things; but actually there is nothing else like it on earth.

The mystery of its origin and of its improbable survival has teased speculation for as long as there have been human minds around to speculate about it. Prehistoric man accounted for it in legends of a Great Bird and Great Serpent. Geologists dig at its secrets, but many are still unsolved, which leaves you room to make your own discoveries and project your own theories, such as: When they blasted away enough cliff to make a highway down the north side, uncovering pockets of queer blue underground ice, was that stuff really a leftover from the Ice Age?

Perhaps the most useful metaphor for the Mesa is that it is a huge book lying flat on the table of the continent — indeed, one strata "chapter" swinging north and west toward Utah has been named the Book Cliffs, not because of their geological table of contents but because they have eroded with such vertical regularity that they resemble a shelf of standing books. The Grand Mesa "book" is bound in black: Lava for the top cover, lignite coal on the bottom. Between these covers lie strata pages that record what happened in this mile-thick volume during the millions of years it took to lay down what geologists dub the Cretaceous and Cenozoic periods. The book is written not in words but in things — sea shells, coral, fossil foot prints, teeth, bones, fig leaves that have turned to stone — so that scientists who want to talk about what they see have had to invent words like Cenozoic to let each other know what page they're looking at.

But you don't have to be a scientist to enjoy the guessing game — for instance those little pimples of reddish rock that picot-fringe the bottom of the mountain along the highway for a hundred miles or so between Hotchkiss and Grand Junction. Geodes and fossil shark teeth are discovered by almost everybody who prowls these bumps which scientists have relegated to the lower Upper Cretaceous Period. Was that ancient ocean simply seething with sharks, or did the creatures shed teeth like a horse sheds hair?

Some chapters of the book are cliffhangers. In the roof of a North Fork coal mine sixteen dinosaurs left tracks that testify the herd was running scared and fast. What could panic anything that big?

The Grand Mesa "book" is just part of a set, like one volume of the Encyclopedia Americana. The rest of the set lies tumbled all over the four-state Four Corners area where continental buckling, volcanic spewing, and the mouse-gnawing of erosion made a fascinating attic mess for scientists to sort out and catalog. But in few places does geology stand up and let itself be counted as it does in the layers that were exposed when Sky Island shucked off the surrounding scenery to become an open textbook on all sides.

————

It is a book without names.

Ute place names didn't count. Indians had no written language to record on maps, and it was hard for white men to pronounce and alphabetize spoken syllables that could mean one thing or another depending on a flip of the pallet or placement high or low on the musical scale. *Thigunawat* is only an English translation.

Two Spanish priests gave this mountain its first written name. That was in 1776, a few weeks after some Englishmen on the east coast signed the

Declaration of Independence — but lacking TV or fax the priests wouldn't hear about that for a year or so. Nor would they have cared. Barefoot and exaltedly humble, Fathers Dominguez and Escalante represented Spain, at its height the most globe-engulfing nation on earth, "owning" most of South America, a third or so of the North American continent, plus home base in Europe, pieces of Africa, and numerous islands here and there.

The priests led a party of eight men, horses, packmules, and Indian guides picked up and dropped off as they entered and left tribal ranging grounds. Their assignment was to find a route linking Santa Fe with California missions, and to put Spanish names on prominent pieces of geography, thereby underscoring Spain's right to everything west of the Mississippi. Getting in a little preaching on the way was their own idea. When they reached this mountain Escalante's callused soles had trod 500 miles of earth and stone.

They must have been down in jagged Hubbard Creek canyon looking at summer-brown fawns when Father Dominguez instructed his map-maker to name the mesa Sierra del Vanado Alazan "Saw-toothed Mountain of the Chestnut- colored Deer." That tag didn't stick, perhaps because they came out on top and saw how flat it is. They crested at Balm of Gilead Park, named straight out of the Bible for the rare species of poplar growing there.

Coming upon a Sabuagana Ute camp of thirty or so tipis, the Fathers washed, preached, and ate the chokecherries and lemitas that three Ute ladies and their children had gathered and prepared. Then, after trading white beads for a supply of jerked bison meat, they went on a little way further to set up their own camp called the "king's camp," since they represented the King of Spain.

The Tabeguache Utes, who had guided the party across the Uncompahgre Plateau, had come as far as their trail-knowledge extended, so it was necessary to engage new ones on this mountain. Guides were needed because Grand Mesa, like the rest of what would be Colorado and Utah, was confusingly criss-crossed with Indian trails accessing routes to favored hunting and food-gathering areas, to festivity and horseracing rendezvouses, and to health spots such as the hot sulphur spring on the North Fork of the Gunnison, or the bigger one, now called Glenwood Springs, which was — a hundred years later — Chief Ouray's favorite spot to soak away his rheumatism. There were no maps, except the one the Fathers were making as they went. No road signs–at least none the Fathers could read, though some folks have since dubbed petroglyths pecked on the walls of Plateau Canyon a kind of prehistoric road sign.

The Sabaguana Utes weren't noticeably eager to guide outlanders deeper into their territory. They opined there weren't any trails headed toward that salty lake, and even if there was one nobody in camp knew where it was, and if somebody did know the route it was too late in the year to start, and furthermore it went right through fierce Comanche territory.

The offer of a blanket and a skinning knife turned the trick, but weather forced guide and party to swing south before reaching Salt Lake — let alone California. The Fathers had run out of summer.

———

Ninety-eight summers later almost to the week another party representing another nation was camped in a flowery meadow on this mountain, scratching its collective head for names to call things by. The flag flying from the tent pole was the Stars (thirty-four) and Stripes.

The Civil War out of the way, and manpower again available, the U.S. Government had set out to fill in the blank paper politely called "map" of the western territories it had acquired, unaware of or disregarding the names the priests had applied to things. To make for speed and precision the survey crews were working under rival departments: War Department survey parties led by Maj. John W. Powell, and Department of the Interior teams headed by Dr. Ferdinand V. Hayden vied to see which could explore, map, and "explain" the largest chunks of the little-known Rocky Mountain West. Bureaucratic rivalry reached such ridiculous (not to mention expensive) proportions that, to quote Dick and Vera Dunham's *Flaming Gorge Country*, we see "teams from both sides storming up the same peak." Supposedly whichever crew did the best job fastest would get the prize — the proposed U.S. Geological Survey. Powell ignored the Mesa or it wasn't in his assigned territory.

What right did the United States have to sic its surveyors onto lands that belonged to the Utes? None. No more than the Romans had in England, the Huns in China, Alexander in Babylonia. On the other hand, they had every right. The U.S. had just purchased all land west of the Mississippi and owned everything in it including the natives, just as AT&T acquires all Mountain Bell telephone operators if it buys that company out.

Ferdinand Vandeveer Hayden had graduated from medical school, served during the Civil War as a surgeon and abhorred it — what can you do for a kid whose musket exploded along side his jaw and carried away half his face? While enduring the horrors of that war he studied geology, and when the war was over he got a job teaching it at Pennsylvania University. Discovering he

FOLLOWING PAGES: Chart of Toreva Block Slumping. Geologists have mapped 280 Toreva block slumps on Grand Mesa. Most of them cup natural lakes or reservoir-lakes.

5

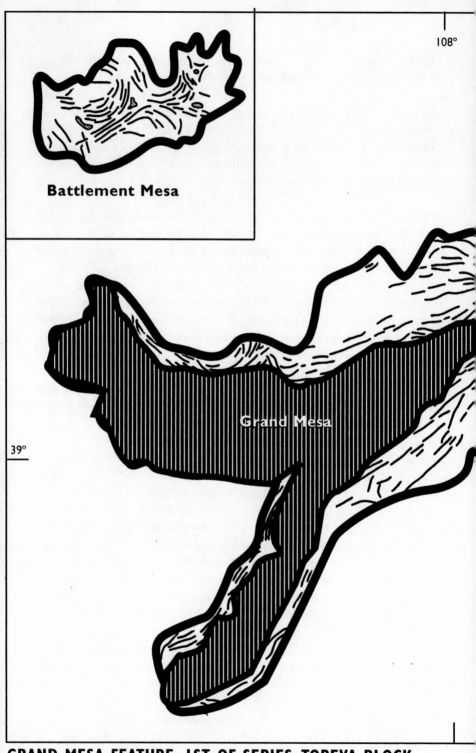

Battlement Mesa

108°

Grand Mesa

39°

GRAND MESA FEATURE, 1ST OF SERIES: TOREVA BLOCK

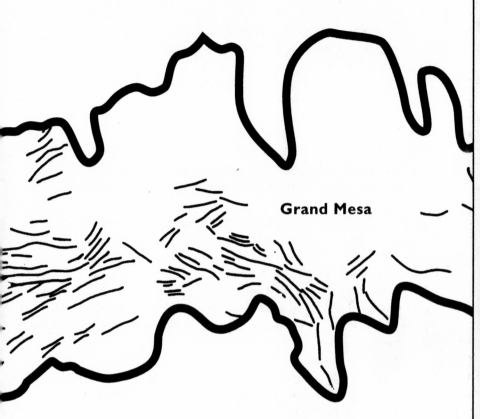

Grand Mesa

Explanation

Area of "in place" basalt

Margin of landslide bench

Trace of slump-block ridge

0   5 MILES

didn't like teaching either, Hayden jumped at the chance when the government offered him a position as head of a survey crew to measure and map U.S. Territories in the West.

Or perhaps he was escaping Mrs. Hayden's tea parties.

Hayden's job was to discover what the scenery was made of geologically, map it geographically, and find names for everything. Like Adam in the Garden of Eden ordered to come up with names for all God's creatures.

This very mountain for instance. In his paperwork, Hayden's topographer Henry Gannett fooled around with names — the place is big and it's flat but Big Flat is gross for such elegance. Great Plateau? Great Mesa? He finally hit on Grand Mesa. That one stuck.

Gannett pursued a life-long career of mapping and applying names to the geography as the country opened up to settlement and people needed labels for what they were headed toward. He was topographer for the United States Geological Survey when it took over Hayden's Survey in 1879, and was a founder and president of the National Geographic Society. In view of all that, it's surprising to find nothing on Grand Mesa named Gannett, but Hayden memorialized Henry in Wyoming — Gannett Peak is the highest point in the Wind River Range.

In the course of squaring off all of Colorado, parts of Utah, Arizona and New Mexico, Dr. Hayden did a thorough job on Grand Mesa. Actually he cubed it off since his maps and charts also measure stratification. The result of his work was published by the U.S. Geological Survey in 1881 — at just the right moment, that being the year the Indians were moved out so whites could move in.

His huge, very thin book includes twenty sheets of Colorado maps — topographical, geological, and economic — along with elevations of strata profiles and line drawings of what the expedition artist was looking at from eminences such as the Mesa rim. An original of the rare book is a part of the wealth of this mountain. It was found by Milo Dick in the attic of a house he was repairing at the foot of Grand Mesa, and donated by him to the nearby Delta County Museum.

Hayden maps show Grand Mesa large-scale, detailed, and amazingly accurate. Plodding on foot or horseback over turbulent terrain, peering through instruments that by modern standards are crudely inadequate, Hayden and his surveyors produced topographical maps that compare very well with today's Geological Survey quad maps made with the aid of aerial survey cameras.

PREVIOUS: Chart of Toreva Block Slumping. Geologists have mapped 280 Toreva block slumps on Grand Mesa. Most of them cup natural lakes or reservoir-lakes.

Hayden's precision would make him seem inhuman except for one incident. Months on end in an all-male bachelor camp, he was perhaps finding the Mesa's flat profile unstimulating. At any rate, contemplating two prominences off to the northeast, he fancied they looked like the mammilary equipment of a well-developed female facing west, and he named them respectively North Mam and South Mam Peaks. The Geological Survey later added a couple of appreciative mm's to make them Mamms.

Among other Grand Mesa features named by him are:

— Leon Peak, where the bony spine of Crag Crest humps up to form the rear end of that prehistoric beast. The name honors a member of his crew, as does Leroux Creek.

— Kannah Creek (Hayden's spelling was Kahnah) for the Ute *Kana-vu* meaning Creek of Willows. Because of the Anglo difficulty with the Ute's tone-variable meanings, this has also been interpreted to mean Creek of Tipis because of the many standing pole-frames found on it, and Creek of the Old Ones because tree-top burial sites were seen there.

— Buzzard Creek, for a colony of raw-neck birds the survey crew saw there, not for the Buzzard family (strangely coincidental for such an unusual name) that would settle nearby a few years later.

— Clear Water Creek, later changed to Bull Creek in honor of that rich tenderfoot aforementioned.

— Grove Creek, for the cottonwoods that grew tall along it. Cottonwoods grow along the lower reaches of most Grand Mesa streams but cottonwoods on this particular creek looked posed, as if consciously setting the stage for picnics.

And speaking of picnics: Somewhere on God's earth, unlocatable as this goes to press, there is a photograph of one of Capt. Hayden's survey sites among the rocks and brambles of a very high mountain top — perhaps the Continental Divide, perhaps Grand Mesa — with alpine ridges low on the horizon beyond. It is tea time. Mrs. Hayden, during one of her rare visits to bring the niceties of civilization to the raw West, is pouring. She is gowned in elegant white. The tea table, balanced among the rocks, is wearing embroidered linen. If this high wild place was indeed Grand Mesa the photographer had discreetly aimed his massive crate of a camera away from those naughty Mamm Peaks.

Hayden's fourth set of maps is geological, showing both laterally and in vertical profile the formations that make up the structure of Grand Mesa, as well as the rest of Colorado. But beyond noting that it is topped with "eruptive granite," he says nothing about that most mysterious feature of the Mesa, its lava cap.

Early explorers, seeing all those lakes and forest-rimmed meadows strangely occupying depressions in the mountain's lava top and sides, explained them by writing that every one of them was caused by a separate volcano. Can you imagine this mountain spouting 280 volcanoes? No real scientist bought that one.

The first geologist-detective who attempted to explain the 500 feet of hard lava on top of a mile or so of soft clays dismissed it with a sentence or so. The cap, he said, is all that's left of a vast sheet of lava that poured out over a vast plain which at the time was lying only one jump above sea level. Every smidgen of plain and lava except the Mesa have eroded away as the land slowly rose.

It sounded reasonable. After all, you had only to look east and south to see immense quantities of lava standing on end in the Elks and San Juan ranges; logical that even more of it would have taken the easy way over level land. And then there are all those relics of the vast lava plain everywhere you look — black rubble peppering the tops of 'dobie benches for miles around.

That geologist was followed by a second who, after concurring with the vast lava-covered plain surmise, stated the lava had come from a spot over near Durango. All of it. Pouring east, west, and north, it went past the piece of plain that would eventually become Grand Mesa, on and on, to peter out somewhere short of Canada.

Geology is an on-going detective story. As the scientist-sleuths dig up new clues in the rocks, they make deductions, and the deductions lead to new clues, revisions, and new mysteries. Educated guesses. But man's changing guesses about his ancient environment are as much a part of history as anything else because they influence his actions.

The Durango-source theory lasted no longer than it took a third geologist-sleuth to discover the intrusive fissure dikes between Chalk and Electric Mountains on the east end of the Mesa. The spewing source of the lava was thus localized to the Mesa itself, but the "vast lava-covered plain" theory still held.

In 1923 a geologist named Junius Henderson rented a pack mule, saddle horse and local guide, Erwine Steward, and spent two weeks nosing into Grand Mesa secrets. At the end of that time he returned the livestock, changed clothes, sat down and wrote a paper stating that the

Mesa had once been buried under about 500 feet of ice, oozing glaciers down off the top in all directions.

The idea that glaciers once covered Grand Mesa flew in the face of reason because everybody knows that mountain-top glaciers scoop out horse-shoe shaped cirques, and Grand Mesa doesn't have any. But Henderson had proof — glacial moraines up on top and grooves in the lava surface cut by stones dragged along the bottom of that weight of ice. The scraped lines show us what direction the glacier was going, and even where the movement originated — a place over on the east end where the surface lava has no such grooves.

At least twice, in separate ice ages, immense icecaps hundreds of feet thick piled up on top of Grand Mesa, so deep and so heavy that though the Mesa is flat they moved outwards of their own weight.

Picture it. As the snows pile up, turning to ice 500 feet thick, great, slow waterfalls of ice bend down off the rims on all sides of the Mesa. The solid sheet creeps down the Mesa sides to about the altitude of Bull Basin and then forks into broad tongues down all the creeks that drain Grand Mesa. Particularly down the creeks on the north side. Spring Creek, Bull Creek, Big Creek and Cottonwood Creek – all were massive rivers of ice inching down, making the turn into Plateau Creek, and getting as far as the vicinity of Healy Bridge before the warmth of lower altitude (5400 feet) melted the ice into a wall of caves from which gravel-bearing outwash streams swept forth.

Between the glacier tongues peninsulas and islands of land stood above the moving ice — Dinkle Hill, the Beehive, Mormon Mesa, Kansas Mesa....

Geologists differ about specific causes for all this solidified water. Most of them account for it conventionally, citing thousands of years of world-wide low temperatures and heavy precipitation equivalent to 400 to 500 inches of rainfall a year. At least one geologist adds a third factor — the unique shape of Grand Mesa, like no other glacier-bearing mountain in the world.

Most mountains at ice-cap altitude and latitude are bulges of granite that glaciers carved into peaks by "frost-picking." In frost-picking, when ice that has frozen fast to granite is pulled down and away by its own weight it brings some of the rock with it, gradually sculpting out great glacier cirques that leave pointed mountains like the Alps and the San Juans. But Grand Mesa was a long flat plain, positioned like a wall crosswise of precipitation-laden winds. According to this theory, an immense "snow-drift," compacting to ice hundreds of feet deep, formed on the mountain

FOLLOWING PAGES: Forest Service air view of west end of Grand Mesa.

11

top and especially its lee side, accounting for the much greater glacial evidence on the north slopes.

But Henderson went further, cantilevering his guesses out in thin air over the rim of the Mesa, postulating that glaciers had gouged out those parallel lake-trapping troughs and ridges down on the Mesa shoulders. The troughs, he theorized, were gouged out by moving ice, and the ridges were glacial moraines left where the conveyor-belt ice melted, dumping the rocks it carried down. Other scientists didn't touch that one.

What caused the cold spell that buried Grand Mesa under ice off and on for many millenia? Scientists have been trying to explain that one ever since they learned about it. Their guesses include: swarms of asteroids which could have blocked out the sun's heat; a Saturn-like ring of tektite particles could have done the same; changes in the earth's tilt, shifting the Arctics here and there....

Latest conjecture, as this book emerges from the computer, is that swarms of house-size snowball ice-comets, melting to clouds on entering the earth's atmosphere, have brought us all the water there is on earth. During times when the comet-clouds got thick enough they darkened the sky, chilled the earth, and allowed the water to pile up in glaciers. This theory, better than any of the others, accounts for periods of tremendous rainfall about the time of the Ice Age — nearly as many feet of rain as fall in inches now.

And on the side, it supports the Bible's account of creation when on the second day God divided the waters above from the waters below. A few years after Junius Henderson a geologist named Reigh — conceding the vast lava plain and ice cap — came up with another explanation for the alternating ridges and troughs below the rims. They were caused by slumping, not glaciers, he said. During pre-ice-age wet spells, when annual precipitation was some 400 inches rather than the present 40, water leached down through cracks in the lava, making slime of a certain deep clay stratum, thus greasing the skids for gravity and causing huge masses of the flat mountain to ease down and out. Not a simple slide — the masses swiveled outward at the bottom while tilting backward at the top. Toreva-block slumping, the process was named. Most of the Mesa's 300 natural lakes and dammed-up reservoirs are waters trapped in crosswise troughs behind these 280 mapped Toreva-block slump ridges.

Reminder of Creation's second workday? Between the repeating patterns of clouds and lakes, a dark firmament of forest separates "the waters above from the waters below."

Weird. How many mountains get their lakes in the process of falling down? It's all laid out below you when you walk Crag Crest Trail that follows the skinny spine of the Mesa mid-section for several miles, weaving side to side around the vertebral humps, threading narrowly across the sags. From a sag on Crest footpath you can look almost straight down a thousand feet to lakes in forested trough-valleys that, once level with where your feet are now, have dropped down and away on either side leaving only this narrow lava wall. The whole Toreva process is illustrated from up here, as if a picture-magazine centerfold had opened down on either side. As you face north, the cliff under your toes ends in a side-ways string of lily ponds twinkling in a crevice-valley nobody has got ten around to naming yet. Beyond and below its far ridge lie Cottonwood Lakes No. 1 and 4 and still lower and farther a glimpse of Neversweat Reservoir. Swing around to face south and your toes are framing Rockland and Butts Lakes, dropping down to Upper Hotel and Baron Lakes, then Kiser Slough down there just this side of infinity.

——— ———

Geologists after Reich supported the slumping theory, the ice cap theory, and the vast plain theory. As late as 1968 geologist Yeend called Grand Mesa and Battlement Mesa "erosional remnants of a large basalt plain," noting that basic lavas — basalt — tend to be more flowing, less explosive as opposed to acidic lavas like the stuff that forms the Cascade Mountains.

The vast lava-sheet theory has been challenged by more recent researchers who believe that at the time lava started flowing from those fissures the Mesa, instead of being a mountain in the sky, was a wide forked valley sloping almost imperceptibly toward the east between confining hills. That the valley was low-lying and marshy is evidenced by fossils — palm leaves, turtles, and other remnants of aquatic life — found just under the lava crust. These strangely misplaced clues — low-land life riding sky high — attracted the attention of the Chicago Museum, which in 1935-38 sent field men to dig up specimens of the prehistoric animal and plant life preserved through the eons by the lava lid.

Erupting again and again — at least twenty times — the hot basalt bubbled from those slits in the earth, flowing out over itself, deepening until the built up surface of the valley floor reversed, slanting gently from east to west as it still does.

Subsequently the soft formations of the surrounding hills eroded away as this part of the continent slowly, slowly rose. Eventually the lava-protected marsh valley up there is all that's left of that geologic episode. Its two forks

A dozen or so of those Toreva-block lakes are visible from almost any point along Crag Crest Trail.

form the great jaws called Indian and Whitewater Points with Kannah Creek wriggling between them like a flicking tongue.

According to this theory the expanse of lava flow was never a great deal larger than it is today. Grand Mesa has always been an island. ❧

2

The Man on the Mare

The man rode an unshod mare accompanied by her colt, purposely leaving sign that would fool Indian or Army trackers into thinking she was merely a riderless stray. Bearded as a prophet he was seeking out the Promised Land, slipping into the Ute Reservation to find and stake out the best piece of ground in it — two years before any white man without employment or business at the Indian Agency had legal right to set foot.

It was summer, the summer of 1879, just a few weeks before the Utes would be pushed into a tragic blunder that would give the U.S. government pretext for taking the other half of Colorado away from them. Getting this man killed might well provide that pretext; any Ute could shoot him at sight for trespass against the Ute Nation. They almost did.

He traveled light, carrying only rifle, ammunition, field glass, and what comforts he could tie on the saddle. He camped cold, lighting no give-away cook fire.

Coming down to the Uncompahgre River valley and following it north, he kept to the bench rims to avoid troops and Indians camped or traveling along the brushy river bottoms. Ute tempers were at the flash point as the pressure of whites around their reservation squeezed it smaller, treaty after treaty.

It was his friend at the fort, Indian Agent McIntyre, who gave him the word that reservation land would be opening soon, both knew that the choicest lands would be almost instantly filed on by the flood of settlers poised along the borders. Even so the man could expect no protection from McIntyre or from the troops the U.S. government sent to prevent exactly the treaty violation he was in the act of committing. The duty of any soldier was to arrest him if intercepted, and shoot if he resisted.

On his third day into the reservation, a band of horsemen spotted him before he could duck for cover. By the way they rode he knew they were Indians. Young Indians. Probably on the prod. By the way they changed course in unison, like a flock of birds, he knew they were after him.

He'd been around Utes long enough to know better than try to run for it. He pulled his rifle from the saddle scabbard and waited.

They slowed as they came on, advancing abreast, stolid-faced, presenting too many targets for his one gun. Suddenly one of the bucks galloped forward alone, pulling his pony to a halt a few feet from the leveled gun.

The Ute's lifted hand was palm forward. To the sign he added the universal code-word of peace, "How."

The man recognized Chief Ouray's nephew, Buckskin Charlie, whom he had once rescued from a band of murderous drunks on the Saguache toll road he had built for Otto Mears.

For that, Buckskin Charlie owed him one. "Where go?" the Ute asked.

"Hunting horses," the man lied.

Not fooled, Buckskin Charlie nevertheless paid his debt: "Go ahead. No see you."

———

When you are reading stories of the past do you like to find your place in history the way you find your own house on a map?

Well, this was seventeen years after Abraham Lincoln signed the first Homestead Act by which a man with no money, or very little, could acquire land by simply living on it and developing it. Passage of the Act hadn't created an immediate rush to settle the West because the Civil War was going on. Men on both sides were tied fast to their military posts. But as soon as it was over many Southern men went West to take up land because they had lost everything during the war. Many Northern men, who had never been more than a dozen miles from home until they'd been yanked onto distant battlefields, got roving fever from that experience, and instead of returning home they headed West toward adventure and opportunity.

Before the Homestead Act the only way to acquire farm or ranchland in newly-opened Indian territories was to buy it from land speculators who acquired county-size or even state-size hunks of the continent "dirt cheap" from the government and resold pieces of it at good profit. Two of these

The Wall. Grand Mesa as seen from the west. Crossing the desert at the foot of the mountain is Highway 50, known at various stages of history as the Old Salt Lake Wagon Road, Ute Slave Trail, Trappers Trail to the Rio Grande.

early land speculators were George Washington and Benjamin Franklin.

———— ————

This man's folks had named him Enos after Adam and Eve's grandson by their third son Seth — the one that didn't get into any trouble. And he was looking for his own Garden of Eden — the pick of the land on the Ute Reservation. He would know it when he saw it, somewhere along the sunny side of The Wall. The Wall, the Mesa — or the Table as some called it — would loom up at the foot of this north-flowing stream he was circumspectly following.

Riding up along the stream's foothills he saw The Wall early, a pale blue-gray chalk mark across the north horizon, stretching smoothly westward from the jagged peaks of the Rockies on the right.

He began scanning the riverbottoms through his field glass, to judge the worth of the earth by what grew wild on it — too alkali if the brush was greasewood, farmable soil if it was sage — and by how hard or easy it would be to divert river to water it.

He noticed the grass growing richer, sweeter. The mare took on sheen, tentatively the colt began substituting grass for tit.

———— ————

Since his teens Enos Hotchkiss, 47, had been seeking gold. Orphaned at nine, he and his brothers and sisters were bonded into foster homes that in those days were actually work-houses where children, no matter how young, were expected to labor for their keep plus profit. He ran away, and at sixteen he walked from Pennsylvania to the Pacific Coast, a '49er in the California gold rush. He was a '58er in the Denver gold rush, and when the Utes were treatied out of the San Juan range in 1874, he really struck it, locating the richest vein in what would become Lake City as soon as the prospectors took time off from digging to do a little building. He sold that vein for a whopping price, several thousand dollars. But, as the Golden Fleece Mine, the lode would soon pay its buyers in millions. As far as we know that's the last time Enos had anything to do with extracting pure gold from the ground; he apparently decided to let corn and cows do it for him.

When he reached the place where the Uncompahgre River butted against the foot of the wall, joined the Gunnison and swung left, the Wall towered overhead; but not threateningly — the black rimrock up there kept its

---

Outwash of glaciers created a mineral-rich soil that drove cultivated crops crazy. Fruits of pioneer orchards swept all the prizes at World Fairs. Here one man's little corn patch is so perfectly photogenic it hurts.

ESCALANTE - DOMINGUEZ
EXPEDITION ROUTE
BALM OF GILEAD PARK
SEPTEMBER 3,
1776

distance. Beyond the merged rivers adobe badlands rose steeply like the gray humps of packed herds of elephants climbing the slopes to where the trees begin. Above the 'dobie breaks the mountain advertised its climates like a billboard in horizontal bands of juniper, then oakbrush, then aspens and pines. Threads of September-gold aspens ribboned down through everything, marking the course of streams. Plenty of water up there!

Was this the place? South-facing wall to cup sun and make spring come sooner, north-towering wall to hold back winter and make autumn last longer. Lofty wall to snag snow and rain out of clouds scraping by, and send water down to your door in mountain streams.

He studied the cottonwoods foresting the flats where the rivers met. Trees that size indicated rich soil, but would demand months of laborious tree-cutting and stump-pulling before plow could find a furrow's length of free ground. A man risking his life to be a first-comer should have his pick of the best, with the fewest drawbacks.

Turning east to ride along the sloping base of the great mesa wall, he followed the Gunnison River, reminded that the stream was named for a railroad surveyor who was killed for doing exactly what Enos aimed to do — driving property stakes in Indian territory. And not too condemn it long ago either!

At a gap in the river bluffs where a creek cracked the mountain open he sighted a well-traveled, hoof-cut trail. Unmistakable and threatening. He recognized what it was, the Ute trail up over The Wall, connecting the Uncompahgre Utes with the White River Utes for ceremonial occasions: war decisions and scouting parties. He spurred up to get out of sight-range of it.

Where the north-flowing Gunnison came out of its black gorge, slammed against The Wall, and was deflected west Enos chose its branch, the North Fork that followed the base of the mountain from the east.

One camp later he came out on a sweep of silver sage covering a gently sloping bench between steep-walled adobe hills and the canyon the North Fork had dug itself into. That sage proclaimed fertile earth, but how many miles upstream would you have to ditch to get a flow of water onto land this high above river level? And how many added miles detouring a canal back into the mountain to maintain the grade around intervening creeks and gulches? Years of miles.

Balm of Gilead Park, named straight out of the Bible, isn't all that far from Holy Terror Reservoir and the place that fell heir to Hotchkiss' favorite cuss word, Condemn It Park.

Beyond the canyon, where the river valley opened out, he rode down a gentle slope to wide bottomland. A patch of Indian corn told him he had found The Place.

Planted in hills not rows, the corn grew in a clearing on the flats at the mouth of a tributary creek. Cupped in the protective arms of sage-silvered bluffs, it was backed by the great sun-trapping Wall.

Green cornstalks, taller than most Indian corn, attested to the soil's fertility. If women could grow corn like that (Ute males did not deign to farm), with nothing better than crooked sticks and water carried in pots, what couldn't a man do with team, plow and irrigation ditch!

Whacking his colt on the rump, he cut loose with his wickedest cussword, "Condemn it! Gold's all right, for a while. But someday this cornfield will be home!"

Enos Hotchkiss' refined brand of cussing got pasted on Grand Mesa maps, the grassy glade that later was summer range for his cattle is still known as Condemn It Park.

As soon as he got his homestead staked out Enos Hotchkiss headed east, off the Reservation to boomer town Gunnison City, there to await the expected "incident" that would make it excusable for the United States, with righteous indignation, to oust the Utes from their lands. By cutting himself off so carefully during his month-long ride, he had also cut himself off from learning that the incident had already happened — the Meeker Massacre. Even as he was pacing off the boundaries of his homestead a Ute chief was holding three American women captive over on the north side of this very mountain. ❧

3

Utes Go, Wheels Come

Cause of the Meeker Massacre, it is written, was Nathan C. Meeker, newly appointed manager of the White River Ute Agency — second river north of Grand Mesa.

An "unmeeker" man than Nathan C. it would be hard to imagine. Squaring his jaw, he set out — in one summer's worth of weeks — to make farmers of Indian men who for thousands of years had been hunters, scorning anything that had to do with food production except killing it. Considering how avidly Americans coveted the Western Slope of the Rockies in Colorado, it is tempting to think that Meeker, with his total ignorance of Indians and his bullheaded do-gooderism, was deliberately chosen as just the man to stir up the needed incident to make confiscation of their land the fault of the Utes themselves.

Playing politics with government money, he informed the Utes they could either farm or draw no rations. The rations were actually Ute property, payment for land lost in treaties, and they knew it. Climax of Meeker's high-handed actions was his order to plow up their horse grazing lands and race track. Ute males, accustomed to a lordly view of the world from the top of the horse, balked at plodding up and down all day staring at the rear end of one. Furthermore, plowing up a race track was close to sacrilege.

They went to war.

At first they were successful. Utes killed Meeker and several of the Agency staff, and ambushed U.S. Army rescue troops, holding them on a waterless flat with no protection but the bloating bodies of their dead horses.

Ute Chief Ouray, well aware that the uprising could cost his people the remainder of their homelands, sent runners to put a halt to it. He himself was unable to make the hard ride from the Uncompahgre Agency across Grand

Mesa and the Roans, being sick in the early stages of a terminal illness. The runners arrived too late, sub-chief Douglas had already committed the kidnapping the press would seize and use to blast the Utes off the map.

Chief Douglas was deferential about the kidnapping, inviting Mrs. Meeker, her grown daughter Josephine, and Mrs. Price (the plowman's wife) to choose what necessities they wanted to take along. Arvilla Delight Meeker chose *Pilgrim's Progress*, Josephine Meeker chose her sewing kit, and Mrs. Price chose her two children. Drinking a little to keep up his bravado, Douglas whipped up the horses that would carry them across the miles of tumbled country between White River and Grand Mesa where he set up camp near a spring and the stream that would someday be called Mesa Creek.

A rescue party led by ex-Indian Agent Carl Adams and Ute War Chief Shavano set out from the Agency on the Uncompahgre. Besides supply wagons, they took an enclosed buggy to protect the sensitivity of captured females. Traveling day and night to reach the women before they too were killed — or what in those days was called worse — they followed the Old Salt Lake road along the Mesa base to its northwest angle. Fearing they would arrive too late, Adams listened when Shavano — one of three Ute chiefs with the party — said he knew a deer-trail short-cut up over the Mesa that would be one sleep shorter than going around by the Hogback. Afraid the white men would panic out of it if they could see where one wrong step would land them, Chief Shavano timed the crossing by moonlight. On upper Kannah Creek the trail became so steep they had to abandon saddle, clawing and scrambling up the last loose-rock vertical mile by hanging to the tails of their horses.

While she waited to be rescued, Nathan's daughter Josephine cut up a brown annuity blanket and stitched together a two-piece, red-cuffed suit for herself which she later wore on a nationwide lecture tour detailing her kidnapping. If TV had been invented then, Josephine Meeker would have been a week-end wonder; as it was she drew crowds for months.

Her mother, Arvila Delight Meeker, spent the time pouring over her copy of *Pilgrim's Progress*. In the reams that have been written about that massacre, neither Josephine nor her mother came out as being all there; it may have been the shock of what happened to them during the Ute uprising or it may have been a lifetime of living with Nathan C.

Aspens admire themselves in Black Pool that was accidentally created when Highway 65 bulldozed its way up the mountainside. Grand Mesa can turn almost anything into beauty.

It was daylight when the rescue party arrived. What they saw was a peaceful camp of thirty white tents among the cedars; horses drowsing near the double race track that made this a favorite Ute camp site; women and children calmly going about their business of drying fall berries and tanning deer hide into buckskin.

Josephine Meeker came out of her tent and greeted the rescuers formally: "I'm very pleased to see you, Mr. Adams."

When questioned as to whether she had suffered indignities to her person she assured him she had not. But Adams had trouble accepting the assurance; from what he'd heard, it was the bounden duty of a Ute captor to properly rape any female captive.

You can see that Ute campsite when you are prowling the north slope of Grand Mesa — beyond Mesa Creek above the town of that name. A juniper called the Meeker Tree marks the spot — about the only tree left when this forested bench was converted to farmland. Undocumented and barely alive because of artificial irrigation water, it corners in a rancher's corrals. Being on private property, permission is required to approach it.

The Meeker Massacre caused panic among people, government, and the military. At the Indian Agency on the Uncompahgre River, the business of soldiers changed from keeping settlers off the Reservation, to keeping the five Ute tribes from getting together and waging a united war on white communities. The agency became a fort as the force was increased by a thousand foot soldiers and cavalry (some authorities say a thousand of each).

Fort Crawford was itself a barrier between the north and south tribes, situated above what is now Montrose, but its position in the wide Uncompahgre Valley made it too easy to bypass. General McKenzie devised another barrier, Grand Mesa.

Because the flat top of the Mesa is so nearly surrounded by sheer cliffs hundreds of feet high, there were very few ways to access and cross it. Station troops where the few trails converge, and you'd keep those Yampa Utes in their place.

Though the iron-rimmed wheels of General McKenzie's supply wagons were probably the first wheels to crease dust and nick rock on Grand Mesa, they were not breaking trail.

The Meeker Tree. Certain tree rings in a dying juniper mark the year Ute Chief Douglas held three women captive on the spot.

Prehistoric eons of moccasins had pressed earth and smoothed stones to a visible trail over this mountain. Within historic times it was the trade link between tribes along northern streams rich in yampa root, and southern bands closer to the source of horses — the Spanish settlements along the Rio Grande. Our modern engineers, like their ancient predecessors, choose the quickest easiest way to get from here to there, consequently most of the Indian tails in this nation are now paved highways — now as then the easiest and shortest way to get somewhere. Colorado State Highway 65 heading north from the Gunnison River more or less follows that Ute "moccasin highway" as far as the Old Road turn off halfway up the mountain. If you turn right at the forks you will stay on that old trail, but only approximately because many switch-backs and detours had to be scraped off to make it climbable by the Model T Ford.

General McKenzie's army wagons ground that hoof-and-moccasin trail into a road — the Military Road. We have a first-hand account of what it was like by a man who drove one of the wagons.

Thomas Bradley came to the West from Alabama when he was nineteen and got a job as a mule skinner with General McKenzie at the Fort. He related:

"We left the Post and came down the Uncompahgre Valley a ways then crossed Garnet Mesa, coming out near where the State Bridge is now, at the mouth of Black Canyon."

Nooning their horses and teams, they stared across at The Wall.

"We forded the Gunnison, and went on up the mountain. We had a large troop of cavalry in front, and more in the rear, and on each side of every team there was a trooper armed to the teeth.

"Several times the mule train came to hills so steep they couldn't climb. They'd be unhitched and taken around a circuitous route while several hundred soldiers grabbed ropes and pulled the wagons to the top of the hill.

"The party camped on top of Grand Mesa for a time, and then returned. We were not informed what the object of the trip was, but I think they were expecting an Indian outbreak.

'"Troopers cut posts and built corrals for their horses and mules up there."

The soldier was in heaven once he made it to the top, surrounded by flowery meadows, lakes, and park-like stretches of forest. Judging by the quantity of shells and bullets early settlers picked up, those army boys got in a lot of target practice, filling the woods with racket and the smell of black powder. They carved their names and the names of back-east sweethearts in black letters on the white bark of aspen trees. For years one tree proclaimed: "O.D.Sullivan, Company D, 14th Infantry USA, 1880." You may still find an antique bullet or two in the part of the Military Park that wasn't put under water when the reservoir dam was raised, but you won't see any of those 1880-81 tree bark carvings. The aspen is not a long-lived tree.

Just because the Military Park encampment sat on top of a mountain eighty or so trail-miles from head-quarters didn't mean it was out of touch with Fort Crawford. The Army had "wireless" long before radio was invented. Curiously, the heliograph wasn't all that different from the Indians' smoke signals which also used line-of-sight. Standing on the highest rim, and using a movable, anchored mirror to flash the sun's rays, an officer skilled

George W. Hawxhurst. (Photo courtesy of Harold Warren).

in Morse Code could send a message by heliograph up to a hundred miles, and to infinity by relay.

During the two summers the Army used the Military Road to keep Indians from fighting whites, the whites were busy fighting each other over who should be in charge of Indians. The Department of Interior claimed charge since the objective was to make farmers out of the nomadic Indians. The War Department demanded charge since the Army was always being sent in to straighten out messes created by the Department of the Interior.

General McKenzie was pretty well out of all that because General Hatch was sent in to handle the hearing to determine which Utes were guilty of the murder of civilians at the Meeker Agency. No guilt was incurred by those Utes who ambushed and slaughtered Major Thornburg's rescue troops because, that being an act of war, it was fair according to the game rules.

The Department of Interior sent in a five-man commission to decide what should be done with the Utes on conclusion of the hearings.

After the treaty negotiations were over, after the hearings, the hours of beautiful but pathetically futile Ute oratory, and the inter-office jockeying for power, General McKenzie's job was to give the order ousting the Utes from the lush mountains of their ancestral home to the arid, alkali Uinta Basin in Utah, and to see it carried out. That he did in the fall of 1881 when he was just past forty, supervising the great trailing, weeping migration down the Uncompahgre River, out around the west foot of Grand Mesa toward the ford across the Grand River and the dry trail into the Utah desert. Grand Mesa was sending smoke signals as the miserable procession crept along its base — smoke from forest fires the Utes had set as the only retribution within their power.

General McKenzie finished the evacuation and resettlement in early winter of 1881. In 1882 he resigned his commission. In 1883 he went insane. To our knowledge, no connection between these events has ever been pointed out.

———— ————

Everybody agrees that the Utes — and all Indians on this continent — were given a raw deal by the incoming government. And worse deals by some citizens whose villainy the government was unable to prevent — such as infecting trading post blankets with smallpox, a disease for which the redman had no immunity, and getting rich by selling whiskey to a people genetically unable to cope with alcohol.

But before you damn yourself and your forebears to eternal guilt, look at another side:

Since the dawn of time nations have been invading other nations, taking over lands, displacing and debasing the people they conquered.

But the pioneers who crossed the ocean from crowded Europe to begin settling a piece of the world that was by comparison practically empty were the only people who had ever made any governmental provision for the folks they conquered. To set aside lands for a conquered people — our self-governing Indian Reservations — and to provide consulting and financial restitution right up to this minute (our Bureau of Indian Affairs) may not be perfect in concept and operation but they are original with us. The Romans didn't do anything like that when they conquered most of Europe, nor did the conquering French and Spanish on the Western Hemisphere until after our example. We can feel proud, not guilty. 🐟

4

Getting Things Named

The moment it was legal, practically in the dust-wake of evicted Utes, Enos Hotchkiss headed back to that corn patch to make his surreptitious stakes official. This time he came with friends and on wheels, piloting a string of covered wagons that with their iron tires, iron-shod horses, and cloven-hoofed oxen created a road as they came.

The wagons were heavily loaded. In addition to the usual living and farming necessities, Sam Wade was bringing enough young trees to start an orchard; the Duke boys — George and William, just out of their teens — had piled their ox-drawn wagons with merchandise to profit on the host of settlers pouring over all the passes. Blacksmith Sanborn brought anvil, hammers, and iron for shoeing all those horses. Ed Duke joined his kid brother, bringing wheelwright equipment to keep the incoming flood of wagons running.

Because of steep rims and deep clefts the few crow-fly miles from Gunnison via Black Mesa took ten days, giving the wagoneers practice in handling the kind of obstacles wheels would encounter on even more road-resistant Grand Mesa. Climbing the rims was slow but simple, if your horsepower couldn't do it, you borrowed enough teams from co-travelers to get to the top, then unhooked and went back for the next wagon. Going down steep grades was something else.

Wagons came equipped with brakes, a tall lever just behind your right shoulder. You engaged it by pulling the rope on top which rammed two blocks of wood against the iron tires of the rear wheels. The harder you pulled, the more braking you got. If the grade was so steep the back wheels slid, you jerked into Second Brake. This was a breeching, a wide, thick strap around the horses' rumps (something like a slipped diaper) that was connected by harness straps running along both sides of each horse to the yoke at the front end of the wagon tongue. You engaged it by yanking hard on the reins. The horses braced their legs and sat back against that breeching strap, the braking force went forward along the harness to the yoke and back along the tongue to the wheels. (Second Brake was an add-on accessory that you didn't need if you lived in flat country. It was heavy, adding to the horses' load — and messy.) If the slope was so steep the loaded wagon threatened to pile down on top of the team, you kicked into Third Brake by cutting down a tree to drag along behind, the bigger the tree the better the braking. On much-traveled roads disengaged Third Brakes accumulated at the bottom, resulting in such grades being named Log Hill, like the one on the Uncompahgre Plateau, between Montrose and Ridgway.

Almost as soon as Enos got his one-room claim-cabin built he secured a U.S. Post Office designation which he set up in one corner. The Duke boys did likewise with their cabin, calling it Dukes Mercantile. Thus was created the town of Hotchkiss.

Hotchkiss was one of eight or ten almost "instant" towns that circled the base of this mountain about a week after the Utes were driven out.

To help people and to build up the new community, and perhaps for pay, Enos led other parties of homesteaders. Like the first-comers they spread along the river, staking out their claims. All but one.

Though plenty of rich, riverbottom land remained, George Hawxhurst set off to homestead on the other side of Grand Mesa. Either he wasn't finished with challenging roadless mountain steeps, or he couldn't bear second-fiddling a town-founder, and wanted to make a town of his own.

Many years later son Alex Hawxhurst tried to explain his father's nature:

"There was the old man Hawxhurst. He can best be described as always mad. He was quick to take offense, had an abusive tongue, and an arrogant manner. The fact that he was always the same, and had no favorites, kept him from being unpopular."

Perhaps losing three of his children in one winter changed George Hawxhurst for life.

There were seven people in the Hawxhurst wagon and cattle train: George and his wife, their daughter Mary and her husband, their sons Tom and John, twenty-three and twenty-one, and Alex who was only five. That gap between John and Alex marked tragedy. While the family was living in South Park where Hawxhurst was placer mining they were struck by the diphtheria epidemic that killed so many children in Denver. That winter, the winter of 1880-81, the Hawxhursts buried three of their children.

They had moved on from that dreadful place and were headed for New Mexico when they got word the Utes were being evacuated from Western Colorado, releasing millions of acres to homestead filing. Heading back, they were in Lake City at the time the Utes were being gathered up to go.

Some Ute women, wailing, their prideful long hair slashed short in mourning, kissed the ground in farewell. Tom Hawxhurst remembered in his diary, "It is little wonder the renegade Colorow staged a few raids after seeing the alkali Uinta Basin they were forced into."

———— ————

George Hawxhurst passed up all the good riverbottom land that Hotchkiss was settling, and led his family's party of wagons down along North Fork and the Gunnison to intercept the wheel ruts known as the "Military Road" up over the mountain. His son's diary continues, "The trail was fresh up Surface Creek, so we followed it to Leon Creek. Some of the Indian campfires were still warm."

The Military Road ended at Military Park. Beyond was just the old Ute Trail, worn easy for hoof and moccasin but formidable to wheels. They took down Leon Creek. Sounds simple; just follow the creek bed. But Leon, like the other streams cutting down through the varied layers of this mountain, is wide and easy going where a soft stratum had been eroded back forming a bench, then becomes a tight squeeze jumping down through a hard cliff-like stratum to the next easy stretch. Again and again. No creek bed in those tight squeezes except what the water is using.

According to the diary George didn't engage Third Brake. To cut and drag tree after tree, wagon after wagon, every time they came to one of those jump-offs would be too slow. It was October, winter was coming on, they still had shelter to build. Instead, he doubled up on Second Brake, hitching teams behind the wagon so that, sitting back against breeching, they could help inch a wagon down the bluff, one lifted hoof at a time.

"The trip down Leon was rough and steep," the diary goes on, "and we had to hook teams on the back of the wagons, and chuck rocks under the wheels. Little Alex tried to help, and the wagon ran over his finger and cut it off. Mother stuck it back on and bandaged it good, but did not look at it for several days. When she took the bandage off, she was horrified to find it full of maggots, but they had kept the wound clean and the finger was grown on fine.

"We landed in the Meadows October 7th. There was high grass and fine soil, so we built a cabin put together with oak pegs, 16x16 feet with oiled flour sacks for windows."

Though the Meadows is many miles from the top, it is still eight thousand feet high. At that north-slope altitude on October 7th, real winter could be only one dawn away. Even with four men working at it from "kin to kaint see," the pressure of getting that cabin built must have been formidable. Four walls' worth of aspen logs to fell, trim, double v-notch on each end, and drill for pegs. Scrub oak to cut and shape into those pegs. Mud chinking to stuff between logs. Grass mat and earth roof to hoist and spread.

At 16x16 feet the Hawxhurst cabin was brag-size compared with most settlers' first cabins, but measure off a sixteen-foot square on your living room rug (that's five good strides and a little bit), and imagine four men, two women, and a five-year-old living, cooking, eating, shaving and sleeping in that space. Lack of privacy and the fact that there wasn't a doctor within two hundred miles didn't deter young Mary's pregnancy.

———

No other settlers came over the Hill or up from the Canyon of the Grand River that year. The Hawxhursts had the entire north side of the mountain to themselves. In that vast isolation Mary Hawxhurst Dunlap gave birth.

Mary's mother wasn't the only experienced midwife present. All the men in the family had assisted in the birthing of calves and colts. But there is a difference: Four-legged creatures tend to slide into the world tentatively front feet first, but because of their ridiculously big brains humans butt into life head on.

Little Hattie made it, and was known the rest of her life as the FWCB (First White Child Born) in what would be Mesa County as soon as newly formed Gunnison County was broken into more manageable size by splitting off Mesa, Delta, and Montrose counties. She was also FWCB on Grand Mesa, but the Hawxhurst family was not overly impressed, her mother Mary was the FWCB in Denver.

Supplies ran low; for one thing a bear rooted out and ate up all the potatoes they planted that first year. Don't puzzle over where those potato-eye starts came from; most pioneers brought seed and starts of food plants they liked and would need. Samuel Wade even brought starts of his favorite flower, the peony, and chose its Latin name, Paeonia, for the "instant" town

---

Bent by prevailing southwest winds, rooted in cliff rocks hundreds of feet above nothing, this tree finally gave up the battle but not before carving its life-story on the sky. If it has a message it is probably that a tree, when it finds itself in a tough situation, cannot just walk away.

he fathered east of Hotchkiss along the base of the of the Mesa. The post office department shortened it to Paonia.

Though their supplies thinned down the Hawxhursts were in no danger of going hungry. There was plenty of meat — deer were described as browsing thick as bands of sheep that have spread out to graze. Elk, antelope, and rabbit abounded. But man cannot live by meat alone. He needs salt, flour and the occasional blast of a spoonful of sugar in the wild Mormon tea he has gathered and brewed.

Young Tom and John Hawxhurst headed back toward Gunnison, a string of pack horses in tow. Long before they reached the top of Grand Mesa the lingering snow was too deep for the horses, so they swung back down over the Hog Back toward the Grand River (Colorado) looping out around the west end of the mountain.

"We were greatly surprised when we came out to find Grand Junction, Delta, and Montrose on the map. We had to go by way of Delta, Montrose and Lake City to get to Gunnison on account of the snow."

Other "instant" towns would have sprung into view if they had taken the North Fork route to Gunnison — Whitewater, Halfway, Pride, Read, Austin, Midway, Paonia. And mountainside chimney smoke proclaiming Cedaredge.

———— ————

The Meadow, a flat expanse covered with stirrup-high grass provided wonderful summer range for the stock, but on the north side of the mountain at that altitude winter came too soon and stayed too late. House and barns had better be lower down. George Hawxhurst moved his family to the mouth of the creek that bears his name, settling where Hawxhurst Creek joins Buzzard Creek and where both fall to join Plateau Creek which flows parallel just on the other side of the peculiar, narrow strip of highland known as the Peninsula.

The Peninsula slants down off the mountain, race-track flat, and a couple of hundred feet higher that the creeks on either side. Six miles in length, it is never more than half a mile wide, and in places pinched so narrow a good arm can toss a rock from rim to rim. As if the Peninsula weren't spooky enough already, settlers squared off some of it in grave-plots and started burying their dead up there.

The post office and instant town that sprang up at the tip of the Peninsula were named Hawxhurst for George, the first homesteader on the north half

Not all of Grand Mesa's beasts are mobile. Puppy-Dog Rock gazes and sniffs at the Teapot without getting any closer.

of the mountain. Having a town named Hawxhurst put George one up on John D. Rockefeller, with whom he'd attended grammar school back in Elmyra, New York. For all the stir John D. was creating in the industrial world at the time, he hadn't had a town named after him yet.

————

Putting labels on scenery items was one of the must pressing jobs for the first settlers. There it stood, a vast mountain full of humps, dips, slopes, cliffs, point, flats — each unique but all ubiquitous — lakes reflecting each other, creeks twisting into each other, forests turning into meadows and back again. And almost none with a name you could get a handle on to tell your partner where in tarnation you cached that haunch of elk.

Surveyor Hayden, with features of three states to find names for, hadn't gone into particulars about this one mountain, he tagged geological oddities such as Forked Tongue Creek, Chair Mountain, and Surface Creek and moved on.

There are more than a thousand named places on the fifty U.S. Geological quad maps it takes to cover Grand Mesa from base to top, end to end. Most of them were thought up in the first five years of settlement although a few, such as Airway Beacon, have been added as times changed.

Five years to get everything named? No wonder a couple of the reservoir lakes are know as Cold Sore and Neversweat.

Every stream, every knob, every lake and lily pond name is a clue to a story of living and struggles, of good, evil and funny. Only another *Encyclopedia Britannica* has room enough for the stories this mesa illustrates. We are forced to pick and choose.

Some places were named for what happened there. Dead Man's Gulch where lies the body of an unknown hermit, killed by another hermit, lugged that far down the mountain, and buried because he was in no condition to be carried farther. Holy Terror Creek was named by consensus of those living with or traveling through its rampages; Hell's Kitchen for how hard it is to find a cow in that Toreva-slump mess.

Bulls didn't have it all their way in getting their version of the bovine equation on the map, there are Milk Creeks on three sides of the Mesa named for the product of the lady cows.

Meadow-grassy Milk Creek above Cedaredge is one of many places on the Mesa where families summered their milk cows in charge of older sons and daughters — teenagers or younger. Because of early practice in being prideful contributors to the family welfare, these kids could take on the job of being summer "dairy managers" from age twelve on up. Cabined in near heaven, all the siblings had to do was drive the cows to and from pasture morning and evening, milk, skim cream, churn once in a while, and keep the butter chilled in icy creek water before wrapping it in green leaves to pack via horse back down to the grocery store at Cedaredge. Some families also made cheese up there.

Farmers at the town of Eckert formed the Surface Creek Creamery Co-operative, built a powered oak churn, and began making butter. Product of all that mountain herbage, Challenge Butter was so superior, that its sweet, delicious flavor made it a gourmet must-have as far away as Los Angeles, at least when we were living there. Though at its peak Surface Creek creamery produced a million pounds a year, it couldn't begin to keep up with demand. Albuquerque alone ordered more than twenty thousand pounds a day. During the crest of the anti-butter health fad, Challenge, like most other creameries, was forced out of business.

Using altitude as a refrigerator was not limited to diary products on the mountain's Milk Creeks. In the early days the Wilkinson brothers killed enough deer to last them through the winter and into the next summer. The mountain cabin they built to "cache" this meat gave Cache Creek its name. If they had brought the meat down to the ranch it would have spoiled in a matter of weeks.

New York Spring was named for five ladies from that city — the record politely doesn't call them spinsters. During the upsurge of women's lib in the 1880s they built their own cabins and had their own summer resort there. New York Spring runs abut two cubic feet of water, very cold, and does not vary summer or winter. Many of the lakes are interlocked by way of surface streams or underground channels. Where a chain of lakes like Mesa Lakes and Grand Mesa Lakes at Alexander was near the Toreva block slumping, they drained into each other by way of streams or underground springs.

Kansas Mesa, the story goes, was named for where first settler Bill Stites came from. Straight-faced postscript to the story to the story is that he brought the Kansas grasshopper with him in his mighty head of long curly hair.

Pete and Bill's Gulch? Why, the place where a couple of young fellows set up cow-keeping. Quicker and friendlier than designating the spot by their last names — Kerney and Tanny. And permanent. A lot of people have owned and profited on that run, but on the map it still belongs to Pete and Bill.

There! was named by the Carpenter, complete with capital T, italics, and exclamation point.

"Hooked this one *There!*" he would say pulling a beauty from the creel in the back of his classic old pickup.

Or setting out afoot from our favorite picnic nook, he'd call back, "If you need me I'll be *There!*" giving specific meaning to that sweet old song.

You won't find *There!* on any Grand Mesa map. Fishing is so good on *There!* that the Carpenter was pretty selective about revealing its known name.

———— ————

How did Fool's Hill get such a name? It's a cliff-hung dugway on the old Salt Lake Wagon Road (now U.S. Highway 50) that heaves and sags across the ridges between the creeks worming down off Grand Mesa. Where Wells Gulch becomes a canyon the heave was too much for the early automobiles whose two and four cylinders were trying to take the place of real horsepower. The county had to gouge out a car's width up Wells Gulch cliff. The two-rut dirt road squeezed around a blind corner with no room to meet an oncoming vehicle. After a couple of head-ons the county put up a sign guaranteed to get attention: "Honk your horn, fool! You may meet another one."

It's been Fool's Hill ever since.

As for the Fool's Hill Christmas Tree, it made national television, because it was growing in the wrong place. Actually the chief mystery about the tree is the mystery of the human heart. Half a century or so ago a road crew was widening the Fool's Hill dugway slightly to keep a few more people from killing each other on this unexpected kink in a long straight road. While nooning, graderman Pat Springer noticed a small juniper that would be in the path of his blade. The tree was only a few inches high, but had a valiant look that touched his heart. After he'd finished his sandwich he dug it up, planted it behind the blade, watered it from his thermos, and went on with his day's work. Thereafter, when maintaining the road, he detoured his blade to miss it.

The tiny tree, perilously within touching distance of wheels, grew and thrived because of runoff water in the borrow pit. People began to look for it and bless it with their eyes as they swished past. No one knows who first got the idea of putting Christmas pretties on a little lone tree out there on the "Stinking Desert" miles and miles from anybody. The decorations — one star and a single strand of tinsel was all it could hold at first — just appeared as if by magic. No club or individual stood up and claimed credit.

By the late 1960s the Fool's Hill Tree, man-tall and annually twinkling all over with Yule glitter, had become a Western Slope institution — as the highway department found.

———————————————————————————————————————

The original Fool's Hill Christmas Tree crowds Highway 50 on the Stinking Desert. Each year tinsel decorations magically appeared as if blossoming from its needles.

At that time they were laying a third lane (on the long since asphalt federal highway) and the Tree stood in the way. When *Delta County Independent* editor Paul Hathaway got word, he rushed to the rescue, argued the bulldozer to temporary standstill, and returned to write an editorial that sent Highway Engineer Dick Procence's phone ringing off the wall.

"Stop!" Procence pleaded, "Call your people off! We aren't going to touch their tree!"

The Tree stayed right where it was, growing in size and fame. Charles Kuralt wanted to use it as his "Christmas On the Road" feature. He had caught the article we wrote about the tree's history and he called asking how to find it.

That was in October. By then the decorations people had hung on the tree the previous Christmas would be in tatters or blown half-way to Canada, what with windy weather and the blast-suction created by semi-trucks flipping the tree inside out twice every time one whizzed by. Knowing this, and realizing that television features by most producers are carefully pre-arranged, we told him the situation and suggested he might want to bring a few decorations to hang on the tree before he aimed his camera at it.

It speaks for the writing integrity of the late Charles Kuralt that he didn't fudge, but waited — not only until decorations had appeared "miraculously" on the tree as they always did, but waited for a miraculous rare snowfall to cover the surrounding desert emptiness.

The Tree stayed until it died of natural causes. One cause — getting whipped to pieces in the wind of passing trucks as traffic on the highway thickened and speeded up. It was replaced a little farther off the road by an alien pine tree faithfully watered by the highway department. Sweet and tender though, but not quite the same.

———

Most of the places, like Hawxhurst Creek, were named in sober tribute to the man who first built a cabin or dam there, first lumbered trees there or ran cattle there. Ward Creek, Atchison Reservoir, Alexander Lake. Getting your name on a map gives you a more permanent place in history that getting elected to Congress.

But the town named for George Hawxhurst didn't stay Hawxhurst very long.

Another man, who coveted having a town named after him as much as George did had more moxie and could impress people in four languages. Dr. W. A. E. DeBeque, who was high in the New York Life Insurance Company, elegantly married French near-royalty, Mlle. Louise de Lavillete, in Mexico

City about the time when Napoleon III was throwing his weight around in that country. DeBeque's only connection with railroads was that he traveled a lot.

Railroads, during this year, had to come up with even more new names than government surveyors did. They were laying through-lines and branch routes in all directions, platting named section houses every ten miles, and real towns in those spots that promised to generate needs and products to freight in and out, as well as people to haul back and forth. When the scattering of homesteads, cattle ranches, and orchards on the north side of Grand Mesa produced enough trade to warrant it, the Denver & Rio Grande Railroad gouged room for a track up the canyon alongside the river whose name had been changed from Grand River to Colorado River.

One way a railroad could incite an employee or financier to more productive zeal — without costing anything — was to name a brand new town after him. DeBeque put up his name for a site where the canyon widened scenically allowing room for the proposed town. The place was already an ancient thoroughfare. Here, within the stand-back walls, the river widened and shallowed into a *pagayvay* where Indians on the Ute trail could wade their horses across on inter-tribal visits. Railroad officials told DeBeque the place had already been named Collbran after a prominent wealthy railroad man in Denver.

During the ensuing face-off with Collbran, Dr. DeBeque slipped to Hawxhurst and persuaded the townspeople to change the name of their town to Collbran. The place wasn't even on the railroad, but Mr. Collbran had to accept it. You can't have two towns in one state with the same name, the mail gets mixed up. That, according to Alex Hawxhurst's memoirs, is how Dr. DeBeque got his name permanently attached to a town, to a canyon of the Colorado River, to the D&RG railroad, U.S. Highway 70, and the pages of seventh-grade geography books all over the English-speaking world. So far nobody has taken Hawxhurst Creek away from George. There are several other stories about how the town of DeBeque was named, including one by Forest Ranger Peck, but neither Peck nor any of the other recounters was there at the time, Alex Hawxhurst was.

(Sometimes railroad planners seemed to take grim fun in naming places along the track. During the thirty-one years when the Denver & Rio Grande and the Denver Salt Lake railroads were fighting over the laying of thirty-eight miles of cutoff rail that would save 175 miles of ride, the D&RG dug in its heels at a point on the track above DeBeque, tagging the spot Dot Zero. The other end, if ever the cutoff track were laid, would be Orez Tod, Dot Zero in reverse. The post office, however, did a little editing and the towns became Dotsero and Orestod.)

Then George Hawxhurst almost had the town itself stolen out from under him.

It started at the 4th of July picnic — the big community event all over the nation in those days. It was held in Sam Kiggins grove a mile and a half downstream; George Hawxhurst refused to attend. As son Alex said later, "He was mad because it wasn't held in Collbran, and wouldn't go."

By this time Kiggins had a fine new house, a big improvement over the cabin Patrick McCafferty described in telling of a dance held in it: "Sam's doors were gunnysacks and his windows flour sacks, and his ballroom floor was the bare breast of mother earth. As we right-handed-to-your partner, alamand-right, swing-your-partner — the old oil lamp looked through dust like the sun at noon through a San Francisco fog."

After the picnic, while the women were clearing and stowing, the men lolled around in the cottonwood shade fiddling with the idea of getting even with old George by starting a river town a mile and a half down the creek from George's Collbran. Sam Kiggins suggested it, pointing out that the canyon is wider there, more room for streets and buildings, and for a railroad. Why, if the D&RG ever decided to build a spur up Plateau Canyon it would squeeze Collbran right up against the walls!

They did it. Kiggins donated the land, and they named the place Plateau City. Babcocks built a brick kiln, Donahue built a meat packing plant and raised berries on the side (sound like a pemmican factory?), Skinner built a lumber yard fed by his own sawmill up in Grand Mesa timber, Townsend set up a pencil factory to use the cedars that grew on his Mesa bench, Mrs. Jones ran a millinery shop, Koch ran a pool hall and ice cream parlor while his wife and sister-in-law ran a cigar factory next door making hand-rolled Annie Laurie cigars from tobacco grown in the bays of Plateau Canyon. Many more, but never as many or as varied as Collbran boasted. Gradually most of the Plateau City businesses and industries moved to the larger, upstream location — the villages were just too close together.

Grand Mesa's only mapped "city" is still on the map, though you glimpse a few houses clustered around a store when you skim past.

———

When the Hawxhurst family pioneered over the top of Grand Mesa they were trailing so close on the heels of the departing Utes that the Indians' cook-fire rocks were still warm to the touch. As they moved on down into the canyons of Buzzard and Plateau creeks they noted picture-messages pecked into the tan and reddish sandstone walls — antlered deer, horsemen with feather headdresses, the carefully toe-complete tracks of bear. Ranchers riding after their cattle came onto clusters of wickiup poles marking a Ute summer camp. Whole and broken arrowheads, bits of pottery abounded and were, in fact, so prevalent they were scarcely noticed.

By 1923 such finds were rare enough that the *Grand Junction News* was reporting discoveries made decades earlier: Dr. A. R. Craig described a find on Sunny Side where he had been hunting — a village of two hundred cedar-bark tipis. In one he found a pottery jar containing an ear of corn. He tried planting some kernels, but they didn't grow.

Even the *Los Angeles Times* took notice when somebody, digging for gold or something along Plateau Canyon, came onto an ancient cave floored with man-made tile. Gertrude Exner, retired U.S. Geological survey secretary, tells what happened.

"The discoverer was so concerned lest vandals, by carrying away souvenir tiles, destroy the evidence before scientists could verify and date the find, that he disguised the place and kept its location secret. So secret, in fact, that he took it with him to his grave. The cave, if indeed it exists, will have to be discovered all over again."

Those tiles don't fit anything this continent's archeologists ever heard of, so they propose that the clay in a pond, pulling apart as it dried, formed symmetrical shapes (as it sometimes does), and that the heat of some kind — perhaps a coal seam burn-back — kilned it into ceramics. About as far-fetched as the find itself, since the tile was flooring in a cave when discovered, not wedged against a heat-slacked coal seam. Another of this mountain's mysteries.

———

When Alex Hawxhurst found a cedar tree decorated with living, growing basketry he was so impressed he tried to tell the world, through the Forest Service.

On December 30, 1943, Alex Hawxhurst wrote Forest Service Ranger Peck that he had found "a very outstanding specimen of Indian work." Pliant withes of green cedar had been cut and woven into a braided design about two and one-half feet long, and then the cut-ends of the withes had been inserted into cuts in a living cedar tree.

"To me it was very astonishing," Alex wrote, "that a graft of such proportions could be made in so dry and sapless a thing as cedar.

"The braided work has grown somewhat out of proportion, some of the parts having grown faster than others. Sometime when you're up I would like to have you see it."

Apparently the Forest Service didn't respond, because Alex wrote again later: "I removed the part of the cedar that has the specimen attached and have it here at the house. If you are going to be up sometime. Or if not I could bring it down to your office when I come." A.P. Hawxhurst.

That was a long time ago, more than half a century, and Forest Service personnel change frequently. No one now knows where that one-of-a-kind piece of Ute live-and-growing basketry is.

Indian graphics, wickiups, cave tile, tree-graft basketry? What are your chances of making a "find" on Grand Mesa such as any of these.

Fairly good.

And if you are that lucky, you are invited to tell the Forest Service about it, so the site can be documented by its archeologist. ✤

Graffiti? Or record of a prehistoric people? Both. The five-toed bear tracks are an ancient message of a successful kill or a hopeful cure. But the figure whose moving limbs show perspective is by an imitator unaware the Old Ones didn't use that device.

5

Whose Tracks Are You Walking In?

Just supposing you come out onto a wide bench of autumn-tawny browse, patterned with sunflowers and purple asters, framed in junipers and pinyon pine. Nearby, under gold-turning aspen trees, a small stream flows quietly in a lull between its strata-leaps down off the mountainside. Nothing special. Like scores of other such terrace places overlooking the river valleys far below.

Nothing special until, looking back into the junipers beyond the creek you make out a cone-shape of old, gray poles.

A dozen or so weathered tree branches spaced wider at the bottom where they are wedged into the earth, slanting inward to interlock at the top, tipi style. A camp shelter of some kind. Put up quite awhile ago, you guess, judging by the soft gray texture of the wood. Maybe a generation ago.

Something glitters in the sun. Purple glass. The thick bottom of an old-fashioned pop bottle. How long does it take sunlight to bring out that much purple? With that artifact clue, you set time back another generation; that's about when the Boy Scout movement was big and new, and groups of youngsters prided themselves in living off the wilds. You visualize boys buzzing about, saluting whenever possible, keeping the knees of their knickerbocker uniforms neat while they scoop water from the brook, skin out a rabbit, interweave branches to weather-proof their pole hut, squat to flip flapjacks.

Then you notice an off-colored rock, creamy red, unlike the black lava boulders that, having washed down from the Mesa top, pepper all these terraces. But this is sandstone, brought in from elsewhere. You turn it over, see its deep oval hollow and know what you are looking at — a "metate," a grain-grinding stone.

Indian!

Could this cone of poles have been a Ute wickiup? But it's been more than a hundred years since Utes were reservationed off Grand Mesa and out of western Colorado. Could wooden poles stand in place that long? Possibly, if they are cedar as these seem to be. Small summer-camp wickiups were usually made of nearby cedar boughs that were twisty and twiggy enough to hold the "roofing" of leafy boughs.

You turn your guess-clock backward another century or so, and visualize the Ute woman bent over this very stone just beyond the doorway of her brush-covered wickiup. The fringes on her buckskin dress sway as she grates the mano back and forth on the metate,

Hazel Austin Finke, whose "Know Your Neighbor" articles are a treasure of Grand Mesa history, sits within the poles of a Ute hunting camp wickiup. Some twenty-two such camp-sites have been found on the mesa. (Hazel's camera took this picture.)

making meal of the wild seed she has gathered and brought back to camp. *Tupu kucogway* "stone that chews" she would have called it.

Something is naggingly wrong about the picture. That stone was upside down.

But of course! This wickiup was just what it looks like — quick-built, temporary, a seasonal camp. And, as she prepares to leave this midway camp to go down to the valley for the winter, she carefully turns it upside down so that water will not collect and, freeze-expanding, break her cooking utensil. Your guess-clock eases backward a couple of centuries, before Ute Indians had the pack horse. When everything a family owned must be carried on the human back in the ceaseless, ranging scrounge for food, she wouldn't lug that rock. She'd have a *tupu kucogway* handy at each of her seasonal campsites. That explains why so many metates are seen in areas where nomadic tribes came and went with the seasons.

Satisfied you've got it figured out, you tuck the metate back where it was — you're after the saga of this place, not its artifacts. In smoothing the earth you uncover a sherd, the broken rim of a pot. Blackish-brown, with fingernail dents forming a pattern where fingers pressed the moist clay coils together. You recognize the ceramics known to museum people as Uncompahgre Brownware, and your clock wavers, groping back into a great gap of time and place vaguely labeled Desert Culture — thousands of years before there were people known as Ute. Yet somebody was making crude Uncompahgre Brownware pots back then and right on up to the 1700s when Utes stopped making clay cooking pots because they could barter for kettles from a trading post.

Frustrated by the history gap, you've turned to go on up the creek when your shoe scuffs something out of the pinyon needle duff. A small piece of metal, rusty yet a bit glittery, crudely folded into a tiny horn shape with a glob of something heavy on one side. A tinkler! One of the ornaments knotted into the fringe of her dress. It had been cut from a tin can and curled around a twig or something; the glob was the drop of hot lead used to seal tin cans back in the days when — Your clock stops guessing and does a fast forward targeting a single decade: The tin can wasn't invented until 1810, it wasn't in general use until the Civil War, and wasn't available in western trading posts until that war was out of the way and life resumed — along about 1870. The Utes were moved out of here into Utah in 1881.

Neat!

Then, half-protruding from the clay cutbank of the creek, you see a fragment of shaped flint, part of a spearhead. Enough is left to show that it was fluted — one long flake had been pried cleanly the length of each side. A Folsom point? Aimed and thrown by somebody standing on this very mountain? Before Columbus, before Christ, before the Pyramids? Your clock throws up its hands and quits.

You straighten, gaze around the ancient campsite glade. The time-spread of what you're looking at hits home.

Deliberately, but grinning, you reach into your jeans for a penny and drop the piece of worked copper alloy into the dust between your shoe tracks, bringing the wickiup's artifact story up to date.

———

If this dream of an archeological jackpot should actually happen to you — and it could on this mountain! — your Folsom find wouldn't be a first, either in this state or on Grand Mesa. In his *Archeology of Colorado*, E. Steve Cassells cites eight documented Folsom sites and "hundreds of isolated surface finds." It is known that a Folsom spear point was found on Grand Mesa a few years ago, but it walked away anonymously and so was not — and now can never be — recorded in the time-place doings of prehistoric man. Charles States found a section of the tusk of a mastodon — the usual target of a Folsom spear. He proclaimed his find and displayed it in his little coal mine museum near Cedaredge. But by moving it before scientific in situ study he unhooked it from its place in the sequence of events on Grand Mesa. That tusk fragment, like the teeth of woolly mammoths found near Montrose, is a relic of the late glacial era when rainfall was heavy, vegetation was lush, and hairy elephants were hunted on these very mesa terraces where you are standing now.

Wickiups still exist on Grand Mesa. How many no one knows for sure, but in 1988 Robert N. Nykamp, writing for a symposium of the Colorado Council of Professional Archeologists , noted sixty-eight sites then existing in the two counties — Mesa and Delta — that border each other the length of Grand Mesa. Most of Mesa County's known wickiup sites are on the Uncompahgre Plateau, but the seven Delta County sites are all on the south slopes of Grand Mesa. Because Indians did their food hunting and gathering in bands of several families, a "site" includes a number of wickiups either still in place or evident in clusters of hearth stones, carbon-datable ash deposits, remnants of cedar bark floor mat or some other sign of habitation.

In spite of weathering, of brat-vandals, and of wood-gatherers the actual number of wickiups is probably more than the symposium's list because archeologists had admittedly made little effort to find them all. In fact the main point made by the sixteen scientists contributing papers to the symposium was that they themselves had been remiss in locating and studying wickiup sites.

They blame their neglect on the fact that at wickiup sites the artifacts are bewilderingly horizontal — just as you found them. An archeologist could spend a couple of summers fingering a thousand square yards of surface and end up with only half a dozen lithics (worked stone weapons or tools) and sherds (pieces of pottery) all spread out at the same dateless level no matter how old they might be. "Material Scatter Sites" they label wickiup camps — with cussword quotation marks — and go off to dig history at Mesa Verde where the cliff dwellers tossed their lithic and sherd trash over the edge of the cliff, along with the cook-hearth ashes, forming a layer-cake dump, every fragment of which can be assigned a specific time-niche by carbon-dating the ashes above and below it.

Some archeologists have labeled the entire Desert Culture intermountain basin (Western Colorado, Utah and Nevada) one gigantic "Material Scatter Site" because of the leavings of nomadic hunter-gatherers through the course of some eleven millennia. Owing to the dry climate the objects stayed on the surface, not buried out of sight by runoff and vegetation as happened farther east. When homesteaders took over, arrowheads were prevalent and despised. Rubbish of savages. Even the next generation could take them or leave them. Cowboy Brownie Blumberg remembered, "You saw so dang many points. Got so it wasn't worth gettin' off your horse to pick one up."

A generation later, before it became illegal to pick up artifacts, groups of "head-hunters" roamed the range all day, eyes on the ground, adding to the collections of arrowheads, flint tools, and pottery fragments in framed-glass arrangements on their walls.

——— ———

One of the reasons the source of Utes and their Brownware pottery, are so lost in the vast unknowable past is that they and the nameless people they sprang from left few burial sites. For archeologists exploring pre-history the world over, the items chosen to accompany the dead on that final journey are a kind of racial recording, an obituary of artifacts left by people lacking a written language. Baskets, pottery, tools and weapons either whole or "killed" by breaking; beads, ceremonial or decorative; bones of sacrificial animals, have much to say about a people and their ways. But pre-historic Ute peoples apparently so feared death that they disposed of bodies as quickly as their customs allowed, and fled the place.

True, they killed horses during rites for Chief Ouray, the last chief of their freedom, when they placed his body in the cleft of a cliff in New Mexico. But this was a couple of hundred years after contact with whites had changed many of their ways, as they themselves have since written in *The Southern Utes, a Tribal History* (1972).

Some burial clefts have been found in the cliffs of Grand Mesa, but so few that archeologists are puzzled to know how Desert Culture people disposed of their dead during the eons before a portion of them became known as Ute. With only stone and bone handtools, it is unlikely Utes would have dug graves in the hard semi-desert earth of the Colorado-Utah basin or the stony clays of Grand Mesa slopes. And anyhow, to put the dead underground, spirit and body held down by a weight of earth, would probably have seemed evil and cruel. Instead, they lifted them up.

"Sooner" pioneer, William McGinley described what he saw on his ride to check on Grand River homestead possibilities before returning to the Uncompahgre confluence to stake his claim. The four young men had camped for the night at Kannah Creek and were headed for the Whitewater divide when they spotted a group of trees with pole platforms. By this time, what with his detention at Fort Crawford, teenager McGinley had been around Utes long enough to know what he was looking at.

"There was a burying ground used by the Utes on Kannah Creek between the old ford and Grand Mesa. The Indians did not bury their dead, but wrapped them up in blankets and laid them on poles on top of oak trees. In several places poles had been tied with thongs in the trees and rough platforms made upon which dead Utes were placed. Probably ravens, magpies and other birds would make quick work of the bodies, and all evidence of these burying places would disappear in a comparatively short time."

He knew what he was looking at, but surely not what it meant, adding, "The Utes were too lazy to dig graves, and apparently got rid of the dead in the easiest way."

To cut or gather poles and build a tree-platform conforming with tradition — high enough to put the body out of the reach of earth creatures but available to sky creatures — wasn't easy work. Nor safe. As soon as they finished the Utes left the fearful place to the spirits they felt were honing in on visible and invisible wings. Most terrifying of spirits on visible wing was the Eagle.

A mile in the sky higher than the Kannah Creek Ute burial place, just under the Mesa rim, two great white slides scar the west side of Grand Mesa. They are glacial scars where ice grabbed and dragged away pieces of mountain. In white-folks' mythology the slides are called "21" for their shape; to the Utes they were the sloughing filth — bones and *paa-kwica-pu* — of death-eating Eagle. The story accounts for all that Toreva-block slumping: Eagle did it.

Forest Supervisor Ray Peck wrote:

"According to an Indian myth Grand Mesa was called "Thigunawat" or the home of the spirits. In olden times it was the abode of great eagles known as "Bahaa-Niehe" or Thunder Birds that built their aeries along the rim. Three pairs of these great birds nested along the north rim of Whitewater Creek, and the large slides that are so conspicuous on Whitewater Point were formed by bones of the victims and droppings from the nests. Even the water of the creek turned white and was called "Nunachaa."

"These birds not only packed deer, antelope, and other animals to their nests, but captured Indian children. An Indian village was located on Kannah, or Tepee Pole Creek, and a young chieftain, Sehiwuq, or Weasel Bear, and his beautiful squaw, Nagaw, or Morning Star, were very proud of their young son who was just learning to hunt.

"One day a great Bahaa-Niehe seized the boy while he was hunting rabbits and carried him to its nest on Whitewater Point. Sehiwuq, bent on revenge,

disguised himself by wrapping his body in the bark of the Basthina, or sacred cedar tree, and carrying a strong crook and branches of a tree, started up the Mesa.

"The Indians ascribe a mystic sacredness to the cedar tree from its never-dying green which renders it so conspicuous a feature of the desert landscape, from the aromatic fragrance of its twigs which are burned as incense in sacred ceremonies, from the desirability and fine texture of the wood which makes it good for tepee poles and lance shafts. According to Indian myth, the first cedar was a pole to the top of which they fastened the freshly killed scalps of their enemies, and the heartwood was stained red by the blood that trickled down through the wood.

"It took Sehiwuq all day to reach the rim, as he had to stand still every time one of the Thunder Birds came over him. At last he reached the first nest, and with his crook of cedar pulled the young birds from the nests, and they rolled down the side of the mountain. He did not give up until he had reached the other nests, and tumbled out the young.

"A large serpent Batiqtuba dwelt near a small lake near the foot of the slides (by the white man called Cliff Lake), and as the young birds rolled down the mountain he captured and ate them all.

"When the Bahaa-Niehe returned to their nests with food for their young, they were distracted with grief, and suspecting the serpent, they fell upon him and carried him to a great height in the sky. They took turns biting pieces off the serpent, and as these pieces fell and hit the earth they made large deep holes in the ground. In their rage, the Thunder Birds shot fire from their eyes, and thunder shook the mountain; rain fell and filled the holes forming the many lakes on Grand Mesa."

———

A child alone, out hunting on this vast mountain? Except for the supernatual such as Eagle, Sehiwuq's son could take care of himself, and knew it.

At somewhere between age six and eight Ute children were considered adults, with the right to make their own decisions and stand the consequences thereof. They still are. When Ione Tyler of Delta was in charge of the school lunch program in Cortez in the 1970s many children bused in off the Indian reservation carried wads of money in their pants pockets. When the school principal complained to the parents that the rolls of cash might be lost or stolen, the response was usually a shrug: It was the child's own money, his

Aspens write in flowing long-hand on sheets of snow.

share of the current earnings from reservation oil wells. If he wanted to carry it around with him, that was his business.

There's no record that any small Ute lost any of his oil well income, but to keep itself out of trouble the school gathered up the cash as the children got off the bus, locked it up, and returned it when the bus took off for the reservation in the evening. ❧

6

Drugstore on the Hill

Restocked fresh every spring, the shelf-like shoulders and table top of Grand Mesa provided Utes and earlier people with a rich variety of edible and medicinal plants, of which Utes are known to have used at least a hundred different kinds — many in several different ways. For instance, more than twenty varieties of roots were eaten raw, boiled, or roasted; and one plant, sage, was used in twenty ways — from making rope, to curing rheumatism, to preventing gray hair.

Indian women used dock leaves, a favorite pot herb green, to tenderize meat, having discovered that its tart juices considerably reduced the cooking time of a tough old rabbit, or brisket of ancient buck.

Men smoked dock leaves, mixed with kinnikinnick or willow when they ran out of the real tobacco (leaves of nicotiana flower) which they themselves had gathered and cured — only men had anything to do with sacred tobacco.

Both women and men used dock-stem tea as an after-shampoo rinse, to increase hair strength and sheen.

Dock root steeped in water was taken as a laxative. The number of plants used for laxative purposes was only exceeded by the number used to treat diarrhea, indicating that the "natural" diet was not as conducive to regularity without medical intervention as it is now touted to be.

Dock seed, hand-rubbed free of hulls, winnowed, toasted and ground to meal, was used in making bread or was boiled as mush.

The Indian cook's bread and cereal menu was anything but monotonous. She gathered, parched, winnowed and stone-ground flour and meal from fifteen or twenty kinds of seed including buttercup, primrose, Indian millet, sunflower, rice grass, saltbush and, of course, the *ugwi-vu* called squaw grass.

To do all this harvesting, she manufactured her own "machinery," coiling a wide, flat basket to catch the seed, and weaving a seed-beater on a split and rejoined withe that looked something like a light snowshoe. To truck the produce home, she wove a large conical basket (holding about a bushel) which was strapped to her back and had a third strap (tumpline forehead yoke), letting her neck muscles help with the load.

Some of the best sources of flour required special treatment. Acorns, for example, are plentiful (and rewardingly big to gather compared to grass seed), but bitter with tannin — even Grand Mesa's relatively sweet gambrel oak acorns. The tannin could be leached out by pouring several changes of boiling water over the meal, but hot water in such quantities was hard to come by when it could only be produced by putting heated rocks into the clay-pot or basket-pot of cold brook water; so a prevalent method was to put the acorn meal in a porous basket made especially for the purpose (a cloth bag was used after the Utes got cloth along with other appurtenances of civilization), and then sink the glob of dough-like stuff in creek or lake, turning and kneading it three or four times a day for about a week.

Sweet-tasting at last, the dough was seasoned with flax seed or spicy wallflower seed, patted into flat cakes, and baked on a hot rock. Treated acorn meal was also dried for winter use.

Oak bark, a handful in a quart of water boiled down to half its volume, was used to treat ailments at both ends — as a gargle and for dysentery. (Sounds like enough tannin to make leather out of the alimentary canal, but a similar treatment is mentioned in the U.S. Dispensatory of 1833).

Besides grains and seeds, a dozen or so kinds of roots were dried and ground into flour — among them the yampa, cow parsnip, salsify, biscuit root, cattail, yellow pond lily, and sego lily. They were almost pure energy-rich starch; biscuit root, for instance, was one of the plants called "Indian potato," and the yellow yampa was called "Indian carrot."

Dehydrating the juicy roots to flour was the simplest way to keep them; the process also reduced their weight and bulk for carrying and storing.

But the favorite way to eat them was on the spot, roasted.

Children learned the "how-to" of root-roasting by gathering and preparing the root they liked best, the bulbs of the nodding onion that in favored places colors Grand Mesa slopes with sheets of lavender-rose. After digging the bulbs with fire-hardened sticks they built a fire to heat rocks which they tonged with

---

The Lily Ponds—one name for dozens of places—provided the Utes with nourishing roots to cook, and "popping" seeds around the tipi fire.

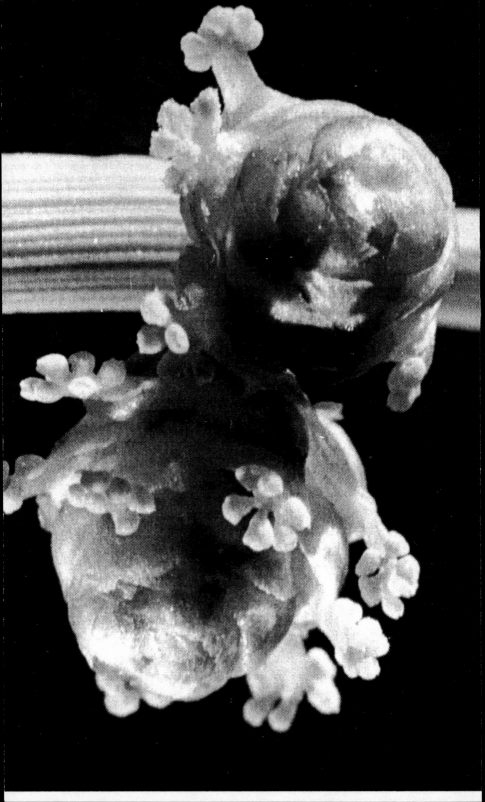

green sticks into the bottom of a small pit. The pit was filled in layers — on the hot rocks a layer of green leaves, then the onions, more green leaves and more hot rocks, more green leaves, more onions.... Finally a layer of earth to keep the heat in.

The process also taught the kids patience because it was two whole days before it was time to scoop off the earth, roll the still-hot rocks away with sticks, get at the treat, and begin the feast.

Onions were strong Indian medicine too. Sniffing onion juice was one way · to clear the nostrils during a cold (there were half a dozen other less jolting ways). Pulped and mixed with grease or honey, onion was applied to snake or mad-dog bites.

Onions were put into meat stews, of course, but so was any of a bewildering variety of other pot herbs, such as lambs quarter, purslane, chickweed, prince's plume (resembling cabbage in taste), fireweed tips, stinging nettle, sorrel, saltbush bracts, water cress, all manner of edible roots. And berries.

The Ute (and other Indian) penchant for combining meat, whether roasted, boiled or dried, with the tart sweetness of berries in a "sweet-sour" cookery is perhaps another bit of evidence (besides the famous "blue spot" birth mark) of their Oriental origin.

Of the nineteen kinds of berries found on Grand Mesa and vicinity, the Utes used fifteen varieties — nine in great quantities: service berries, chokecherries, raspberries, currants, rose hips, squawberries, holly grape, elderberries, and strawberries.

Of the berries they ate right off the bush or vine, they preferred strawberries, and are described as "going on regular strawberry sprees," children and adults happily chattering and skittering at the forest edges in search of red-ripe berries the bears and other creatures hadn't beat them to. A similar chirping, chittering excitement can be observed today among reservation Utes and Navajos gathering pinyon nuts.

Strawberries that survived to be taken back to camp might be made into a thick hot drink called strawberry soup. But the favorite way to eat strawberries anywhere was fresh and sweetened by shaking over them the dew collected overnight on pink milkweed flowers.

Strawberry leaf tea was supposed to be good for the liver and aching joints. This may well be, since the leaves contain iron and salicylic acid (the

---

Nature still in finger-paint kindergarten? Herbal ephedra (Mormon tea), perhaps the oldest flower on earth, apparently got stuck half way between the idea of pine cones and the idea of flowers— and stayed there. To get this intimate with a pinhead ephedra blossom we had to hunker down with magnifying lens.

basis of our aspirin). Utes also discovered that rubbing their teeth with raw strawberries removed tartar build-up.

Main-crop fruit such as service berries, currants, chokecherries, and raspberries, were mashed and dried into large cakes or disks that could weigh up to twenty pounds each and, after the Ute got the horse, were shaped with a hole in the middle for tying onto the pack saddle.

During non-berry season, a chunk of dried berry disk would be broken off and added to stew or boiling meat.

It is said the early Ute (before picking up ideas from the Plains Indians) did not make true pemmican — a mixture of berries, pounded dried meat and fat. But they did knead dried berries and fat together, producing a traveling ration, which they put into buckskin pouch "lunch boxes" along with pieces of jerky for their men to carry while hunting.

An infusion of raspberry leaves was given women during labor to make the process more comfortable, but since babies were often born out of leaf-season, the usual method of making birth easier was half a cup of juniper-twig tea taken daily beginning about a month before the birth was expected, then to speed things up during actual labor a decoction of ground juniper berries.

———

Several plants were used as contraceptives.

Settlers had big families; but Indians, it was noticed, didn't. Puzzling over that, some scientists theorized that in the stark, hand-to-mouth economy of primitive life, Indian girl babies simply came equipped with fewer eggs lest population exceed food supply, wiping out the race. This might have been an operating factor in Paiute and Goshute country, the deserts of eastern Utah and Nevada, where food was so scarce that grasshoppers and ants were staples. It could hardly have been a factor among tribes with access to the plant and animal wealth of the Rocky Mountains. Observant game hunters had another theory: Maybe Indian women were like doe deer, able to halt the growth of an embryo, and hold it in the womb until food prospects improved — a bad weather cycle was over, and the range got better.

Actually they were practicing birth control.

Nurse Lola Loss of Delta learned about one Indian contraceptive substance while working in a hospital on the Southern Ute Reservation not long ago:

Three generations back, instead of the arm-holed cotton blouse this grandmother is wearing, she would be robed in deer hide she had tanned and flat–cut herself. Shaping garments to the in-curves of the human body only arrived on this continent with the trousered European. In turn he adapted the Indian's long, belt-hung leggings to create cowboy chaps.

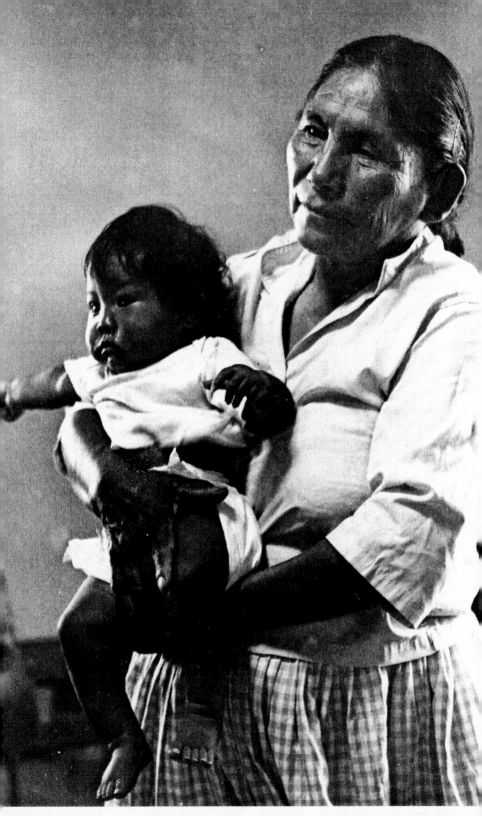

gypsum crystals brought up from the White Sands in New Mexico. It was ancient usage, her patients told her, taught to the People by the Old Ones.

Utes frequenting Grand Mesa didn't have to travel that far, or barter tanned buckskin for white sands gypsum from southern Indians passing through. They had their own contraceptives — a carefully measured tea of a dangerous substance, *poni-yi kaaavaci*, or steeped juniper berries taken on "appropriate days."

Population control was indeed exercised, not by numbers of ova in baby girls but on the judgment of the shaman. He had the power to decide when an abortion should be done, and did it herbally; and whether a man or woman should be sterilized for life, and he could accomplish that also with plants growing on Grand Mesa. His power was absolute, but his wisdom not necessarily so — as was demonstrated when Agency physicians down at Ignacio had to stand back while tribal medicine men unsuccessfully took over treatment of terminally ill Chief Ouray. Ouray was dying of kidney failure and hernia, the medicine men treated his condition by incantations, pounding his belly with their fists, and butting their heads against his chest to drive the evil spirit out.

———

Indian knowledge of the medicinal properties of plants was ancient, a lore handed down from eons of experiment and experience. And the effectiveness of a great deal of it has been verified by scientists isolating the chemical agent in each plant, and its effect on the human body. Of those Indian remedies that still elude scientific endorsement, many were so disagreeable to take that they doubtless "worked" simply because they tasted so bad they must be good for you, as do some modern remedies for the same psychological reason.

But when the white man came, he brought diseases the Indian had never had, and possessed no treatment for. At least four of them were deadly plagues to a people completely lacking immunity: syphilis, smallpox, measles and tuberculosis.

As these plagues wiped out whole villages and tribes, the Indians' desperate casting about for something to treat them is heart-breaking. For venereal disease alone, they cited fifty-eight plants that would cure it — some, it was said, in less than a week. Among these were teas made of locoweed, paintbrush root, sage leaves, yucca roots, kinnikinnick and dock. Other plants were dried, powdered, and applied to the lesions. Our beautiful blue penstemen was thought to be so effective all of it was used in all ways, the leaves, flowers, stems and roots, as teas, poultice, powder and wash; a kind of shotgun treatment for the scourge first called "French disease."

Nature is tricky. Among the hundreds of edible and medicinal plants on Grand Mesa are at least fourteen poison ones, some of which look almost exactly like food plants — cow parsnip and deadly water hemlock, for instance. Some are poisonous at one time of the year and not at another — the elderberry when still red, the lupine peas just before ripening. Some are poisonous only when raw — the groundcherry. Some are poisonous in one part and not in another — wild rhubarb stalks are a fine tonic food, the leaves can kill you.

In the case of the false hellebore (what we call skunk cabbage) the Indian used the body's rejection of a poison to effect a cure. A man suffering from hernia took a good pinch of snuff made from the ground root, and during the ensuing fit of sneezing a friend pushed back the rupture with his fist.

All of the monkshood plant is poison all the time, but the Indian used it and datura and the other hallucinogenic plant poisons that produce visions just before delirium, coma, and death. One can only imagine by how many fatal experiments the tribes learned exactly how much the medicine man could take to create the visions he used in achieving a faith cure, and still live to take the credit for it.

When the rains come right, Grand Mesa forest floor grows a wide variety of mushrooms, some of which are poisonous. The Ute ate none of them, apparently never trusting herself to know the difference every time.

Like their modern counterparts, Ute children roving Grand Mesa had their "entertainment" foods. Half a dozen plants produced chewing gum for them in half a dozen flavors. Mountain dandelion, cactus, pussy toes, chicory and rabbitbrush yield milky sap that on drying hardens to a satisfying chew. Chewing gum was not just for children, it was used by adults to reduce thirst during long treks through dry country.

Other Ute "fun foods" were flowers. They delighted to eat cottonwood catkins raw. They dipped elderberry blossom-heads in meal-batter and fried them in grease on a heated rock. They flavored acorn soup with lupin flowers. They thickened soup with the flowers and buds of the pink milkweed. They shook flowering cattails in a buckskin bag to collect pollen for an especially rich flour. They simmered violet flowers to make a syrup flavoring for porridge.

Other syrups were made from cactus, rose hips, and aspen sap — the latter dripping into little square buckskin "buckets" just as maple sap is collected now. The syrups could be further boiled down to make candy.

They had "pop corn."

This fun food was a product of the yellow pond lily so prevalent on Grand Mesa. Earlier in each Mesa season the yellow pond lily had already provided a rich harvest of "root-bread" which the Ute woman secured by wading out waist-deep and, with a hooked stick, yanking up the tubers that snaked over the pond floor. Then in late July or August, she waded in again to gather the globe-shaped pods filled with large black seeds.

Back in camp and supper over, the seeds were spread on a flat rock and heated till they jumped and popped open. Then everybody sat around munching and watching the dancing flames in the firepit while the family Story Teller recounted another of the shady adventures of that x-rated tribal cartoon character, Coyote — as now recalled for us by *pusari-niya-mi-ti* the Story Rememberer:

Yogovuci, that Coyote, had him a yellow shirt in those days. *Yogovuci*, he went that-a-way along the water edge. He had a yellow shirt, a buckskin shirt, and he kept moving way up high. And right there he saw some people sitting, two of them, *Tsupuyci tuaciu*, Rock Children. So he approached them, and right there and then he peed on them.

"What does she let you drink, *Piaciamu*, your dear mother?" he asked as he proceeded to pee on them. And then he took off, having done that to them.

Later on their mother came back, "*Kwa-kwanay* How come you smell so bad?" she asked them. "Coyote *v-int-su* on us," they told her, "And then he went up this-a-way."

She got real angry, their mother, and she took off after him. Rolling up the hill, she went real fast, and she caught up with him way up there. She dragged him over there and threw him in the water. She threw his yellow shirt into the water.

And that was that.

———

Prowling the Mesa slopes afoot, ahorse, by ski or snowmobile you may find your way blocked by a drift fence made of piled-up tree branches. Laid up by early settlers, you surmise, for containing cattle. In most cases you would be right, but if the fence is so old it is sagging earthward, its twigs and small branches rotted away, it is probably one of several deer-drifts put up by Indians to nudge feeding bands of deer to where hunters were waiting in ambush. If the "fence" is laid in a circle, you are not looking at a corral — as early settlers thought — but at a Ute Bear Dance site.

Mama-kwa-nhka-kwi-a-pu is the Ute name. Notably lacking kava, the word for horse, it can be translated: "Fenced-in, Woman winning dance step." The five-day hypnotically repetitive dance was held in very early spring to give power to She Bear, to help her and the whole winter-dead earth come alive. Holed up somewhere underground She Bear had been dead to the world since autumn. During those cold gaunt months she comatosely gave birth a cub or two. Her appearance in the spring with two new lives, presaging the renewal of life once more on earth, was so miraculous and vital it took everything the tribe could do to help bring it about.

After brush and tree branches had been dragged up to form the encircling fence (called the Bear Dance Cave in one translation) the drummer started sending She Bear the word: It's time to wake up. He did this by rhymically scraping a notched stick (morache), its end resting on a hide stretched tight over an amplifying hole in the ground. The rumbling beat of it would travel through the earth and reach her wherever She Bear was. The dance gave her power to come forth.

Forward and back the two lines of women and men danced toward and away from each other. Hours on end. For five days. In olden times a *ta-waa-vi* with a whip lashed sluggards into line. Anybody who passed out lay there until treated by the shaman making healing passes with a morache rather than the usual feather fan.

On the last day of the dance a man and a woman dressed in bear skin robes impersonate the male and female bear that are now awake. A new song starts, "He is singing. His fur is swaying as he dances." Now even He Bear, siring but unfathering, is awake and out eating "the round grass down by the willow creek." The song includes the rather hetero-fauna line: "He is going to get away with Buffalo's wife."

That last line is the token of what the Bear Dance eventually became — the occasion for the gathering of bands in the spring of each year so that young people could meet non-relatives, fall in love, have affairs, and make the financial arrangements (usually measured in horses) required in getting a mate.

Of late years the Utes have been holding regular annual Pow Wows at their immemorial Ute Council tree at the confluence of the Uncompahgre and Gunnison Rivers at the foot of Grand Mesa. The pow wow, at least so far, has not included the Bear Dance. It may be so sacred they do not wish to make a general-admission show-piece of it. ✿

7

Big and Little Beasts

The first "money crop" on Grand Mesa was beaver pelt. Half a century before any settlers came onto Ute lands, mountain men were running trap lines on the Mesa streams, stretching the hides, and packing them by mule or burro down to the trading post at the base of the mountain.

Antoine Robidoux brought five trappers — among them Sacajawea's son Jean Baptiste Charbonneau — up from the Taos-Santa Fe area where trappers had almost annihilated the beaver population. In fact, because of a fad for men's top-hats made of the silky felt that only beaver fur produces, beavers all over the continent were getting scarce. The west slope of the Rockies was still beaver-rich, and early in the 1830s Robidoux made a special arrangement with Tabeguache Ute chiefs to build a trading post at the confluence of the Uncompahgre and Gunnison Rivers to serve trappers working on the steep geography that would later be named Grand Mesa, the Uncompahgre Plateau, and the West Elks.

Robidoux's Fort Uncompahgre was unique, the Utes had never made such a concession before within territory that hadn't been treatied out of their hands. They allowed it with the understanding that the post would carry "Indian trade-goods:" supplies such as sugar, salt, flour, beads, blankets, kettles, knives, guns, and whiskey; thus saving them the long trek to the Rio Grande for commodities that were becoming necessities as contact with whiteskins made them more and more "civilized."

Robidoux didn't fully comply. He was a fur buyer supplying trappers with their needs — most of the above items plus traps and bait for those mountain men who didn't make their own bait out of beaver glands, plus sugar and spice. He had enough to do carting in trapper supplies and carting out the bales of dried pelts he bought and put through his baler. And trappers were more understandable customers. They came in from a year of solitude famished for fun, and got it by spending most of their pelt-money on whiskey, then took off for the mountains again to trap more beavers.

Indians, on the other hand, hung around, couldn't handle whiskey (nor guns when they'd had whiskey) and required extra watching to keep property from walking off. Utes, like most Indians, were a communistic society — within limits such as horses and wives. If something wasn't being used, and you could use it, there was no wrong and no stigma whatsoever in appropriating it.

Robidoux decided to expand his trapper territory by building another trading post to serve trappers in the Uinta mountains. His pack-train route took him up over Grand Mesa via that old Ute trail and down the other side. A day or so beyond the big river he unintentionally struck oil.

At the mouth of a canyon he came onto a place where black oily stuff was oozing from the ground. In the 1830s there was no use or market for petroleum — even kerosene wouldn't be produced for another fifteen years, people were still burning whale-oil or whatever in their lamps. But Antoine, always the opportunist, found use for it. Dipping stick in the black goo, and turning to the blank rock wall, he wrote what if anybody did it today would be considered graffiti:

> ANTOINE ROBIDOUX
> PASSE ICI LE 13 NOVEMBRE
> 1837
> POUR ETABLIRE MAISON
> TRAITTE A LA
> RY. VERT OU WIYTE

Tar is a lasting substance, the writing is still visible on a rock cliff at the mouth of Westwater Canyon. If you know mongrel French (as "real" Frenchmen term Antoine's grammar) you can read: "Antoine Robidoux passed here Nov. 13, 1837 to establish a trading post on the Green or White Rivers." The Utes destroyed both trading posts, angry that Robidoux hadn't set up the Indian-goods outlet he had promised. Neither post was replaced; the market for beaver pelts crashed about that time, as the style in men's top-hats changed from felt to silk. The nearly exterminated beaver were free to stage a come-back.

Grand Mesa is beaver heaven. Uncounted streams flow between almost countless lakes and pools. Creeks take off in all directions down the mountainside through glades of aspen trees — the beaver's favorite food and construction material. So why don't you see more evidence of them when you are exploring this mountain? A beaver couldn't care less where the water goes after it spills across his dam — straight on down or over toward Joneses. But towns and farmers care. Every trickle of runoff from Grand Mesa is apportioned and makes a programmed detour through city water pipes or country irrigation ditches before final debouch in the Gunnison or the Colorado. You can't have four-legged engineers messing up the system, so when an over-zealous beaver picks out the wrong dam site he is trapped. A few years ago he would have been killed, but not now. Instead he is transplanted to the West Elks or San Juans to work from his genetic blueprint on less critical sources of water.

Some early settlers supplemented their farm or ranch income by trapping and selling pelts, and beaver was among their take. Negro Creek, on the south slope of Grand Mesa, is named for the black homesteader who laid up his stone cabin nearby. The Trapper, they called him.

———

Next biggest "money crop" on Grand Mesa (not counting naturalized aliens such as the cow and horse) was game — deer and elk. First settlers, like the Hawxhursts, reported deer as plentiful as "flocks of sheep spread out to pasture."

Because the supply seemed inexhaustible, there was no restriction on how many, when, or what kind of big game a man could kill. At first hunters slaughtered them solely for hides to sell, there being little market for meat since every family could restock the screened meat-house with fresh venison in less than a half day's ride.

Then as the valleys and lower foothills thickened with people, and as wildlife pulled deeper into the wilderness, professional hunters supplied butcher shops with venison, elk, bear, turkey, and other game, bringing it down off the Mesa and other nearby mountains by pack-train. About this time, too, the iced railroad car became available and tons of wild meat were shipped East, passing west-headed carloads of barreled oysters, providing gourmet fad foods on each end of the line — a gourmet food being any edible that is common to someplace expensively distant from your own table.

Fishing was just as wide-open and commercial. "William Pollett came in with 280 pounds of speckled trout from fishing on Grand Mesa." "Fishing" in quantities that large was usually done by dynamite blasting.

The first Colorado game law was passed in 1884. It stated "no person shall kill, wound, ensnare, or entrap any deer, elk, buffalo or bison, fawn, antelope, or mountain sheep within this state between Jan. 1 and Sept. 1 in each and every year."

There being no restriction on how much game a man could take within season, the *Delta County Independent* noted Jan. 4, 1887, "A load of 27 deer, the last of this season, were brought into town last week, and were offered for sale at 1 3/4 cents a pound, with no takers."

By 1890 the season was limited to three months and one each: "one deer, elk, antelope per person for food only."

Barely in time. In the nine years since the first settler came, antelope and mountain sheep had disappeared. Deer and elk were almost nonexistent on the Mesa. A man and all his sons could hunt a week, prowling game trails, blind-stalking springs, without drawing bead on buck or doe. For a while there was no open hunting season at all; it was illegal to have a piece of deer or elk in your possession any month of the year.

Families had been accustomed to using the best cuts of quarters hanging in the screened meat-house on the north side of the cabin, throwing the rest to the hogs as it inevitably spoiled, then going off to the woods for fresh. But now, with game so scarce they had to find ways to save and use it all. They salted, smoked, corned, and jerked it, and in the process discovered that jerked venison, hammered to powder on a cottonwood stump, made a roux that out-savored anything the French had come up with.

Hunting, when there was again any game to hunt, had changed. It became a family affair, unlike the greedy shoot-'em-for-their-pelts drives that preceded it, and unlike the bag-the-biggest-antlers sporting events that hunting later became. In this interim, with game still scarce, father taught son the ways of deer and elk and bear, the family's winter larder depended on it:

"If you come onto a herd of deer and they're gone," James Fennel wrote, "bouncing out of sight before you can raise gun. Watch how they go. If they all light out in one direction, forget it. Go look somewhere else. But if they scatter, hunker down and wait. They'll be back. They don't like to be alone, and the only way they can get back together is to return to where they broke. How do they know how to get back? By smell. A gland between their split hooves leaks smelly oil, they'll follow their own tracks back. Just wait."

The Carpenter took down the old WWI Winchester and — with Son learning by watching not lecture — counted out half a dozen bullets, expecting to return with game and only one less bullet than he left home with. Which he usually did.

They camped pioneer style, tentless, rolled in blankets on the pine-needle forest floor beneath the hunters' moon. If in those food-gathering, son-tutoring adventures they got cliff-hung with night coming on, were confronted by bear and mountain lion, or lost brakes and skidded a wheel-and-a-half over Crater

View, the roused adrenlin wasn't enough to stick the event in son's memory. A tinier creature did that for life. It happened when the lad was less than hunting-license old. He woke, something other than blanket had touched his face, and there he was, staring nose to nose with a wood mouse.

As the enforcement of hunting laws gradually brought the game back, and science found a way to make cold without waiting for winter to do it, the screened meat-house behind the cabin went out of use. A new industry had developed — freeze locker rentals. Every town encircling the base of Grand Mesa acquired one or more of the frigid places, sawdust floored aisles along stacks of wire mesh compartments, their padlocks guarding pre-cut, paper-wrapped roasts, steaks, and innards of deer, elk, cow, and hog. You could dress out and package your own meat, or the owner would do it for a small charge in cash or kind. No longer must meat be salted, smoked, pickled, or corned to make it keep.

From a basic family food source hunting is now a recreation industry, keeping the state in license money and outfitters in business. Even grocery stores profit as parties of hunters, headed for a camp food binge, buy twice the poundage in goodies they can possibly bag in game.

Of late newspapers warn that hunting is becoming a threatened activity. Deer are getting scarce, forest rangers say. Evidently the rangers haven't looked lower down where towns are pushing suburban lawns and gardens up the mountain side. There deer by threes and fives delicately nibble your rosebuds off, eat your tulips to the ground, and, bedding down on your lawn, watch their reflections chewing cud in your patio windows. Obviously they've learned where the hunting boundaries are and stay clear of them.

———

When Ark Hall was pointing his rifle at his thirty-first bear it failed to fire, and she charged. Dropping the gun, he made up the nearest tree and stayed there while she snuffed the gun over, sat down beside it, and called her cub out of hiding for some timely education in the wiles and weaknesses of the two-legged predator.

Getting tired of looking up at Ark, the two ambled off into the brush. He eased down the tree and was sneaking toward his gun when she came charging back.

Taming deer by hand-feeding—in some cases to the point of mouth-to-mouth refreshments as demonstrated by George Norris—became such a popular hobby that deer herds caught on and relocated. Formerly they were so rare in the lower valleys that a deertrack was something to call the kids to see; now they munch on your tulips while watching TV through your glass doors.

He re-shinnied.

After regarding him thoughtfully for a while she climbed a tree of her own nearby and sat straddling a limb where she could keep an eye on him.

Eventually Ark got hands on his gun, got the bad cartridge out, a good one in, and raw material for another bearskin rug.

A week or so later the editor of the *Tribune,* for whom Ark was always good comic copy, noted that nothing like this would ever happen to Ark Hall again because he had tied a 30-foot buckskin tether between him and his rifle.

Ark, for "Arkansaw" Hall, was one of the colony from that state who, settling the slope of mountain between Austin and Tongue Creek, caused the lower end of Surface Creek Mesa to be called "Arkansaw Mesa" for a time. Ark was the epitome of Arkansawishness of his day, full of jokes, brag, and with an infinite capacity for getting into trouble and out again, on his feet and grinning. Before bridges, and during bridge wash-outs, he ran the North Fork Ferry at the mouth of Black Canyon, providing reliable access to towns and farms along the North Fork, but he tried not to let the job get too serious. Somewhere between his third grandchild and his third wife, Ark jumped off his ferry into the ice-clotted Gunnison with his clothes on just to prove he could still do it without dying of pneumonia.

Ark wasn't the only one to get his name in the paper for being treed by a bear on Grand Mesa — or to prove the immense patience of a mama bear once she has put a man in that fix.

Ed Duke, owner of Duke Mercantile and most of the Hotchkiss Bank, with friend Will Barrows was on the Mesa hunting bear. They found one, emptied their guns into or at it without slowing it much, climbed a tree one jump ahead, and stayed there all night.

It rained. Lacking their jailer's waterproof bearskin gear, they took sick. Dr. Levi Todd treated them for "scare and hanging from a limb for ten hours." The medication was the usual mixture of capsicum, camphor, chloroform, and opium, which he spooned into them himself but probably not from the family's heirloom tablespoon that had emigrated to America — and eventually Grand Mesa — via the Mayflower and Mary Todd Lincoln.

The Duke-Barrows hunting experience, climaxing similar fiascoes, resulted in a female sequel, according to hunter-trapper Robert Head.

"Two young ladies of the North Fork, Miss Edith Hammond and a lady visitor named Miss Shaw, rode out to capture a bear alive. They found a full grown cub, lassoed him and brought him part way back between two taut ropes, one riding ahead, one behind. The rope slacked a little and he clawed it off and escaped."

Head described the ladies as "daring riders, expert with lasso and rifle," who performed this feat "to put to shame some of the young men who have spent hours roosting in a tree while an able-bodied bear stood guard beneath, or have torn up the earth in a mad stampede to get away from same." The ladies, of course, roped their bear from the sidesaddle, those being the days when the genteel world was keeping it secret that women have two legs.

Alex Hawxhurst's diary-memoirs give us a picture of what sidesaddles were like:

"They are a padded affair with a low cantle which extends clear along the right side. There are two padded horns, one of which the lady's right leg hangs over and the other curves downward and the left leg is shoved under this horn. This device prevents the lady from bouncing up and down in the saddle.

"There was a strict code of etiquette always observed. The gentleman would request permission to assist the lady to mount her horse. She may have milked a cow or two, carried water and cut wood that morning but she affected great helplessness about the horse. She was not supposed to know how to untie him. The gentleman would hold the horse with his left hand and take the lady's foot with his right hand and lift her on in that manner.

"When the lady was on her horse and had a good whip in her right hand the assumption of helplessness ended abruptly. If she had a better horse than yours she would run off and leave you. In fact, their idea of a common road gait was a good fast gallop.... Owing to unequal distribution of weight those side saddles very frequently turned, giving the lady a spill, but this was no discouragement to them."

———— ————

Most animals feed either on plants or each other. A few of them — notably man and bear — feed on both. Omnivorous, we call ourselves. And bear seems to be the only other herbivore that turns criminal, killing for nothing but the cold, mad hell of it. Criminal bears are usually hermits, loners, rovers; perhaps exiled by their own "people" for their sins.

Such was Old Club Foot, or Two-Toes. He got his name from the three toes he left behind when he tore himself out of a trap in the fall of 1890. For years that footprint, like a monogram, left no doubt who was raiding the cattle and horse herds on Grand Mesa and nearby mountain ranges. He killed for a meal, killing again the next time he was hungry, never returning to stale meat. Sometimes he killed just to be killing.

A couple of cattlemen caught him in the act of killing a fine large cow and, being armed, they drove him away. Usually when insulted by gunfire he just kept coming on, but this time he ambled off. While they were dressing out the cow to save the meat, Club Foot strolled down the trail a couple of hundred yards and killed another cow, just to show them.

Bullets didn't faze him, except to make him more determined. Smart men stopped shooting at him. Authorities called in Moccasin Bill who had killed more than a hundred bears and was "one of the best hunters that ever lived in Colorado," according to E.M. Getts who wrote about Old Clubfoot for Outdoor Life in 1903, "but when he saw this one he was afraid to tackle him."

Old Clubfoot was killed by a tenderfoot who didn't know he was bullet-proof. The tenderfoot put twelve bullets in him, and not all at a panicky once, either.

F. Mange, recently of Nebraska, was on his first hunting trip ever, and probably because of that had been left in camp by the group of hunters. He was described as "sixty-one years old, a strong, active, very quiet, and cool-headed old gentleman."

The first Mange knew of Old Club Foot was a "woof" behind him, he turned and there the huge animal was coming right toward him. Not knowing enough to be terrified, Mange let the bear go on past "so close he could have touched him with the end of his gun" and shot when he was about sixty feet beyond. Following the bloody tracks, he shot a couple more times, then again just before the bear retreated into some willows. Stamping on the ground to make him come out, he shot twice more, so effectively this time that the bear lay apparently dead. He went over and rubbed the wonderful soft, silky hair before returning to camp to report. When the hunting party went with him to see what he'd bagged, the bear was gone. They tracked him to a hole-up where he lay watching. Mange, never man to take advantage, leaned his gun against a tree and stamped the ground in fair warning. When the bear tried to struggle up he gave him two more shots. The one through the ear finally did the trick.

The reason Old Club Foot was so bullet proof came to light when they dressed him out. He was padded with fat. Getts marveled that "a shot from a Winchester .30-30 at a distance of fifty to seventy-five feet would not penetrate the fat but would simply lodge on the outside of the body. The old animal weighed about sixteen hundred pounds. It measured twenty inches between the ears, and its front legs measured as large around as a man's body. When it stood on its hind feet it was fully ten feet high. The fat on the body was between five and six inches thick." Getts, who eventually owned the rug that Old Clubfoot became, concluded, "The hide was taken to the World's Fair at St. Louis. The bear was one of the largest that was ever known in the Rocky Mountain region."

Grand Mesa's most famous bear hunter was President Theodore Roosevelt, whose hunting prowess was so widely known that toymakers had invented the "teddy bear" to profit on his name and exploits.

Teddy Roosevelt and two friends arrived — by private railroad car, of course — at New Castle in March of 1905. This was only a few months after a presidential campaign which he won by the unprecedented margin of two and a half million votes.

One whole chapter of his book *The Wilderness Hunter* was devoted to that hunt on Grand Mesa without ever once mentioning its name. But we know where he was by the creeks where he bagged bear: Divide Creeks, both East and West, and Alkali Creek, and by where he conducted church services — The Little Blue Hen Schoolhouse. Roosevelt describes the hunting entourage:

"As guides and hunters we had John Goff and Jake Borah, than whom there are no better men at their work of hunting bear in the mountains with hounds. Each brought his own dogs; all told there were twenty-six hounds, and four half-blood terriers to help worry the bear when at bay. We traveled in comfort, with a big pack-train, spare horses for each of us, and a cook, packers and horse-wranglers. I carried one of the new model Springfield military rifles; a 30-40, with a soft-nosed bullet — a very accurate and hard-hitting gun."

What did a president wear while hunting high on Grand Mesa in winter? "...heavy flannels, buckskin shirt, jacket lined with sheepskin, overalls, cap which drew down entirely over the ears, and on our feet heavy ordinary socks, German socks, and overshoes."

He describes that first camp on East Divide: Tents pitched in snowdrifts under leafless aspens beside the ice-rimmed brook. "Fry, the cook, a most competent man, had rigged up a table, and we had folding camp chairs — luxuries utterly unknown in my former camping trips." (This is saying a lot because Roosevelt had hunted almost all over the world by the time he got around to Grand Mesa.) Also it was his first experience in hunting with hounds which put the hunter at a distance from prey and process by forging ahead and barking "bayed!" or "treed!" when they'd found and surrounded the critter.

Doing his own houndless stalking earlier had given Roosevelt some close-up views of the bears' way of life:

"On one occasion the bear was hard at work digging up squirrel or gopher caches — he looked rather like a big badger. On another the bear was fussing around a carcass preparatory to burying it lost his grip and rolled over. This made him angry and he struck the carcass a savage whack, just as a pettish child will strike a table against which it has knocked itself."

Naturalist first, politician second, Roosevelt noted all the growing things he saw — vegetable and animal: "the tiny four-striped chipmunks were plentiful and tame; they are cheerful, attractive animals. We also saw white-footed mice, a big meadow-mouse, and a brush-tailed pack-rat. The snowshoe rabbits were still white on the mountains, but in the lower valleys they had changed to the summer pelage. The long-crested jays came familiarly around camp, but on this occasion we only saw the whiskey-jacks, Clark's nutcrackers, and magpies."

On and on, page after page: Hawks, eagles, grouse — Teddy Roosevelt didn't leave anybody out, and he knew them all by name.

"On Sunday we rode down some six miles from camp to a little blue schoolhouse and attended service. The preacher was in the habit of riding over every alternate Sunday from Rifle, a little town twenty or twenty-five miles away. Ranchmen with their wives and children, some on horseback, some in wagons, had gathered from thirty miles round to attend the service. The crowd was so large that the exercises had to take place in the open air, and it was pleasant to look at the strong frames and rugged, weather-beaten faces."

We can only guess how Little Blue Hen Schoolhouse on Divide Creek got its name. We know it was painted blue, the U.S. President said so. (Probably with some unwanted paint because nobody painted a house or barn blue in those days.) Squatting there all by itself on a brushy bank with its lifted belfry looking around, it probably did resemble just what they called it.

Hunting guide John Goff had told Roosevelt he could count on bagging between eight and twelve bears, but Teddy had a bout of the Cuban fever he had suffered intermittently ever since climbing San Juan Hill. He had to waste several of the assigned hunting days moping around playing whist. In spite of that, and some unusual spring snowstorms, Roosevelt shot three bears, one on each of the three named creeks. In deference, the hunting party shot the babes of the mama bears, leaving the glory of bagging the Big Ones to their president.

Because of the pressure of admirers Roosevelt had to retreat to his railroad car to get some rest, but was wakened by the serenading of New Castle's irrepressible Mayor Parkinson and the Mandolin Boys.

Carved autographs cause wounds that aspens tortuously try to heal. But the larger one was probably caused by a clawing bear leaving his mark.

————

Bears, like other predators, are on the increase because of wildlife protection rulings that in many places favor the eater over the eaten. If a bear ambles up and seems interested in the chokecherries you are picking, let him have them, and avoid eye contact as you back off. According to wildlife specialists, if you look a bear straight in the eye he takes it as a challenge to match muscles and teeth with you.

How many bears roam Grand Mesa today? Nobody really knows. Tallies are made now and then by setting up bear count traps — baited and grated sections of culvert pipe. But the bear — except for its "criminal" loners — is a gregarious animal frequenting hang-out spots where the eating is good. If half a dozen bears are caught and tagged in a given locale the bear population of the mountain can't be estimated by multiplying its square miles by six — you could end up with about as many bears as squirrels! Actually, bears are relatively scarce on Grand Mesa because its dense "black forests" provide little for them to eat. So count yourself lucky if you glimpse a bear, not many people do.

————

Before settlers Grand Mesa was presumably in ecological balance (we can only presume this since nobody then was tabulating plant and animal population booms and busts). It was adequately provided with predators — bears, mountain lions, wolves, coyotes, eagles, owls, falcons, and hawks — and with plentiful creatures for them to eat and control by eating.

Hunting deer and elk almost to extinction had an unexpected and near disastrous effect on the cattle and sheep industry. Predators that had lived safe and easy on the aged, frail and young of deer and elk, were forced to risk their lives raiding guarded herds of livestock. They quickly developed taste and craving for calf, lamb, and colt. Even before wild game played out stockmen organized a war to extinction on wolves, bears, mountain lions, coyotes and eagles.

The wolves went first. None are noted in the newspapers beyond the initial years of settlement. One early camp on the Mesa was besieged by wolves already smart enough to stay out of range of the guns of that day. Lions took longer, and they developed a taste for the sweeter, less gamy flavor of horsemeat.

In early days, when the slopes and shoulders of Grand Mesa were deep-furred with grass, cattle were not trekked up the mountain; instead the flat top was used as a kind of "attic storehouse" for saddle horses not needed at the time. There they turned into wild, stallion-ruled harem bands that increased very rapidly considering that it takes a mare nearly a year to make a foal and only half of the them are mares. As needed for work they were roped and saddle broken with as much resistance as if they'd never seen man before. Some young fellows made a few bucks by noose-trapping, bronc-breaking, and selling those wild horses that belonged to nobody because they belonged to everybody.

Grand Mesa summers were horse-heaven, but winters were cold hell. Like deer, elk, and all other Mesa-top creatures that don't go to sleep or underground, the horses drifted down to sheltered glades at tolerable elevations where they could paw through to grass. Their worst enemy was the mountain lion. Pioneer rancher Edgar Rider described that beast's cleverness in hunting them.

"The dead horses were usually found in downed timber," Rider noted. Apparently the mountain lions would herd horses into a swath of downed trees knowing the hooved animal could only stumble through the maze of fallen logs, one lifted foot at a time. "The horses were hemmed in the tangle, while the lions could jump from log to log and kill the horses quite easily."

As part of their job, ranchhands tracked down mountain lions, working alone or with packs of trained hounds. The hides were his to trade for cash down at the Hawxhurst Grocery or over at Duke's Mercantile.

Ark Hall got into the lion hunting game by copying the two-rope trick used by those ladies on side saddles. He and a friend tracked a lion through a fresh snowfall, treed it, and lassoed it while their dogs held it at bay. Each getting a rope over its neck they stretched the ropes tight, tied one to a tree while the other was held by a horse. A chain was fastened to the animal's neck and it was dragged into town. They held it stretched out on the floor of a saloon while carpenters built a cage around it.

At DeBeque lion hunting went commercial. The DeBeque Lion Hunt became Western Colorado's first big money tourist attraction. For $500 Sam Perry participated in a melange that included "forty horses, many saddles, a grub wagon and cook, two horse wranglers, two packs of hounds, and guides who had what it took."

Hartel Morris trapped mountain lions for zoos. At that time every town big enough to have two grocery stores also had a zoo in the city park. Coyote, bear, lion, antelope, paced all day long in their six-by-six cages, exchanging scents with an imported tiger if the town was big enough to afford it. Highway service stations attracted customers by chaining a bear by the collar out where passing motorists could see him.

The government helped with predator eradication, paying $10 bounty per scalp, stockmen paid another $15. This bounty, plus the sale of the hide, made bear-hunting much more profitable than hiring yourself out to dig post holes.

The bear-bounty industry began to damage the ecology though people didn't use that term, what they said was: "It stinks up the place."

Sheriff Doc Shores noted: "A number of parties engage in this business in summer when meat and pelts are worthless, chiefly for the bounty. Most bears are killed by dead-fall traps, which have to be baited with fresh meat every day; and a great many does, elk, fawns, and mountain sheep are killed to bait the trap these carcasses (along with those of the bears) are left to putrefy on the hillsides and in the gulches."

———— ————

Little Alex Hawxhurst, whose severed finger was saved by the natural cleansing of maggots eating away the rot of infection, grew up to be a man who had an instinctive rapport with wild creatures.

Alex trapped coyotes, he raised them, he studied them.

"To make clear my contention that all animals have a means of making themselves understood among one another I will be obliged to deal extensively with the coyote," he wrote in 1942.

"I would go out in a little district where no one but myself trapped, and I would kill two or three horses every winter to keep the coyotes collected. I would catch some that were simply dumb or nonresident coyotes, but the fifteen or twenty that I couldn't catch or poison were specialists. I would go out when it was snowing hard and set traps in their trails where traps had never been before. The snow would cover the traps and obliterate all signs. About a hundred feet from the first trap they would detour, and after they passed the last trap they would take the trail again. Once in expectation of a good fall of snow I set six traps along a narrow ditch bank, expecting them to snow under. It only snowed about an inch , so the next day I looked the situation over. The coyote had sprung all of the six traps. The tracks in the snow clearly proved that. The only way they could spring them was to lift up the free jaw of the trap and touch the pan. Now to do this they must have understood the mechanism of a trap, which I know they do because once a trap is sprung they ignore it completely. That may not require a reasoning mind, but it is getting along in the borders of it."

With scarcity of big game, the "free" meat of the poor and the thrifty changed from venison to cottontail rabbit, usually supplied with a .22 rifle by the little boy of the family who prided himself on shooting "only through the head," even "only through the eye," or on especially braggy days "through both eyes at once."

There were plenty of rabbits. Almost everything that preyed on them was gone or going via gun, trap or poison. Even hawks — ladies with chickens kept a loaded light-gauge shotgun beside the kitchen door.

Fate handed the world to the rabbits, and they took over. The permanent range deterioration — the barrenness we see on the adobe bench-flats and lower shoulders of Grand Mesa which old-timers remembered as once being stirrup-high with grass — the barrenness that was blamed on early-day overgrazing by cattle and sheep, may have been caused as much by a plague of rabbits.

The rabbit population might have been kept in check or decimated by the diminishing foodstuff to carry them through the winters, but something new was developing in their favor — miles and miles of young fruit tree bark to nibble.

The world had discovered the wonderful fruit that could be produced in the river valleys that encircle this mountain. Virgin soil, as yet pest-free, and watered by purest snowmelt off Grand Mesa. Fruit from these valleys swept prizes at national fairs, was shipped to Europe and as far away as Australia after the advent of ice refrigeration in railroad car and steamship. So much of the valley farmland was converted to orchard that grain and hay for livestock had to be imported. The wide valleys on two sides of Grand Mesa were carpeted wall to wall with fruit trees; strips of orchard stretched up the canyon rivers on the east like hall rugs.

Rabbits had it made. The inner bark of fruit trees is delicious (to rabbits) and very nourishing. With free banqueting like that, summer and winter, they could have babies ad infinitum. One rabbit in just one night can fatally girdle a young peach tree.

"Rabbits and orchards can't exist together!" newspapers headlines screamed.

Communities organized day-long rabbit drives, women served plank-table dinners for the scores of men and boys who elbow-to-elbow swathed the brush in one area after another, their guns sounding like war. A drive that netted only 300 rabbits was dubbed a failure.

"Pest" game hunting was an organized annual event on the north side of Grand Mesa, with Hank Tomlinson and Fred Maigatter as rival captains. Coyotes counted 10 points, bob cats 10, weasels 5, jack rabbits 3, and cottontails 2. Losers treated winners to an oyster supper. The rabbits eventually thinned out, whether from drives, disease, the aging and pulling of orchards or a growing sentiment against poisoning coyotes, eagles, and other predators. Game laws tightened and narrowed, the poisoning of predators was forbidden, and trapping restricted to designated persons.

By the time Chuck Worley was having trouble with mountain lions — last week — the whole scene had changed. What with Colorado Division of Wildlife, the Sierra Club and the animals' version of OSHA (if there is such a thing) coyote and lion now have the upper hand. Luckily there aren't all that many.

Chuck lives on the Grand Mesa bench known as Cedar Mesa; his letters to the editor have occurred with such regularity for so many decades that he is known as the "Unsalaried Columnist." In October of 1996 he wrote that a mountain lion had killed his milk goats in his own pasture. Though the wildlife officer saw to it that Worley was reimbursed for the animals, he said the lion would not be killed, nor even trapped and moved. Under the law she apparently has her own unfenced territorial rights. But a milkoat and her kid are not just reimbursable property, they are beloved pets. Worley quoted an equally unhappy neighbor: "This is an accident waiting to happen. When it has eaten all the available sheep, goats, cats, and dogs, what's to prevent it from going after little people?"

———————

With all the to-do about game and predators, Grand Mesa and its slopes is still chiefly the domain of little rather than large creatures.

Estimating how many kinds and numbers of small animals live on the Mesa is done by area-count; a wildlife officer notes what creatures and how many appear in the area he is watching, and multiplies the count by the acreage of similar areas. Something like figuring out how many mosquitoes are on Grand Mesa by counting the number parking on one square inch of your anatomy, and multiplying by the number of square inches of lake-spangled mountain. Your calculator won't handle it.

If you sit on a log still enough and long enough to become scenery to the creatures, here are a few of the folks who will resume their day's business (or continue their day's dozing unseen) around you:

Beaver, raccoon and muskrat along streams; red squirrels, voles, and snowshoe hares in dense spruce-fir forest; marmots on rock slides; martens, mink, rock squirrels, deer mice, porcupine, badgers and skunks almost anywhere on the mountain; Colorado and Least chipmunks — the later at lower, hotter elevations.

And those are just the wingless. In their spendid Grand Mesa guidebook James and Christine Keener use five of their seventy pages

T.S. Chipmunk and A. Niemand converse in sign lanuage over snacks at Land's End. (Photo by WInfried Niemand.)

just to call the roll on this mountain's feathered fold from hummingbird to eagle.

Though you may never see one, that winged beast, the bat, is numerous. Since Grand Mesa lacks large caves for bats to hang upside down in, they are inclined to bed down (up?) for the day in the rafters of vacant cabins.

"We evacuated more than a hundred bats out of one cabin on the north side," recalls Fred Wild of the Wildlife Commission.

You are not scenery to the chipmunk. You are a vital part of the food supply for whole colonies around camp, picnic, and overlook grounds, such as Land's End where people pause regularly to nibble and share peanuts or sunflower seed while admiring the view.

The chipmunk cannot put on fat enough to hibernate through the winter as bear and marmot do; he must store up enough seed to outlast seven or so months of snow. In an enlarged section of his burrow (which he digs mysteriously without piling any dirt outside) he lays down layers of hulled seed under and around what will be his winter bed which he finishes off with a lining of flower-seed down.

Only as many chipmunks can live in a given area as there are seed producing plants to stock those pantries. When you see a "mean" or "bossy" chipmunk you are looking at a fellow defending his food source, fighting for survival.

Now into this war zone a ranger sets up picnic tables. At once the whole picture changes, you with your sack of sunflower seed have become a part of the assets of the territory; the "boss" chipmunk and all his sub bosses will try to drive others away from you.

When, a few seasons later, the chipmunk population at this table-area has tripled or quadrupled, it's not because the word has got around among forest freeloaders, it's because the added food made it possible for more chipmunks in this favored spot to outlive winter until spring and breeding time. Your peanuts are now vital links in the food chain.

When the site is closed to visitors, picnic tables moved elsewhere, its chipmunk population quickly dwindles — not because the surplus munks have dug burrows elsewhere (territorial "rights" of other colonies would prevent) but because survival has returned to what the plantlife here will support.

If you doubt that the chipmunk has a proprietary attitude toward you, regards you as put there for his benefit, try teasing him — offering but not releasing that peanut. He'll show you who's boss by biting you.

8

Stairway of Flowers

"Roof Garden of the World." Sheets and swales and hills of flowers framed by forests framing countless lakes. Mile after mile after mile. There's nothing like it anywhere else on earth, much-traveled visitors exclaim. From about the first of June to just after the first of October the thousands of meadows are like pretty girls dressed up for a prom.

Because the season is so short the blooming is massive and intense. And diverse — each variety taking its turn at enticing the pollenizing insects. Come up every Sunday and you'll see a different garden every time.

How many varieties of flowers bloom on Grand Mesa? Probably no one knows for sure.

During one afternoon in an acre-size glade near Rim Drive Forks we counted 107 different kinds of flowers. Well all right, some of them were merely different colors of the same thing, such as four hues of Indian paint brush, and some were so small we had to lay flat and use a magnifying lens to properly admire them. But all of the 107 were classifiably different.

How many flowers bloom at the bottom of the Mesa? In some places absolutely none, which in nature is so rare a thing it requires special effort such as creating tight clay-pan flats too rigid for roots, or steep adobe slopes that won't stand still long enough for roots to catch hold.

There are so many kinds of flowers, trees and shrubs on Grand Mesa and its slopes that in the space of one page it would be impossible to list their names and nicknames. To include descriptions, families, genera, and life-habits would take a whole book; and in fact you could go up on Grand Mesa, with illustrated botany book in hand (preferably *Colorado West, Land of Geology and Wildflowers* by two locals, Robert and Joann Young), and discover dozens of little beauties that you can't match up by mug-shot, name, rank and serial number in their book — or any book, there isn't room enough.

In addition to collaborating on books Joann Young, a botany instructor at Mesa State College, and geologist husband Bob conducted June-time wildflower tours of Grand Mesa every Saturday for many years.

But unless getting things classified into slots is your business or forte, not knowing flowers by their given names needn't hinder your intimacy with them. A flower is itself, and was itself millions of years before somebody christened it Convolvulus Linne (an obscenity meaning Bindweed). Naming it hasn't changed it or its way of being itself, which in the case of C. Linne is to spread onto and strangle everything in reach, or conversely to clothe barren roadsides with devilishly beautiful sheets of pink or white blossoms several times a summer. Scientific flower names are solely for the use of the namers; among the uses is creating a selective herbicide that will pick on just one plant such as the decorative but unloved C. Linne.

Grand Mesa has been called a stairway of climates; its one vertical mile stretches from near hundred-degree temperatures at the bottom, to below zero at the top, from less than eight inches of annual precipitation at the bottom to more than forty inches at the top, from barren desert to lush flowery forest.

A president of the United States gave a most vivid description of Grand Mesa's stairway of climates. In 1905 Theodore Roosevelt and his party had just finished a high-country bear hunt in three-foot snow the horses could barely negotiate, killing bear so soon out of hibernation they had empty stomachs. In his The Wilderness Hunter Teddy Roosevelt wrote:

"As we left ever farther behind us the wintry desolation of our high hunting-grounds we rode into full spring. The green of the valley was a delight to the eye; bird songs sounded on every side, from the fields and from the trees and bushes beside the brooks and irrigation ditches; the air was sweet with the springtime breath of many budding things. The service bushes were white with bloom, like shadblow on the Hudson; the blossoms of the Oregon grape made yellow mats on the ground."

———

But Grand Mesa is only a partial stairway.

In the structure of climates, if the basement is tropical and the penthouse is alpine — above timberline but not on the roof of the world where nothing livelier than lichen grows — then Grand Mesa's stairway of climates starts somewhere about the third floor, the valley-bottom altitude at which you might be able to persuade a fig tree to stay alive (as some of the first pioneers did) but couldn't coax it to stop pouting about the chill long enough to produce figs. And the stairway ends a couple of stories short of the height at which a forget-me-not (alpine variety) feels it must put out flower simultaneous with first leaf in order to be sure of getting the reproduction job done in the few days of uncertain summer.

In general each step of the Grand Mesa climate stairway has plant inhabitants specific to it — bottom slopes of sage and greasewood among the elephant-bare adobes; the band of juniper and pinyon that in turn yields to scrub oak and mountain mahogany just below the swath of quaking aspens which give place to spruce and fir on top.

But some plants by drastically changing themselves manage to make a living all up and down the climate stairs; for instance the wild vine called Virgin's Bower or sweet summer clematis.

Along streams and irrigation ditches at the foot of Grand Mesa, clematis sprawls over trees and fences, covering them with feathery mounds in fall. The same plant on of the Mesa top, where it is called Old Man's Hair, grows only a foot high. Old Man's Hair is found in abundance along the western part of Crater View. In alpine passes east of Grand Mesa clematis is so tiny that an inch-high feather sticking out of the quartz gravel is all there is of it.

How heavy the flowering is, and which varieties predominate, all up and down Grand Mesa's climate stairs, depend on how much snow fell in winter, and just when (or if) spring and summer rains come.

On top there is usually plenty of water for all, and in any year there will be a progression of avalanche lily, marsh marigold, buttercup, geranium, scarlet gilia flower, columbine and fireweed etc., from one end of the Mesa to the other — ampler in some places than others but all reliably there.

On the lower rungs of the Mesa ladder, however, mass-blooming flowers are inclined to take turns at the limited moisture available. The seeds or rootstocks of each variety seem to be programmed to a different time-moisture trigger, and will sprout or sit this year out depending on whether the crucial rain comes in the middle of March or the middle of April.

In 1996 the slopes rounding the west base of the Mesa between the Uncompahgre and Colorado Rivers were purple-red with dock, but not in 1997. This year (1998) the roadside borrow-pits near Payne's Siding were fairly awash with purple phlox. Some springs the landscape from mid-Mesa on down will be lacy with wild alyssum; other springs the sand verbena has its turn, spacing the doilies of leaves by which it keeps its jeweled and perfumed bouquets of miniature lilies out of the dust.

Irrigation water can change the kinds of flowers that populate the steps of the floral stairway, providing the right conditions for aliens. For instance where Highway 65 crosses canals in the shade of Chinese elm or cottonwood, little chatterbox orchids stick out their tongues at passing motorists.

That count of 107 different flowers within the space of a stone's throw was made in the wet stage of the eleven-year precipitation cycle (as measured by tree-rings). A mid-cycle, lower precipitation year might reduce the varieties, but scarcely affects the volume of floral color on top of this high tableland.

Drought-coping plants that have been waiting their turn take over, painting the scenery in other colors. Anyone lucky enough to be up here when the Mesa experiences the wet crest of that other climactic rhythm, the hundred-year flood-drought cycle, will have something to write home about! It is possible that current doom-criers, concerned about human-caused climate changes, are not taking these recorded natural, but so far inexplicable, rhythms into their calculations.

Though most plants tend to stay put at favored rungs of the climate ladder, their blooming does not. As the northern hemisphere tilts into more sunlight and the great sea of warmer air rises up the mountainside, its "shore" is marked by a moving tide-line of spring blossoming, prolonging by many weeks the spring available to those of us with boots or wheels to overtake it. Dandelion bloom is a kind of moving place-marker indicating how far up the mountain spring has reached; where the dandelion's first flat gold coin opens, hugging the ground to keep from getting clobbered by cold and snow — that's how far spring has climbed. Of course it doesn't stop blooming then — or seeding! — so dandelion blossoming is more like a highwater stage of spring than a line on its ascent.

———— ————

If it annoys you to measure anything but rage by dandelions, there is an even earlier harbinger, the Easter Daisy that can appear as early as February in protected nooks below the Mesa. Rushing the season, it doesn't take time to grow stems but spreads its yellow-centered, lavender-white flowers flat on the mat of gray green leaves, as two-dimensional as if somebody had painted a still life on the rocks. Almost Sunday-School nice, the Easter Daisy — unlike the dandelion — procreates with decent restraint and keeps on smiling if you happen to step on it.

With summers so short up here, yell the yellow flowers, we have to push the snow out of the way to get our blooming done in time!

Later and higher the sego lilies start fluttering. In a good sego year almost every mountain sagebush will sport one of these thread-tethered petal butterflies. A sego growing bare, beyond the reach of sage, is so rare a sight that the relationship would seem to be symbiotic — nature setting up a situation where each plant helps the other chemically, and neither could make it alone. Actually the lily occupies sage space by elimination, not invitation. Sego is one of the most edible native plants. Indians dug the bulbs for special snacks; cattle and sheep nibble the succulent leaves, stems, and flowers. Sego lilies that are not protected by bristly sage disappear.

Trailing this blooming sequence are cactus and yucca. In almost any spring of any year you'll find cactus blooming en masse in a timed advance right up into gravelly glades among highest pinyons and junipers. The several places on the encircling slopes of Grand Mesa and vicinity mapped "Cactus Park" issue their own invitations. Spectacular yucca years are not so reliable. If you don't have your own favorite yucca-watching site, you could try the lava-rubbly bench-flats and back-slants in the 'dobie hills along the Doughspoon Road.

Naturalized foreigners have moved in on the lower slopes of the Mesa — mainly immigrants from Russia: The Russian thistle (tumbleweed), the Russian Olive, and of late the fiendishly beautiful Russian knapweed. They all keep their place on the lower rungs of the climate ladder. But that global rover the dandelion struts its alien stuff right alongside the monkshood up on top.

Of flower varieties that will cover the Mesa after snowmelt the pentstemon is lowest and earliest. Its misty, powder-blue drifts bring sky to ground in glades and roadsides as far down the mountainside as Hotchkiss Meadow among the scrub oaks. This large opening in the oak and aspen forest is so named because pioneer town-founder Enos Hotchkiss regularly halfwayed his sheep here between winter valley range and summer mountain top. At its peak of natural landscaping a few years ago, this meadow was about as near an English manorial scene as America can come up with — deep green grass sloping down to a brook, a few large quaking aspen trees that had clumped themselves as if posing for John Constable's paint brush, clusters of sheep wearing bright new spring woolens.

One day we hunkered on the road-fill above this sheep-starred meadow, camera poised, waiting for an approaching gap between clouds to hit the scene with sun. It was a long wait even up here where mountain rims shoulder the clouds aside with speed and aplomb. The designated patch of sunlight crawled

These ADCI blossoms (see text for unexpurgated meaning) face all one way just as they should, but about half at this high altitude. The puzzle is, without muscles how does the flower make the swing?

down the hill beyond the brook, crossed, and was inching up into the meadow when somebody in a passing car recognized our vehicle and gave us a friendly shave-and-a-haircut honk. Sheep exploded in all directions toward scrub-oak invisibility. In seconds the only thing living and breathing down there in the sun was a perturbed raven.

There's nothing English about that meadow now. Nature's stage hands are in process of changing the set. Dead-gray aspen clumps demonstrate the shortness of life to their progeny sprouting all down the grassy slope, gaily clapping their quakie leaves in the breeze like spectators at a show. (The root-propagating aspen is a "gay" tree in just about every sense of that word.)

————

On top of Grand Mesa, the first spring flowers bloom just inches from snow. Marsh marigolds and buttercups encroach so close to snowbank it looks as if they are pushing it back, as if the heat of their yellow petals is melting the snow ahead of them. The barest hand-span of mud flowing with ice water separates winter from summer here. The line of flowers follows retreating snowbank right up to where it finally melts away in the shortening shadow of trees that have preserved it.

Buttercups also do this pioneering thing on the banks of Mesa lake-reservoirs all summer long. As water is drained off to irrigate farms below the mountain, and the shoreline slowly recedes to the lake's natural pre-dam level, the buttercups follow it on down the exposed shore, determined sprays of yellow flowers only a couple of feet from the waterline all the way.

Even if you come to the Mesa top after all the snow is gone you can usually tell where snowbanks lasted longest by the blue flowers growing where they were. Whether or not this is merely because blue flowers like shade, and the shade of the pines and spruces is where snow lingers longest, it is notable that drifts of lupines often take just the shape of former snowbanks, with nemophila, gentians, polemonium, and Virginia bluebells scattered through. Unlike its companions in these "blue drifts" however, lupine is found blooming in full hot sun.

Also preferring full hot sun is almost everything that looks like a sunflower, daisy or aster — anything, that is, with petals (usually yellow, but sometimes white, pink or lavender) raying out from a central pad of stuff colored variously from yellow through orange to a brown so dark it is almost black.

At Four Pools, as at thousands of other forest glades up here, flowers yell in full color to attract the caresses of winged inseminators.

A flower built this way is called a Composite because the actual flowers are tiny and packed together to "compose" the glob in the middle — the raying petals are just for show, commercials yelling nectar products at passing bees. A few of the many Composite types on Grand Mesa are groundsel, sneezeweed, coneflower, and a small variety of actual sunflowers which face all one way just as they are supposed to but often in the wrong direction from the sun, as if the cold nights at ten thousand feet had made them too rheumatic and stiff to get the swing-around job done on time.

There are thousands of different kinds of Composites, most of them yellow. There are so many in fact that in scientific circles they have been given their own informal acronym — ADYC.

An eager beaver of a botany student comes up to the professor on a field trip, proudly holding out a hitherto unknown yellow flower for the professor to identify.

He does. "Oh, yes! How intriguing! You've discovered an ADYC!"

Scientific translation of ADYC? Another Damned Yellow Composite.

———

After a few summers up here you learn where to go when in order to see what is at its prime: Out along the prong of Indian Point to Flowing Park for special spreads of gilia flowers and columbine, to Land's End for asters and golden eye, to Crater Overlook for cliff rose and paintbrush, to Four Pools for little elephant and pussy toes, to Trickle Park for glimpses of the shy avalanche lily....

The only end to the opulent color is time and the black cliffs falling away at the Mesa rims.

Plant species on the Mesa find summer living so lush they can bloom in profligate generosity, not needing to forestall extinction by arming themselves against hungry herbivores. Most plants up here don't have thorns, a bitter taste, or self-defensive poison. Those that do are carefully avoided by wild creatures — the bear, for instance, never touches the deadly poisonous water hemlock though it looks exactly like the cow parsnip, one of his favorite foods. Animals that have a history of long association with man, however, aren't that smart. Range cows wolf down larkspur though it kills them — ranchers have lost as much as half the herd by turning their cattle out on Grand Mesa slopes when blue larkspur was at its deadly loveliest. Horses that nibble locoweed become addicts, so hooked on its mind-altering chemicals that they will eat almost nothing else though it gaunts and withers them away.

Profligate as they seem, flowers are picky about who inseminates them. Some flowers, mertensia for instance, tilt their entrance foyers downward to keep out any bastard-pollen toting bugs that are disinclined to walk up hill to reach the goodies. More hospitable varieties such as the pentstemon build protruding-petal landing strips to accommodate flying guests, others such as the snapdragon family are weight-conscious: unless the caller weighs enough to tip down the flower's spring-hung horizontal door he can't get in. This tends to keep family lines pure — the only successful solicitor will be one who has had dealings with another snapdragon. Nor is floral discrimination limited to bugs, some flowers such as the columbine put the nectar bait at the bottom of tubes unreachable for anybody but folks who drink through straws like humming-birds. Few plants carry bias to such extremes as the yucca that closes its petal portals to any suitor except the one with a symbiotic key — the yucca moth.

Message of the Mesa top in summer — meadows glittering with flowers, air shimmering with fliers — is: more flowers make more bugs and vice versa. The more flowers there are the more bugs will have babies; the more bugs there are the more flowers get incidentally pollinated to create more flowers. With the short time-span at human disposal it is impossible to tell whether this Mobius process is on the wax or wane. Does it matter? Fossils in strata beneath us in this very Mesa tell us the earth was green and lush long before floral sex was invented.

———— ————

If all this talk about sweeps of flowering glades and meadows gives the impression of emptiness, that there are no people on Grand Mesa, look again. All summer long — and winters too since the advent of cross-county and down-slope skiing and snow-mobiling — the Mesa has about as many people as chipmunks and deer. But the place is so beautiful it tames almost everybody into flowerlike gentility to match. There are, however, a few exceptions; people who haven't breathed inside this heaven long enough to become mannered.

There was the Brooklyn lady with the little boy.

At that "107 Varieties Forks" we had set up a reformed cardtable holding camera — separated from its lens by a long, sliding micro bellows attachment — mounted within a plastic-covered cube that the Carpenter had made to transmit light but keep the slightest breath of breeze from making a bobbing smudge of the blossom that was going to sceen-size. (The Carpenter wasn't with us. He was off doing his own flower thing — constructing the gigantic wooden morning glory form that would shape the Paonia dam spillway.)

The flower targeted by the long lens was one we've never seen in life or book or since, a pinhead orange globe poking out a purple tongue. We were working against time — who knew how many minutes or seconds the root of this unknown flower could survive separation from its nurturing soil? The long sliding lens was stretching its neck to within kissing distance of the tiny flower

whose camera "smile" was going to be a hundred times larger on film than in life when....

"How int'resting!" somebody jostled us in a Brooklyn accent, "Step ovah, woncha? My son oughtta see this!"

Luckily, when the boy (totally uninterested) had looked as long as she thought he should, the tiny flower was still there, its petal-mouth sagging open as if agape at such manners.

–––––– –––––

Grand Mesa flowers have provided lavish floral backgrounds for many weddings without losing a petal. Both formally — bride wafting gauzy train across a rosy gilia flower meadow to join tuxedoed groom standing on a carpet of blue lupin beneath an altar-like fir tree. And informally — twosome wearing backpacks on cliff-edge rocks embroidered with purple asters, pledging to explore life together; couple on horseback silhouetted against a lakebordered with buttercups, taking vows to ride into the sunset together.

It is illegal to pick flowers in the National Forest but one person, our sister Eileen Kempf, got permission to gather as many as she wanted. Eileen headed the Goodwill Rehabilitation center in Montrose that was established to provide the mentally handicapped with experience in working at useful jobs and getting paid for it. Workers in the Montrose and Grand Junction centers had been doing unstimulating tasks — a few repetitive moves on a piece of something that was sent to Japan for assembly into a recognizable tech product. All day long, day after day. Enough to make anybody mentally woozy. Eileen Kempf wanted work they could do from start to finish, taking pride in what they had completed. She created it — Colorado Wildflower Stationery.

With special permission and the advice of the Botany Department of Colorado State University as to endangered species, she took her workers by bus to the top of Grand Mesa where they snipped flowers, pressed them between the pages of books, and took them back to the shop to make into "flower windowed" stationery. An oval window in each sheet was cut and char-framed with a burning iron, then "paned" with plastic holding a pressed columbine, pensteman, or violet. The workers had the satisfaction — and monetary reward — of seeing their creative work pay off, selling in selected gift shops on both sides of the Great Divide.

––

The mystery of mushrooms living off the fat of the log.

Cerise-purple fireweed closes the season of mass blooming on top of Grand Mesa. When fireweed has finished flowering, and is making ready to pull the ripcord of its pods and release its children in silk floss parachutes to the winds, that's when the on-top aspens briefly blaze up and quickly shed, making a golden carpet of their golden roof. Everywhere up here life-forces pull in — draining juices earthward, twig into stem, stem into root — leaving Sky Island to the evergreen spruce that is winterized with fragrant antifreeze.

Fall comes down the climate stairway just as spring went up, slowly, a step at a time. The highest aspen groves are through with glamor and stripped down to furry winter gray while the lowest quakies are tentatively changing from green to lemon. When the hemisphere's sea of summer warmth has ebbed as far down as scrub oak they flare up red and brief as brush-fire. Lance-leaf trees growing along steep streams cross-thread the ebbing "shore line" of summer, lacing ribbons of yellow down the mountainside.

When autumn reaches valley-floor cottonwoods it lingers, hemming Grand Mesa all around the bottom with two weeks worth of orange-gold ruffles. ✻

9

Forked Tongue Creek

It's altogether fitting that Pack Saddle Jack, who talked himself out of countless criminal charges, lived on Forked Tongue Creek. But that's not how the creek got its name.

U.S. government surveyor Hayden officially named it Forked Tongue Creek because the stream lies oddly straight from its mouth on the Gunnison River to Ward Lake up on top. Into it a great fan of tributaries drain the south side of the mountain from Point Peninsula to Trickle Reservoir — the whole area of natural lakes and reservoirs known as "The Grand Mesa Lakes."

Stand on the Mesa rim, at the first overlook after Highway 65 drops away from Deep Slough, look down and you will see how strikingly straight the creek is, confining all its wiggles inside a trough that looks as if somebody (eons of erosive years ago) had bulldozed an eight-lane highway part way up the mountainside.

Togo-makuti, Indians called it. Literal translation in our Ute dictionary is "Stream Flowing Straight Up to the Top." (Ute names for places are usually explicit descriptions, verbal trail markers, so that the hearer will recognize the place when he comes onto it.) Don't get the Utes wrong, they didn't believe water can run uphill, their double use of "straight" was like our puns, meaning that the channel of the creek is conspicuously straight, and that following it is the straightest, quickest way to put moccasin on top of mountain.

But Forked Tongue Creek itself got cheated.

First it was cheated of half its name. Homesteaders who settled Forked Tongue Creek were still too close to the Indians' use of the term ("Pale face speak with forked tongue") to want to be thus designated to God and the

whole world by address and map. The adjective "Forked" was delicately deleted from Forest Service Maps.

Then it was cheated of half its designation. By rights the name Tongue Creek should have continued right up to the source, the in-line branch, the one that heads straight for where you are standing on the overlook just below Deep Slough. Instead this upper half is called Ward Creek for an early settler.

Much earlier Tongue Creek was cheated of half its water — most of the water that is carried down by tributaries of Young and Milk Creeks.

In good geological tradition, streams converge as they travel toward the sea, brooks flow into creeks, creeks join rivers, digging their orthodox valleys deeper as the eons pass. But not this offshoot of Milk Creek. Separating rather than converging, it splits off from Milk Creek and takes out across country like a teenager with a backpack.

It stymied geologist Hayden. He observed that instead of creating a valley for itself as all the other Mesa streams had done, it hardly made a dent as it traversed the long slant of mesa bench, paralleling Tongue Creek to within two miles of its mouth. Hayden labeled it Surface Creek for this eccentricity, and went on to deeper things.

———

The Tongue Creek mysteries may have changed the life direction of a boy who grew up among them. Gerald Loucks was born and raised on Surface Creek near Eckert. Role models of the day were cowboys riding for the fabulous Bar I cattle ranch and the Figure 4.

The Bar I (pronounced Bar Eye) began with the "sooner" cabin Pierre Settle built before the Indians went out. It grew to take in a whole mountainside of spring and fall grass leading to and from summer range on top of the Mesa. It was a group affair; every time they took in another landed partner they brought a few thousand more cattle up from Texas. As over-grazing decimated the natural forage in the lower valleys, winter feed had to be grown in grain, hay, and alfalfa fields. Hay and alfalfa could be stacked, but silage had to be stored. The three towering silos still stand. Laid up like five-story hogans of squared logs, held together with wooden pins, they form the nucleus for the "Old Town" cluster of pioneer buildings recently formed into an outdoor museum by the town of Cedaredge which now almost surrounds the Bar I silos.

By running faro tables in mine-born Lake City, and running cattle on Grand Mesa Ed Hanson made enough money to build this "Castle" on Leroux Creek. Cornering fireplaces used one chimney to heat three rooms.

ABOVE: This saloon was a part of "old Town" a streetful of pioneer-style buildings built by Don Reed on the mesa bench above Eckert. Old Town moved down and became the basis for Pioneer Town Museum in Cedaredge. LEFT: Bar I Ranch silos, built like Navajo hogan-sided timbering are just as enduring. They are now a part of the Old Town Museum in Cedaredge.

The Bar I ranch was almost a town in itself. Besides those silos there were dwellings for owners and a manager, a long bunkhouse for the crew of twenty or so, a cookhouse putting out three meals a day for the crew and seasonal hands, a huge barn and hayloft for the best horses, sheds for dairy cattle, granary, buildings where butter and cheese were made, an ice house, and a butcher shop — all powered by a water wheel over on the creek.

The Bar I had owners to equal the impressiveness of those silos. The original core of land was homesteaded by Pierre Settle, driving over from the gold-boom town of Lake City in the company of 500 cows with calves. He sold to a group of rich men—one of whom, Henry Kohler, became manager and was a bank director on the side. Henry was a genius at sensing opportunities and getting other men to help attain them. During his leadership the company built those silos and that barn, and acquired not only the earth that now supports the small city of Cedaredge, but "owned" the right to graze cattle in a wide swath to the top of Grand Mesa. When he sold his interest he went to Milwaukee and started the Kohler Paint Co; yes, the same Kohler company you bought that deck-floor paint from last spring. The next owner was a man named Powers whose father was known as "the Quinine King" of Philadelphia at a time when that herb drug — the only known treatment for malaria — was

beginning to be manufactured from salts of coal tar. Powers sold to Zanetti whose claim to fame rests on his daughter's voice which was so wonderful he sent her to Italy for singing lessons. Another owner, banker Stockham, increased the company holdings by siphon-forcing Grand Mesa water to the top of that smaller flat island in the sky, Antelope Hill. He made one huge orchard of its tabletop and rimmed it all around with wind-breaker cottonwoods standing like a fringe of dark picot crochet against the sky up there. When the Great Depression struck Stockham was one of many bankers in the nation who decided not to outlive their failures.

Illustrious bunch. And with crew to match — cowboys riding by, lordly in their saddles....

They awed the socks off most boys, but sixth-grader Gerry Loucks wasn't impressed. Even before he got his hands on his first geology book Gerry had been out exploring the country, poking at Milk Creek fossils, prowling Tongue and Surface Creeks wondering why they were so queer. Why hadn't Surface Creek cut itself a valley like all the other creeks? Why was Tongue Creek bordered by soft adobes on one side and cliffs of hard rock on the other side? All the way up!

By the time he was in the seventh grade Gerry Loucks knew he was going to be a geologist. After graduating from Colorado University he and a partner operated a geological advisory business in Denver for a time, and he is presently consultant geologist for Anschutz there. All without even loosening his roots on Surface Creek. Beside its banks he built the family home, triple decked for views of the fascinating geology of this Island in the Sky. He commutes from the job by private plane to spend his weekends there.

Matching what he read in books with what his eyes beheld, Gerry Loucks soon got Surface Creek figured out: Late in post ice-age history it had been diverted down across Surface Creek Mesa when a glacier dammed Milk and/or Young Creeks. It hasn't carved itself a valley because it is still too young and the ground is too hard. That ground is a long, deep glacial outwash of gravels, earths, and boulders that sweeps down Grand Mesa almost from the top. Many-layered, representing millennia of deposits, it splits around the adobe remnant called The Mounds, rejoins near Cory, and ends in bluffs overlooking the Gunnison River. Tongue Creek flows straight because it scrapes the west side of the outflow, unable to do more than make a line of rubbly bluffs

PREVIOUS LEFT: Moonrise over Quill Pill Hill, during the bluff's transition from a good place to put the barn-lot for drainage, to a beautiful place to put picture windows for viewing.
PREVIOUS RIGHT: Putting the house on the edge of the bluff for the view—instead of the barn for the drainage—started with this house and continued on up the mountain.

because the outflow cap protects the underlying soft shales, just as its lava cap protects the mountain.

Those bluffs above the Gunnison are now dubbed Quill Pill Hill for the writers and doctors (one is actually both, a doctor of divinity who writes) who have built homes on the edge of the cliff overlooking river, peaceful farming valley, and sunset-painted San Juan Range eighty miles away. It wasn't always this way. When the Carpenter began building the first house on the cliff-bluff above the river folks were tolerantly amused at his ignorant misuse of a natural resource. A sensible person would put the house back a ways like everybody else, leaving the edge for barns and pigpens where the drainage of the fall-off would do your dung chores for you. And he was warned that a crack could develop behind his house, scooting the whole point down into the river, and was shown places where this had happened. Invariably these sites were not boulder-strong glacial outflow buildup, but a bench-rim of adobe Mancos shales, subject to small-scale Toreva-block slumping if a farmer over-irrigated the ground behind it.

The outwash that formed Surface Creek Mesa is only one of many such outflows around Grand Mesa powered by gravity, by the fantastically heavy precipitation of that time, and pushed from above by the slow flow of glacial ice. (If you need to get technical, this is called upper Pleistocene). The grinding movements mingled rock material from all the intervening strata up to and including the lava flow on top, creating rich and easily worked farmlands wherever these outflows occur.

———— ————

Like the whole mountain, Tongue Creek has tended to draw events and personalities to match its odd geology. (Or is it that oddities stuck faster in pioneers' memories than ordinary daily living — like today's newscasts that come up with a new weird murder every morning and have nothing to say about ten million Californians who got through the night without killing anybody.)

There was Tongue Creek Hermit Gray, who at rare intervals of absolute necessity ventured from his crooked side canyon to walk to town, gunnysack over shoulder, for supplies and a fresh look at what the world had been up to in his absence. He was invariably disappointed. In 1889 the situation looked so bad that he felt obliged to come out of seclusion and straighten things up by officially announcing his candidacy for president of the United States. He didn't win.

Then there's George Beckley's two-story house at the mouth of Tongue Creek. The "Haunted House," children called it, making up stories about its tall

loneness to scare each other with. It might better be called the "Indestructible House."

It never did have a foundation, sometimes it has had almost no flooring, sometimes it has had almost no ceilings, often it has had no windows; woodpeckers have perforated it, sunlight has shafted through its shingles, but it stands as firm and foursquare now as the day it was erected a hundred years ago, surviving both the wear and tear of being inhabited and long periods of standing empty to the elements.

You'll have to look for it; it no longer stands alone like a monument on its bare mound. You can see it to your left, when you cross the bridge on Highway 65 headed up into Grand Mesa. Tall and dark, half hidden among newer structures of the present Rozman Ranch.

Pioneer George Beckley came from Tin Cup where he was building cabins for mine-boomers. He took up the first claim on the Forked Tongue, built a cabin which the undammed creek promptly swept into the Gunnison. George resolved the creek wouldn't get the next roof he put over his family. He hewed aspen beams a foot square and as tall as the two-story house was going to be, and fastened them together with mortise and tenon joints pinned with oak. The four walls were assembled flat out on the ground, pointing toward the four directions of the compass. Then with block and tackle and the pulling power of his ox team, the walls were raised one at a time and pinned together by driving oak pins through previously drilled holes.

His son Mort remembered: "Pa drilled those holes on the ground, and when the timbers came together up there you couldn't ask for a better fit.

"We used oxen because they pull steadier than horses. A horse gets excited if he thinks the load is too hard for him to budge, but an ox just lays in there and pulls sure and steady, until something gives, either the load moves or the yoke and chains break."

Over the timber framework Beckley laid outside walls of vertical boards, hauled down from the sawmill by those same oxen. The square nails he pounded are still holding the boards firm. Laying floors and partitions he made eight rooms for his family — seven girls and five boys. Somewhere in there, under tag ends of wallpaper layers is the date George Beckley carved, 1888.

Since the Beckleys the house has been home and shelter for sheepmen, cattlemen, a government hunter-trapper, squatters, and woodpeckers — without in a whit weakening its stolid strength. The "Haunted House" is

The "Haunted House" that George Beckley laid out on the ground and lifted into place with oxen.

probably the oldest unrestored, as-it-was, historical building in this half of Colorado, if not the entire state. The Rozman family aims to keep it that way.

———————

And then there were those two characters on opposite sides of the law — Pack Saddle Jack and Ott Peterson. One quite bad, and the other who started that way but turned out so good people could hardly stand him.

Pack Saddle was a robber by trade, but he homesteaded on the side, taking up land near Brimstone Corner on the Tongue extension called Ward Creek.

A slick worker, he acquired his nickname from stolen goods (mainly money) he packed off, misdeeds that he was occasionally arrested for but seldom convicted of. By practicing his calling outside the county he usually went scott free because in the days before coordination of local, state and national enforcement the power of the law usually stopped short when a sheriff's horse stepped across the county line.

On the homestead, within his home county, he religiously kept the law and a low profile, creating a safe, unsuspect retreat to hole up in after an unsanctioned transfer of property. If he had been able to keep from beating his wife he might never have been arrested for train robbery.

The train was No. 5 passenger train, the year was 1904, the place was Parachute on the north side of Grand Mesa. He got on, got the money, got off, and got away with it as usual. Either the law didn't know Pack Saddle was involved, or it couldn't lay a hand on him. Arrived back home he released post-robbery tension routinely by beating his wife. This time she called the law.

Her action was doubtless taken after long suffering because according to the statutes of the time a woman had to prove she had been subject to beating for at least a year before she could bring charges.

Wife beating was no rarity, but it was rather frowned upon; one judge chided a Russian immigrant at the town of Read for over-disciplining his wife, temporarily crippling her, because she wasn't getting the milking done fast enough. His honor explained that things were different in America and that here the right to hit with fist or club did not as a matter of course go along with other property rights in the female spouse.

Pack Saddle Jack got fifteen days.

The publicity was slight, about three lines of print, but enough to bring him to the notice of Doc Shores, famous Gunnison County sheriff who had escaped the restriction of county lines by becoming a D&RG railroad detective. Doc arrested him for train robbery; he was tried and, as usual with Pack Saddle, turned loose for lack of evidence.

The Humane Society took Jack's children away from him and put them in the Grand Junction Indian School. When it was discovered they hadn't a drop of Indian blood, they were denied this advantage and sent to the State Home. Jack's wife stayed with him — whether foolishly because she loved him, or desperately because she feared he would kill her if she tried to leave.

If Pack Saddle Jack hadn't so vigorously defended his God-given right to beat his wife he might never have been tried for murder.

By now his hidey-hole was Taos, New Mexico. The Taos justice of the peace who found him guilty of "family disturbance," who not only fined him but had the gall to lecture him, was so thoroughly righteous, outstanding, and well-liked that Pack Saddle couldn't bear it. With 40-70 Winchester in hand, he slipped up to the uncurtained window where Justice R.C. Pooler sat reading by lamplight, and shot him dead.

For this Pack Saddle Jack got 99 years. He would have been hanged by the mob if the law hadn't slipped him to Albuquerque. He might have been hanged by the law if he hadn't, as usual, convinced the jury the evidence was only circumstantial. ❧

10

Hell and Brimstone Corner

As for Ott Peterson, according to newspaper accounts and his own admission, he didn't start out much better than Packsaddle. The son of pioneer parents, he grew up near Brimstone Corner.

Brimstone Corner? One of the few places on this creek-frayed mountain where two straight roads cross at right angles, the Corner was en route to a couple of country schools. Because of seasonal farm work, boys frequently couldn't put in enough time to graduate from the eighth grade until sixteen or so, well after hormonal belligerence set in. In those days even the tiniest teacher could maintain order in classroom and school ground, so the most a fellow could do was growl under his breath, "I'll beat the hell out of you on the Corner after school!" The same situation applied at dances, which were also held in the schoolhouse. Since fighting at dances was considered gauche, combatants were dispatched to the Corner after which they wended their several ways home battered and beatific. Fights occurred with such regularity that the place became known as "Hell and Brimstone Corner." In mapping the Corner the United States Geological Survey did away with Hell.

"The Peterson boys," recalled one of their descendants, chuckling, "started and starred in most of these events." That was just Saturday nights, during the week the Petersons were a hard-working bunch, successful at their farms, lumber mill, and coal mine. But these seldom made news; Ott did.

What Ott and his father, Otto A., kept getting in trouble for wasn't fighting, it was fishing and hunting. At first they weren't breaking any game laws because there were none to break.

From Hell and Brimstone Corner the old Colby store was the closest source of cut plug chawin' tabacca. Time and disuse, not rowdy misuse, accounts for its sad condition.

In 1896 when Ott was nineteen the paper reported as a matter of community pride: "The elder Peterson and his sons caught 200 lbs of fish out of the Gunnison." This was done with seining and trout lines. On Grand Mesa it was often done by dynamiting the lakes. Fishing and hunting were commercial. Iced trout, elk and deer meat, as well as hides, went eastbound from Delta and Grand Junction depots by the carloads.

By the time game laws were in force, there was almost no game left. As Forest Ranger Bill Kreutzer said, "A haunch of venison was almost as much of a curiosity as one of the new-fangled automobiles."

———

The Peterson family were bedrock pioneers — that is, they came in early and by the door. Other settlers climbed in over mountain passes from the east and south, but the Petersons came in at ground level — from Utah by way of the Stinking Desert and the ancient salt Lake Wagon Road. (Nobody knows why the fifty miles of flats along the bottom of Grand Mesa between Grand Junction and Delta is called the Stinking Desert. Hot it is, but grassless it was not at the time of naming — perhaps the infrequency of creeks put bath water too far apart.)

When they came wagoning in — Ott was barely four at the time — the family was already experienced at pioneering. Twenty-five years earlier Petersons had been part of the Mormon Migration, pushing handcarts across the plains from the Missouri to the Kingdom of Deseret on Great Salt Lake, and they had driven Mormon "stakes" into new country at intervals thereafter.

Coming so soon that they met the straggler Utes trailing out, the Petersons felt possessive about fishing, hunting and timbering. Defiant of upstart government meddling they went right on doing what came natural even after the U.S. Forest Service was created. The whole county felt the same. Even before the Grand Mesa feud, when Radcliffe had the Petersons arrested for using seine and grab hooks on Mesa lakes, but they were acquitted though the evidence was clear. Significantly, Womack, who was later killed in that feud, was one of the jurors in the Peterson case.

Usually law-breaking hunters weren't even arrested. And if so, Ranger Kreutzer had a hard time getting anybody prosecuted, especially a Peterson. "Civil authorities couldn't or didn't cope with the situation," he complained later in fellow ranger's book, *Saga of a Forest Ranger*.

Following a tip, Kreutzer found five deer carcasses hanging on the back of the Peterson cabin. This was during the time when, to restore wiped-out game herds, there was no open hunting season at all, the killed meat was pure thumb-nose illegal. But when Ranger Kreutzer called the law, Sheriff Hunt refused to come, saying he couldn't get Justice of the Peace Colonel Boyd to issue warrants for hunting and fishing violations.

The common and official view was that hunting and fishing are a natural right. A man had a duty to defend that right by defying pushy laws, even if he didn't need meat at the moment.

Then suddenly we find Ott on the other side of the law.

When Otto C. Peterson became a game warden, it was like a religious conversion. All the zeal he had used in outwitting and defying game wardens, he now used against violators. He went at the job with a kind of controlled rage as if every creature in the forest was under his personal protection, as if the whole structure of the law would collapse unless he enforced every wisp of it.

What changed him? Well, for one thing he had shot and wounded a man in defending his rights in a ditch-water dispute; and though he was acquitted, it was disquieting to see how far things could go in one reflex moment when a man took the law in his own hands. For another thing his father, whose Old-World stubborn-mindedness he always adored, had died but not before backing down to one lawman — Ranger Kreutzer.

As Ott explained to Kreutzer when they finally met as colleagues rather than adversaries, "In those days back in Cedaredge, I always admired your way of going straight down the line without fear or favor. I couldn't forget it. One day I decided maybe you were right and I was wrong. I had to find out, so I applied for a game warden's commission."

One of the things he couldn't forget was the incident of the Co-op telephone poles.

Ranger Kreutzer found them, piles of fresh cut Douglas fir poles along the newly surveyed Co-op telephone line from Delta to Cedaredge. He hadn't issued any timber-cutting permits so he knew they'd been cut in defiant trespass. He tagged them government property, and waited. The Petersons stormed in demanding to know by what right he claimed their telephone poles. He informed them the tags would stay until the fine, plus stumpage, was paid.

"After considerable argument the elder Peterson offered to settle."

This involved going up into the wilds of upper Ward Creek with three Petersons to count the stumps. The sons were not visibly armed, but the elder Peterson carried a rifle which at odd moments was pointed at Kreutzer.

The Ranger noted later, "He was a good shot, and the gun might go off accidentally.... The old man had recently shot a gun and two fingers from the hand of George Hyder of the Bar I Ranch. Hyder had attempted to draw on him but had been too slow."

While the elder Peterson was crouched down drinking at the stream, Kreutzer picked up the gun, extracted the cartridges, handed it back to him, and told him not to reload. The old man cursed, threatened, but obeyed.

The back-down appears to have had a great effect on son Ott looking on. Years later a friend of the family, Ulan Austin, said, "Those Petersons! They were all out, completely one way or another, no in between. And not afraid of anything!" Young Ott was looking at a man, unarmed, who wasn't afraid of a Peterson.

Once he switched sides, Ott set out to be "the best damn warden there ever was or would be — and he damn well was," Kreutzer said, adding "and the most hated."

Though he hounded violators in an area from Lake City to Rifle (game wardens were not subject to county line restraints) Ott always seemed to be exactly where any one violator had just bagged illegal game. It wasn't sixth sense, it was thirty years of woodsmanship and hunting tricks learned on the far side of the law.

"Don't pull the trigger," George Huff's father advised his small son, "till you're sure you can kill the deer with your first shot. If you have to shoot again, Ott'll triangulate the sound and he'll get you."

George was ten at the time. His job was to keep the Huff family in meat — older brothers with more size were helping the old man force crops out of difficult adobe land west of Tongue Creek. The only meat they could afford was free (and illegal) venison.

One day, the Huff pantry being desperately bare, little George was so nervous he shot two or three times. Sure enough, Ott got his trail. George dismounted, whipped his pony toward home, and hid in the brush. Ott Peterson, grim and tenacious in dealing with adult violators, was not one to pick on a kid. Seeing the pony couldn't have carried anyone very big, he didn't trail it home.

In spite of Ott's apparent ubiquity, he wasn't a full-time game warden. On the side he was a stockman-farmer over in Cactus Park — where else, with a personality like that? By building reservoirs on the mountain top and ditching miles of flowing water down, he turned the whole expanse from cactus thorns to lush alfalfa, but the Park stubbornly retained its prickly name.

Newspapers wasted little space on reporting Ott's innumerable arrests for routine poaching. An item had to be something peculiarly Ottish:

"Otto Peterson arrests 4 men, 10 dogs, and 4 dead bears. Hunting with dogs is illegal."

The paper didn't explain whether the arrested dogs served time. The bears, presumably, were well out of it.

Ott could smell out illegal meat even after it was processed. Suspecting that some of the smoked hams hanging in Ellis Blackman's meat shed might be venison, he took down and sniffed each one. Ellis passed the test, and then — level-eyed — advised Ott never to meet him in the woods.

Dynamiting fish outraged Ott to the point that merely apprehending a man wasn't enough:

"Otto Peterson arrested some six Leadville men in Lake City for having too many fish of two little size, said to have been taken by dynamiting. One of the men (perhaps) resisted arrest, at any rate he claimed Otto poked him in the jaw and knocked out a tooth."

But Ott's zeal in enforcing the letter of the law is best exemplified in the taking of smaller game.

On a day in May, 1929, Ott arrested W. H. Dickison for catching suckers in the Gunnison. Suckers! And Dickison had a permit, too, from the Fish and Game to seine-fish for a distance of three and a half miles below Delta. A permit, but no fishing license. $25 and costs.

And then there was the matter of the prairie dogs.

At this time these rodents were so numerous and so busy perforating irrigation laterals that prairie dog poison was advertised and advised.

One farmer preferred to shoot the ones on his land, and Ott caught him doing it. Did the farmer have a hunting license? No. $25 and costs.

The judge in this case demurred, but Ott Peterson read the law to him too.

———

Unrestricted hunting for elk meat, hide and horns virtually wiped out the herds on Grand Mesa and the Elk and West Elk Ranges which had been named for their large elk population. After the passage of laws that made it illegal to kill elk anywhere anytime, the herds were just beginning to make a noticeable comeback when they were hit by a new species of hunter. All this species wanted was their two front teeth.

This was at the height of the fraternal lodge era, when lodges had become social and status organizations rather than merely insurance providers for groups of immigrants. Most males belonged to one or another brotherhood and wore insignia to proclaim them Knight, Oddfellow, Eagle, Moose or Elk. For members of the Benevolent and Protective Order of Elks the totem insignia was a couple of gold-mounted elk teeth dangling from the watch fob.

The newspaper noted: "Though there has been no open season for elk in twenty years, in the past season wardens have discovered bodies of sixteen elk from which teeth only, and no part of meat or horns, had been removed."

Ott, of course, was right there. A later issue states: "Ott Peterson arrested Tony for unlawful killing of elk and possessing four sets of elk teeth... four beautiful sets which Peterson will send to Game Commissioners as they are now state property."

Elk teeth were ridiculously valuable, several thousand dollars for a perfect pair. (To get an idea of how much money that was, one thousand dollars at that time would buy two brand new automobiles.) With stakes that high not even the law could stay legal.

"Otto Peterson," the paper noted, "pinched another Gunnison County deputy sheriff for killing elk on the Muddy."

A man didn't have to actually kill elk himself to get Game Warden Ott Peterson on his trail. Apparently Ott could scent elk teeth right through a combination lock. Taking Warden Jennings along as witness, Ott entered the Paonia jewelry store and demanded to look into the safe. Jeweler P.C. Curtis obediently opened it and seemed as surprised as anybody at what he beheld — a tray holding thirteen sets of elk teeth. The newspaper commented, "The officers took possession and told the thoroughly mystified jeweler he was under arrest."

You wonder where all those confiscated elk teeth are now. With no Ott Peterson to guard government property from government employees did they melt away? Or are they still locked in a bureaucratic vault somewhere? If so, will a future archeologist come along — after the mountains have done their rising-sinking, take-it-on shake-it-off act a time or two — and while poking around with his pick discover elk teeth fossils lying in a certain strata near some vault-shaped iron stains in the rock, and try to reconstruct an ancient civilization where the antlered beast *Cervus canadensis* had free run of the office? ❧

//

Goodies in the Layers

Old Man Moore discovered oil on Grand Mesa by lighting his pipe. He happened to be standing over a gas leak and almost got his beard seared off.

Schoolboy Gary Thompson discovered a sea-going version of the dinosaur just above town.

Red Davis, using a kettle for retort, made patties of Grand Mesa gold in his backyard.

Ira Sanborne, first to drive a pick into the Mesa's eleven billion tons of coal, was so unimpressed with his find that he rode off, telling blacksmiths to come get it.

Strata formations involved in the above episodes are fairly recent in the Grand Mesa geological soap opera. (Definition of a soap opera? A cliff-hanger story that just goes on and on and on, cliff after cliff. Sure fits geology!)

Oldest visible layer of the Mesa is the Dakota Sandstone at the bottom. Like the names tacked onto the other five formations that compose the mountain, it has nothing to do with Grand Mesa or anything contained in the strata. If Utes had done the naming the layers would have descriptive designations such as *oa-gama-ti* "Tasting of Salt" and *kaa-pawiya-vi* "White Clay for Grinding into Body Paint." Instead, the usual mode is to tag a stratum by the place where the geological sleuth happens to be when he first identifies it — which in this case was the Dakota Black Hills. The name does serve to remind us that this whole section of the continent was absolutely flat when those sands settled out. The Rockies hadn't invented themselves yet.

Dakota Sandstone contains a little coal but it is so near low-calorie lignite that blacksmiths complained it couldn't get hot enough to make iron blush.

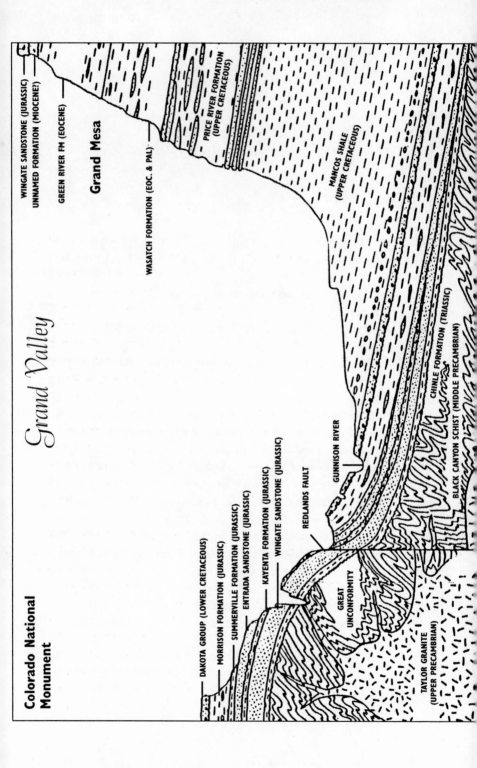

Colorado National Monument

Grand Valley

Grand Mesa

WINGATE SANDSTONE (JURASSIC)
UNNAMED FORMATION (MIOCENE?)
GREEN RIVER FM (EOCENE)
PRICE RIVER FORMATION (UPPER CRETACEOUS)
WASATCH FORMATION (EOC. & PAL.)
MANCOS SHALE (UPPER CRETACEOUS)
CHINLE FORMATION (TRIASSIC)
BLACK CANYON SCHIST (MIDDLE PRECAMBRIAN)
GUNNISON RIVER
DAKOTA GROUP (LOWER CRETACEOUS)
MORRISON FORMATION (JURASSIC)
SUMMERVILLE FORMATION (JURASSIC)
ENTRADA SANDSTONE (JURASSIC)
KAYENTA FORMATION (JURASSIC)
WINGATE SANDSTONE (JURASSIC)
REDLANDS FAULT
GREAT UNCONFORMITY
TAYLOR GRANITE (UPPER PRECAMBRIAN)

The most impressive layers of Grand Mesa are its top and bottom — the lava that crowns it and the deep Mancos Shale Formation that, just as spectacularly, forms its base. The 'dobie badlands, Grand Mesa moonscape.

Mancos Shales are not old geologically speaking. Before them are some three and a half billion (±) years of continental construction and destruction. If the Creator had been making movies of His work from satellite height, and were to run the film by you speeded up to get it all into a two-hour flick, the pieces of this part of Colorado would look like wood chips bobbing up and down on a sloshing pond.

The Continental Divide was alternately that, or a sea-filled trough from end to end. Every time a mountain range pushed up into the weather (which was much wetter then than now) it eroded into the inland ocean deepening and enriching those Mancos clays.

With so much input and practically no outflow the mid-continent body of water became a salty sea with shores taking in parts of today's Utah, Colordo, New Mexico, and Arizona. A great bottomless basin. Bottomless because it obligingly sank at about the rate the silty sediment flowed in from surrounding mountains. This process went on for five thousand feet of strata depth or thirty-seven million years of time, whichever you find easiest to visualize. And that's just the bottom layer of this mountain.

The 'dobie badlands are mainly composed of clays colored blackish-gray by the unoxidized iron they contain. In early days when settlers were graduating out of their cabins into real houses, there was a brickyard in almost every town at the base of the Mesa. Surprisingly, brick made from gray 'dobie mud fired with black Grand Mesa coal produces creamy yellow brick, as heat oxidizes the iron.

Gypsum found in the clays was burned for plaster by early settlers, and where ancient lava heat has turned gypsum into alabaster — such as on the rim of Black Canyon — it was mined and carved into small sculptures. By ingestion sheep turn the shale's rich minerals into wool and lamb cutlets as they graze the grassy flat benches that drop off into tumbled badlands.

The most profitable thing Mancos Shale does is what it does naturally — erode. Softly yielding to wind and rain, the steep hills slowly shuck down to enlarge rich farmlands in the floor of valleys that widen inch by inch imperceptibly.

There's fun in all that chaos. People who like to prove how near to straight up they can drive their vehicles without chickening out or flipping over

The chart constructed by Dr. Robert G. Young, geologist, makes it easy to find your place in the Grand Mesa layer cake.

backwards have carved scars up the steepest slopes with four-and two-wheeled contrivances.

But the favorite fun activity in the 'dobe badlands is fossil hunting.

Mancos Shales lie in layers representing different deposit levels in that vast inland sea. Fossils differ from layer to layer. You may find pelecypods and gastropods — Greek names meaning respectively ax-foot and stomach-foot, which doesn't give you too clear a mental picture to keep in mine while looking. High on Point Cliff where Highway 50 swings out around The Horn, a thin layer is studded with scallop-shaped shells. Not stone casts or imprints, but the actual shells still pearly with iridescent nacre.

"Fossil turtles were found on the flats below The Horn," Welland States remembered, "where a ditch was being dug. Shell plates and all, but so fragile they went to pieces once they were out of the ground."

To which Arnold Hood added, "In certain layers that you learn to recognize as ancient shorelines, you find petrified wood. It's jet black inside with a tan exterior. North of Cedaredge are stone petrified trees still standing, but covered with overburden."

In 1912 coal geologist Willis T. Lee identified thirty-five different kinds of fossils in Mancos Shales, not counting "Inoceramus problematicus" near the top of the formation nor "Ostrea lugubris" near the bottom. Since Ostrea lugubris translates into "sad shell" and problematicus hardly needs translating to reveal the discoverer's state of mind, one must assume that what a first-finder paleontologist ate for breakfast had a lot to do with the labels he chose for the long-dead, defenseless creatures he dug up that day.

Mancos Shales were laid down during the heyday of the dinosaur, but you probably won't find dinosaur bone in them because, except for isolated strips of shoreline, everything at this level was under salty sea water. It was rife with sharks. You can find shark teeth at almost any level of the Mancos, once you learn to recognize the triangular shape. Good place to look is on a desert ant hill where ant construction workers have brought up shark teeth to help shingle the company domicile. Some scientists say these are not shark teeth at all, but belong to prehistoric toothed birds or flying serpents.

And there were Plesiosaurs, sea monsters that paleontologists sketch as long-necked, long-tailed lizards with flippers instead of fingers. A Cedaredge high school boy found one on the hill overlooking the town's rodeo grounds.

Dinosaur Jim (Dr. James Jensen) unearths the fossil skeleton of a mosasaur discovered by high school student Gary Thompson just above the Cedaredge town rodeo grounds.

Gary Thompson was walking along the road on the bluff east of town when he glimpsed a piece of bone the road grader had slightly uncovered.

A science student, Gary not only had a good idea what he was looking at, but the good sense to leave it undisturbed until it could be excavated by someone capable of understanding the bones in relation to the matrix of stone and time they were nestled in.

Dr. James Jensen — who has found so many prehistoric creatures that he is known in the paleontological world as Dinosaur Jim — came from Brigham Young University and with trowel and toothbrush separated the bones from the earth that had held them for 80 million (±) years. Though not all of the tail was found the five-foot jawbone indicated the size of the animal.

Jensen described the fossil vertebrate as "a marine reptile," a Mosasaur, common to the late Mancos seas.

Speaking to students who had trooped up from school to watch the dig, Jensen encouraged them to use their young muscles, scrambling over the scenery, hunting clues that would help explain the history of their world.

"Where that red rock meets shale — like those knobs on the Mesa slope beyond town — the hunting is good. Watch for spots of rusty-colored earth or rock," he advised, and then complimented the kids by getting technical. "Iron has always been present in the oceans of the earth, and since iron in solution has an affinity for organic materials, marine fossils are often chemically enriched by it. It sometimes occurs as pyrites in invertebrate fossils, but generally it is in an oxidized — reddish or yellowish — form."

Ray Bigham, whose grader revealed the bone Gary found, had the last word:

"There's a certain layer along here that every time you break open a rock it's got a bone or clam or fossil fish."

———

Grand Mesa contains an estimated eleven billion tons of coal. One whole strata-seam, side to side of the mountain, is bituminous and anthracite coal, but you'd never know it by looking at the slopes. Coal doesn't weather out, it weathers in — slacking back out of sight just a little faster than erosion can expose it. Sly stuff.

The "bookmark" that geologists use to find the coal chapter in the Grand Mesa story is called Rollins Sandstone, a white cliff-forming layer that is most impressively seen at The Eye midway up the south side of the mountain. Rollins Sandstone marks the end of Mancos Shale and the beginning of a conglomeration of strata that geologists named the Mesa Verde Group because they found it best exposed on the rim-slopes leading to the Anasazi Cliff Dwellings.

Using the Rollins "bookmark," experienced coal-locaters from England, Nova Scotia, and the Appalachians opened mines along the hidden outcrop. A lot of mines. By 1912 when geologists Willis T. Lee mapped coal resources in the Grand Mesa - West Elks fields, there were forty named mines in a horizontally-straight line around the mountain from Somerset to Cameo. Most of the mines were tram-and-burro outfits. A few were wheelbarrow enterprises — a rancher finding coal on his land used pick, shovel, wheelbarrow, and muscle to mine enough fuel for his own stove. Roof-slumps and erosion have removed most of these tiny, low-ceiling mines, but one wheelbarrow coal dig in Cactus Park was still there in the 1970s when we were researching coal. We couldn't wedge into it. Clever pack rats had sealed the public out of their residence by dragging in heaps of cactus.

Some of those forty mines became company-owned towns — Bowie, Somerset, and Cameo.

Of these the town of Bowie kept its original look the longest because it shut down before modern methods struck the industry. You can still see the steep slant of the tramcar track from the mine mouth down to the loading bins on the railroad, the coal-fired power plant, the elegant mine-owner's dwelling in it landscaped grounds, the schoolhouse provided by the company for miners' children. Until a few years ago you would have seen the company town itself: two streets of identical, pointy-roofed houses, each with matching backhouse along the alley behind. But when Coors beer money bought Bowie those miner-houses were razed to keep drifters from annoyingly camping in them. Coors hired watchmen to guard the other buildings; if they had done the same for the miners' homes America might have its own only remaining example of a complete "company minetown" as was.

In canyon-jammed Somerset the big three-story company store office was razed to make room for an even bigger coal silo. Miners' houses, now individually owned, are no longer identical but still retain identifiably similar roof lines. With their fenced gardens crowding the highway, they epitomize minetown spirit. When authorities wanted to straighten and widen Main by moving those houses or bypassing the town altogether, the miner-owners voted to keep things just the way they are. So now when you zoom down off McClure Pass you get to slow down at Somerset, make a sharp right and take a good look at what is the nearest thing to a company minetown you're likely to see anywhere today.

Changes in Somerset reflect changes in methods of coal extraction. Longwall mining has replaced pick, shovel, and dynamite. Coal conveyors have replaced the tram cars that we rode in the company of U.S. Steel mine superintendent Lloyd R. Miller when we visited the back end of Somerset mine in the 1970s.

Because Grand Mesa coal has the advantage of being sulphur-free, it is preferred to others and is shipped all over the world. For more than a century, in good times and bad, coal mining here has never closed completely down. Currently mile-long trains — three to five a day — thread down the North Fork with loads headed for as far away as Japan.

Eleven billion tons of coal on this one mesa? Those mile-long trains can just about run forever, right?

Actually only a fraction of the tonnage is mineable. When a mine is dug back under a mountain to a point where the overburden of mass above it exceeds two or three thousand feet (depends on the kind of formation) the weight of gravity invincibly crushes any tunnel shut. Only the fringes of the Grand Mesa coal layer can ever be mined by digging it out. Several ways to outmaneuver gravity have been proposed. One is to drill down to the coal strata from anywhere above it, set in on fire by supplying oxygen, and use the resulting heat to generate electric power.

Things haven't come to that yet.

How did all that coal get there? The great basin that received the Mancos sediments stopped sinking. Such floods of muck built up that lakes and lagoons were created everywhere, pushing the seas eastward and creating wonderfully lush marsh-grazing for wonderfully unlikely beasts. Ceilings of almost every coal mine in the area have the "potrocks" that are the swamp-filled footprints of dinosaurs. These souvenirs of another age are unloved because they have a tendency to fall out of the tunnel roof and kill miners.

Charles States saved the biggest dinosaur tracks from his coal mine near Cedaredge — thirty-eight inches across with a stride of sixteen feet. They were part of the exhibit when he turned the mine's original entry into a dark "mine-museum," displaying fossils of plants and creatures found in the mine and on the surrounding mountainside. Dark is the word; your flashlight pokes a tunnel through blackness, suddenly framing still-lifes on floor, wall, glass case. The exhibits included flint tools, stones patterned in fern fronds, a piece of mastodon tusk, a stuffed rattlesnake, and a bare-naked human skull, which Charles was careful to explain did not come from the same stratum as the dinosaur tracks. When Smithsonian Institute heard the size of those tracks they traded him out of them, leaving cast duplicates instead.

Old Man Moore wasn't looking for oil. He had come in over the top and was headed down the north side to where the altitude was low enough to provide range grass year-round. Preparing to set up camp for the night near the top he lit his pipe. The tossed match landed near a gas leak creating a big flare that singed his long whiskers.

That was in 1883, forty-six years after Antoine Robidoux knew of no better use for petroleum than to write on rock with it. A lot had happened in the meantime: kerosene was lighting the civilized world, Grandpa's Tar Soap was sanitizing it, and some nerd back east had applied for a patent on a horseless road vehicle that would propel itself by exploding gasoline in its cylindrical innards.

Old Man Moore knew what he'd found. He looked around, located the oil ooze, and sat tight on his claim even though it is so high up Buzzard Creek that winter is nine months long. Heating with gas hadn't been invented yet so he adjusted to those winters by building an out-sized fireplace in his cabin. It almost cost him his life, or at least his liberty when the settlers suspected he had got rid of Johnnie Owens in it.

Trapper John Owens was a young loner who disappeared. A lot of early comers were loners — including Old Man Moore himself. They came West on their own to achieve something or to escape something; and many disappeared when the trouble they'd escaped caught up with them. It was easy to disappear in those days — no Social Securiy number, no drivers license, and no nosiness among lawmen and neighbors. It was discreetly recognized that some people had a right to disappear if they wanted to.

But a man who disappears on purpose takes his rifle with him. Johnnie's Sharps rifle and his pack were found on the creek that was later named Owens Creek for that reason. Folks really looked for Johnnie.

Someone remembered that soldiers from Fort Crawford reported they smelled human flesh burning when they passed down Buzzard Creek.

How did the soldiers know it was human flesh they smelled burning?

They explained they had smelled human flesh burning before, knew it when they smelled it, because they had assisted at the cremation of a fellow soldier. Which opened more questions than it closed: Why had someone at the Fort been burned, not buried? By his own wish, because of some disease, to destroy evidence? And who?

Hermit Moore had few friends and didn't trust the ones he had, so it was naturally assumed that the old recluse, fearing Johnnie planned to jump his oil claim, killed him and burned him up in that big fireplace. The case never came to trial except in court of public conjecture where Old Man Moore stood convicted even though he could prove he'd been over on Cache Creek at the time.

No trace of Johnnie was ever found.

Did Old Man Moore himself react by disappearing? He did not. He rode it out; hunting, fishing, waiting until enough uses were found for oil to make it wealth.

The first of Grnad Mesa's oil booms began on Buzzard Creek in 1892, and there has scarcely been a decade since without one, especially during wars. That year they were planning to build a railroad to the oil, not realizing that oil was destined not only to put the horse out of the transportation business on the road and on farm and battlefield, but would just about finish off railroads as well.

Only God and the secret records of drilling companies know how many holes have been sunk on Grand Mesa and its slopes, or what was discovered in them before the wells and their drillers' mouths were sealed.

Oil Well Camp and Oil Well Mountain on Forest Service maps mark Moore's discovery site and later drilling booms.

The natural gas that singed Old Man Moore's beard hides in porous pockets in that jumble of clay and sandstone called the Mesa Verde Formation. There seems to be a lot of it, but until the driller's bore has sunk down through thousands of dollars worth of hole he can't tell whether he has hit or missed one of those rich pockets.

In 1969 the Atomic Energy Commission, seeking peaceful uses for atomic energy, set off a 4-kiloton atomic bomb 8500 feet underground over by Rulison. The idea was to see if the blast would fracture the tight sands making one big gas reservoir of separated pockets. If it worked at Rulison the technique would be repeated in gas-bearing strata elsewhere. It may have worked but it was never tapped because of the possibility that the blast created radioactive gas, and who wants that piped into the kitchen! Drilling near the site of that blast is still restricted.

And speaking of atomic radiation, among the minerals in this mountain is one nobody wants, a man-made deposit of uranium mill tailings over on the west flank.

Cheny Residual Radioactive disposal site on the mountainside southeast of Whitewater began receiving uranium mill tailings from Climax in the 1950s. But the biggest share of its more than four million tons are from Grand Junction. Uranium ore was mined on the far side of the Uncompahgre Plateau, trucked through Unaweep Canyon, and refined in Grand Junction to produce material for atomic bombs. As the post-war decades passed, and scientific knowledge of the dangers of atomic radiation grew, folks began to worry about those hills of radioactive tailings right in town.

By that time uranium mine tailings were considered so everlastingly lethal that the government decided it would be too risky to run truckloads of the stuff through the traffic of accident-prone federal highways. A two-lane blacktop haulway was constructed, running alongside Highway 50, across a specially-built overpass, and on up the mountainside to what is locally called the Pits.

———— ————

Grand Mesa's next strata — the Ohio Creek Conglomerate — is an orphan in time. Before the Ohio Creek layer was deposited uncountable eons of previous strata washed away into the seas, and after it the same thing happened. Those geological data banks — strata — do a good job of recording how and when the earth's layers were formed, but erosion leaves no time recording. You can't calculate geologic time by what isn't there. Geologists, however, strive gamely. They figure the fifty to 500 feet of Ohio Creek plus the blanks above and below it come to sixty-three [±] million years.

(Geological estimates in millions of years — by far the wildest game in town — are usually followed by the sign [±], meaning plus or minus a million years or so. This mathematical finger-crossing is the scientists' acknowledgement of the vagaries in the present system of dating strata by such things as the radioactive half-life of certain substances they have found in them.)

Ohio Creek Conglomerate got its name about as logically as all the other strata. Men from that state came west looking for gold, didn't find it, but did find coal over in the West Elks. The creek where they mined became known by the place where they came from, and that's where geologists first encountered the frustratingly mixed-up strata. Surprising they didn't name it something worse.

This conglomerate is composed of gravels and rocks cemented together in a sandstone matrix with few if any fossils to reveal what was going on in the living world of its time. It is what geologist term (in cussword tones) "massive," giving them no help by way of time-counting "pages" of stratification. It is all alike straight through, lumpy. And it yields nothing mankind has so far found any commercial use for — well that isn't exactly true. Ohio Creek Conglomerate contains chunks of red and black chert from which prehistoric peoples manufactured weapons and tools by chipping it into spear points, arrowheads, butchering, and skinning knives. Several of these chert "factory sites" have been identified by their rich scattering of chips; probably many more are concealed by the Mesa's rich vegetation.

Because Ohio Creek Conglomerate is harder than the slate formations below and above, it is a cliff-builder. You can see its jutting points on three sides of Grand Mesa.

———

After being twice up where erosion could get at it, the land that was to be Grand Mesa once more sank below water level — an immense lake reaching into Utah — receiving runoff debris from the Uinta Mountains, and laying down what has been called the Wasatch Formation.

Wasatch is the Mesa's rainbow layer. It was first called the Ruby Formation because its color is deepest and most brilliant where it occurs on the Ruby Anthracite Mountains. As it comes west, Wasatch thins and fades until at Land's End it can only be called variegated.

Mainly layered shale and sandstone, the Wasatch is interbedded with conglomerate containing rocks of metamorphic origin, most are rich in iron. The iron oxidized, bleeding into the other layers, producing all tones of red from grape-purple to pale blush.

But the color is tricky. Just when you think if it's red it's Wasatch, if it's Wasatch it's red, you'll come onto a stretch where the iron-bearing mineral is epidot, forming rocks and earths of a milky green ranging from pistachio to olive; or — if the iron has leached out — a stretch where the Wasatch is almost as white as chalk. Even in some of the red beds, nodular masses of green epidot have been found.

Since these rocks were water-hauled in here, it is unlikely that any of the beautiful translucent, two-toned epidot crystals will have arrived intact — but if you are a rockhound you can hope.

As for fossils in the Wasatch, gastropods and pelecypods continue to reveal their coiled shells, but the news now is the mammals who are forging ahead and trying all sorts of weird combinatins of skeleton and accessories. Of these the rhinoceros has preserved the original model up to the present day, though not here. Others changed with the times or phased out.

Bones of the "dawn horse" have been found on the Mesa, with four of his five toes still making tracks whenever his front feet came down — the hind feet were already putting weight on only three. This delicate little foot-high creature went on to develop, with unbroken fossil record, into the full-scale, hoofed horse we know, flourishing all over the continent. Then, like the dinosaur, he suddenly died out. In the case of the horse, scientists have modern criteria for their guessing, and attribute his demise to an epidemic of hoof-and-mouth disease or sleeping sickness. Luckily the horse had previously migrated to Europe by way of the Bering Strait and Asia, survived there, and was brought back to America carrying Spaniards in 150-pound suits of armour.

Incidentally, the straight-faced scientific naming of the "dawn horse" is delightfully onomatopoeic. His Greek name is Eohippus, "eo" meaning early and "hippus" meaning horse. Repeat Eohippus fast enough, and it sounds like a gallop. Another mammalian experiment was not so lucky. They call him Titanoides, and they dug him out of the Wasatch Formation two miles from the town of Mesa. Titanoides (which roughly translates into "like the Titanic") looked like a cross between rhinoceros and horse, having horns on his nose, a shape like a hog, and four toes on the ground per foot. Like the dinosaur he had delusions of grandeur, evolving from hog-size to a mass that stood eight feet at the shoulder and weighed in terms of tons. Doomed perhaps by his dimensions, he passed away without leaving direct descendants or collateral cousins.

Wasatch has one further distinction: Its clays are thought by some geologists to be the slick floor, lubricated by percolating water, that skids hunks of mountainside out and down in the Toreva-block slumping that shaped Grand Mesa's benched, land-slide shoulders, and created the hollows for its lakes.

————

About a hundred million years ago northern Colorado scenery started to sag again. Everything between the Uinta Mountains, the La Sals, the West Elks, and the White River Range began slowly sinking, creating what is called the Piceance River Basin. The basin became a lake, and during the ten (±) million years the bottom collected as much as 2000 feet of strange stuff geologists are calling the Great River Formation.

Besides receiving silt and salt, the lake swarmed with so much life it's a wonder there was room for water. The list of living matter begins with soup-thick algae, rafts of pollen, fin-to-fin fish, clams, bugs, and snails — and might well end with puppy-dog tails. There was so much living and dying guck it couldn't properly rot. Instead it became films of a waxy hydrocarbon kerogen (misnamed oil) clinging around minute particles of marlstone (misnamed shale). Oil shale is very valuable — if you can separate it without going broke.

Though Grand Mesa does have a Green River layer, it missed out on its riches, containing only a remnant of that lake's shoreline. It has a fairly thick Green River strata on the north, pinching to nothing on the south.

In missing out on the wealth, the Mesa may have escaped the trouble and mess. The "oil" in oil shale cannot be pumped, pressured, or flushed out of the ground. Nine hundred degrees of heat are required to break the wedded bonds of marlstone and kerogen, and when you've accomplished that you are still at the bottom of the petroleum refining process, with mere crude oil, and in addition have on hand vast quantities of spent shale waste that has to be put some place. If that isn't bad enough the valuable shale lies beneath two stacked underground lakes of different kinds of salt that farmers and city water departments all down the Colorado River will fight to keep right where it is.

These difficulties and others have stymied entrepreneurs ever since the first oil shale mini-boom at the turn of the century when pioneers sought to refine it, perhaps because it wasn't proving good for much else. The shale rocks were useless as campfire kettle rocks because they caught fire, and useless as fuel because if they burned at all when you wanted them to, they burned with a smoky stench and produced twice their volume in ash.

There has been an average of half an oil shale boom per decade ever since its discovery.

Grand Mesa also has only traces of gilsonite, that other strange petroleum created by rampant life-forms in the Piceance Basin.

Just under the lava that crowns the Mesa is strata of so little significance that nobody bothered to give it a name until recently. The Uinta Formation is made up of gravels, sandstone, and marshland fossils. It is, of course, what's left of the floor of the valley that all this lava poured onto.

The lava itself is basalt, given to flowing rather than erupting into volcanoes, as its cousins, the acidic lavas, are prone to do. The West Elks had gone into an upheaval phase with great hot lacoliths shoving laterally between the strata, pushing them up, making mountains of them. Some of the hot liquid found weak rifts farther west and squirted up through dike-splits flowing out into the stem and forks of a Y-shaped valley. Again and again. Sometimes frothily, cooling to form stone full of bubble-holes. There were great gaps of time between some of the eruptions leaving eons for soil and sediment to build on old flows before new flows burst forth. When you see layers of red in the black basalt they were once iron-rich soil that volcanic heat has oxidized and fused to rock.

"Grand Mesa lava is peculiar. It hates to break straight," John Wetterich said, while conducting us over the Crag Crest trail he and his crew of CCC boys had carved along the mountain's skyline in 1937.

"Hit it with a hammer, blast it with dynamite and it doesn't split, it peels off like an orange."

There is some evidence that other formations once lay on top of the Mesa's present lava crown. Stream-scoured rock deposits near the lily ponds on upper Kannah Creek match nothing anywhere except some rocks over in Unaweep Canyon to the west.

How thick the Mesa's final layer was there is no way of knowing because sometime in there the scenery began to rise and wash away. The part of the lava-protected valley that wasn't eroded into the ocean took to the sky, as you see it now.

12

Gold All Over the Place

Alvin "Red" Davis said, "Gold may be one of the most prevalent minerals. It's just about everywhere — at least everywhere on or in sight of Grand Mesa — but so fine and far apart you spend more money getting it than you'll ever get for it."

Red should know. His hobby was finding and panning gold, refining it in a kettle in his back yard, and giving the resulting gold patties to his friends. What he didn't give away he saved for fall when he and Jeannie took off for Las Vegas to have a blast and perhaps, on the side, maybe, get rich on the slot machines. They never did, but the manager at a gold-silver exchange got so used to Red Davis he didn't even bite the gold patties (or otherwise test them for purity) before translating them into dollars.

This might sound like something from the Gold Rush of 1859 except that along with the gold they took paper cash that Jeannie made creating crossword puzzles for Dell. Until 1990, the year he died, Red Davis spent the free-time of his summers panning gold. From his home base in the juniper forest above Cedaredge he four-wheeled all over Grand Mesa, the Unaweep cleft, and the Uncompahgre Plateau, incidentally wearing out two copies of our *Uncompahgre* in the faint hope he'd find some trail-hint where lay the rainbow's end.

Red Davis and one of those patties have sufficiently strong vibes that "Red" and "gold" were two of several cogent clues "seen" at long distance by psychic astrologists testing their powers at the world-wide Church of Light annual meeting under the stars on top of the Mesa in the fall of 1996.

——— ———

Gold has been found on all sides of Grand Mesa. Spaniards are said to have discovered placer gold on the West Muddy before the Indians went out. During the depression of the 1890s when silver was demonetized, John Roper, a hotel owner in the now ghost town of Red Mountain, decided to get out from under his dying business and investigate those rumors of a Spanish gold strike on Grand Mesa.

"I outfitted thirteen burros and five horses, took a dog, guns and ammunition to go prospecting, trapping and hunting ... went over to the head of the Plateau River and prospected old supposed Spanish diggings."

What with hunting, trapping, and stretching hides, Roper had too many projects going to find gold, or at least enough to talk about. Creek-heads on both sides of the drainage in that area were prospected, but noncommittally; the usual response to queries was a cautious, "Just about making wages."

Flour gold discovered on Clear Creek, drew international attention. A company, organized in Salt Lake City and partly financed in England, sent in mining equipment via ox train over McClure Pass. It was an impressive outfit but it didn't attract much attention because there were still too few settlers to impress. Flour gold floats, and is mighty hard to corral behind sluice-box riffles. The outfit stole away so unimpressively there is no record of their going.

———— ————

Earliest recorded account of gold panning on Grand Mesa — recorded because it involved murder — was in the early 1880s.

Tom Welch, his two teenage sons, a fellow known as Butcher Knife Ed Hardesty, and some unnamed friends, packed in over McClure Pass from the Aspen area where Tom had been placering and jack-packing for several years. The riders trailed up Hubbard and Holy Terror Creeks, test-panning as they came. As an associate of the Ragged Mountain Placer Company of Aspen, Tom knew what he was looking for, a place where a hot mountain had done his refining for him. Particularly promising was a grassy valley on Little Muddy Creek yielding not only colors in the pan but a telltale abundance of lava rubble washed down from above. It takes intense heat to make lava, there must be a gold-refining volcano up there somewhere.

He forayed up from camp, circling Muddy Basin — a steep cirque of mud slides that, slowly undermining the Mesa's lava rim, gives Muddy Creek its name and its texture. He crossed The Burn and No Good Park that crowns Spruce Mountain — no volcano there. The same for Elk Knob and Elk Mountain. Then The Dikes east of Leon Peak.

The Dikes, twenty-seven great basalt ribs, are standing monuments to the inner heat that once squeezed molten lava up through cracks in the earth like hot toothpaste, spewing it out across a valley that would someday, because of its black protection, be mountain top. Dikes are good places to look for gold lodes, metal refined out during the mysterious alchemy of volcanism. A few pure, weighable gold nuggets have been found in the area of the Dikes, but not by Tom Welch. He noted that hot lava had indeed done the trick, but not lavishly. There was enough precious metal downstream from those peaks and dikes to later give Gold Creek its name, but no more than in the grassy valley Tom had already staked, and that wasn't enough to be worth the company's while.

However, the valley had another wealth — grass growing belly-high to a horse, and chemically enriched by minerals brought down from the clay Slide. Animals sheened up and fattened as you watched. Besides, the place was beautiful, forested mountain all around softening down into rolling, aspen-covered hills at the valley edge.

Tom and his boys, Butcher Knife Ed and friends started harvesting the hay — by hand-scythe that first year — bringing in cattle and mine mules to feed out the winter. Downstream, at a lower and warmer altitude, they built three log cabins with such permanent intentions that one of the cabins survives in good shape today, perhaps the oldest building on the east end of Grand Mesa. Next year they purchased a horse-powered mowing machine in Glenwood Springs, took it apart and jack-packed it to the valley they were calling Hay Park before the incident that named it Battle Park.

Using his ribbon of placer claims along the creek as legal base, Tom had never bothered to homestead up there. Each placer claim gave him surface rights to twenty acres, totaling a good-size holding. But a placer claim isn't a homestead. Tom realized that when in the summer of 1890 a rancher challenged his right to the valley hay.

Ed Harbison, of the newly staked out IX ranch lower on the Muddy, sent word he intended to cut grass in Hay Park, adding that Welch had had it to himself long enough. Tom Welch has been described as a red-headed Irishman with sons to match. Sixteen-year-old Tom Jr. rode with him when, armed, he stormed down to the IX and informed Harbison and friends they would cut hay in Hay Park "only over my dead body."

War to the death over hay?

Yes, but maybe not as ridiculous as it sounds. Hay in those days was a much more valuable commodity than we realize now. Powering horseflesh, it was equivalent to gasoline and diesel. Mines "burned" tons of it in their mules and

burros, railroads contracted miles of it along each side of advancing survey lines where new track was being laid by horse and scraper. Town-folks who owned wheels bought it by the rack-load to store in "fuel tank" lofts above the carriage house "garages" that lined the alleys of village and city. The ubiquitous livery stable powered "rentals" with it. Every businessman with anything to move — grocer to mortician — bought hay. Preferably rich, mountain hay.

Hay quality was much more variable than our gasoline and diesel. Poor land produces few calories. Animals that are programmed to produce only milk, meat, and wool have nothing to do all day but graze. They can yield a profit on lean pasture. But an employed horse can only refuel at noon and after working hours (which in those days were ten), food must necessarily be richly nutritious. True, horses can eat at night, which ruminants don't do, but hours spent chewing are taken away from machine-repairing sleep.

Hay Park horse-fuel was high-octane rich.

The morning after that fiery visit to the IX Tom Welch, with Junior, and some of the other men put up a log breastworks to crouch behind. Tom armed himself with a 45-70 rifle, Junior had a 44 Winchester.

Evidently the people at the IX thought Tom Welch was just spouting off. When they came they carried only one gun — Harbison brought his rifle on the chance of sighting a deer. They pulled a mowing machine behind a home-made wagon loaded with camp gear and a plow to take care of impassable pieces of trail along the creek. Peter Small and Charles Purham were riding in the wagon, Alexander LaBelle was horseback — intending to look the place over and stake out a homestead. Ed Harbison was afoot, walking behind the mower to keep it from snagging on rocks.

As the party came in sight, young Tom Welch yelled warning from behind his log barricade. They ignored the kid and came on. Junior fired at Ed Harbison and watched him fall. Tom Welch himself was already in action (it is said but never proven in court that he fired the first shots). With his gun leveled in the crotch of an aspen tree, he got LaBelle and, a few seconds later, Peter Small. Charles Purham was fatally wounded.

In the meantime, Ed Harbison from the ground — he had only pretended to be hit — was watching that log. When he saw the flash of sun on gun above it he fired under the log to make a head come up. It did, and his next shot pierced Tom Junior's hatband front to back.

Top of the mountain, Leon Peak is the highest point on the Mesa. The Dikes beyond is where the gold-retorting lava came from, and where people still occasionally find nuggets.

Tom Welch, unaware his son had been hit, yelled, "Pick up your dead and get out!" then discovered the teenager's body and realized it was he himself who must tragically do that.

Four deaths — Purham lived for nearly a year but never recovered — and no convictions.

To begin with, the law didn't know which county Hay Park — now and forever after called Battle Park — lay in. Which county, which court, which judge had jurisdiction? This was less than a decade after the Indians went out. The original Gunnison County — about half of Western Colorado — had only recently been split into four counties; the survey lines between Mesa and Gunnison were incomplete and hard to find. And still are. Boundary lines of four large counties jostle each other on this mountain — Mesa, Pitkin, Gunnison and Delta. Theoretically the lines follow the crest of the mountain, but crest has little meaning when a mountain is flat, heavily forested, with accidental Toreva slump sags and random-placed lava bumps that are themselves called mountains, "crest" has little meaning. If in this wilderness you see a forest pond sort of leaking off in two directions, you're probably looking at a crest marking a county line.

Moreover, with Teenager Tom dead and unable to testify there was no proof he hadn't done all the shooting. Tom Welch drifted off, out of the country, out of history.

The West is rife with stories of gold discoveries, the location kept secret and lost when the discoverer died or was killed before he could develop his find — the Lost Dutchman in Arizona being the most famous. This happened repeatedly on Grand Mesa, to people everybody knew and neighbored with.

Pete Christian was bringing his cattle over the divide between Roaring Fork and the Muddy when he saw a promising formation. He took samples and had them assayed. They were indeed very rich. Pete didn't tell anybody where he found them, not even his wife. That winter while hauling a load of hay to his cattle, he fell off the load and was killed, taking his secret with him.

Charley Ewing brought some ore samples into Fuzzy Graham's Paonia grocery store, offering a share in the find if Fuzzy would grubstake him. Next time Charley came back to the store he dumped a bagful of ore on the counter and said, "Boys, we it made." And he was right, assay yielded four to five thousand dollars a ton. Not long afterward Charley took sick and died. Not even Fuzzy knew where he dug that ore.

As late as the 1970s a Mexican sheepherder found an odd rock that he brought down to Hotchkiss. The rock was handed around for a while until one rancher had it assayed. It turned out to be almost pure gold, but by that time the Mexican was long gone, and clue to the place where he found that rock gone with him.

One find was secret from the finder himself.

In the fall of 1891 Joseph Johns, an experienced prospector, was hunting game on the upper Muddy when he discovered a ledge of free gold he estimated would yield $5000 to the ton, the richest find he had ever made. He took some samples and marked the ledge. Winter was coming on; he finished his hunting and went home, determined to come back and stake claim to the ledge.

He couldn't find it.

Summer after summer he returned to search among the welter of cliffs along the upper Muddy for that particular outcrop. After his death his son searched just as fruitlessly.

That $5000-to-the-ton ledge is still there. Most likely it is in the vicinity of the Dikes where from time to time a few nuggets, product of nature's hot-lava retorting, are discovered and picked up.

———— ————

If your Mesa-prowling takes you over to the dam that restrains Todd Reservoir water your feet are standing on dirt that pans $5 to $16 in gold per ton — or did at 1905 gold prices when the dam was being built. At that time the newspaper reported: "They immediately sought dam materials from some other points quite a ways removed, and here again they ran into the same yellowish brown rock. They have had it assayed and put up location stakes covering the field."

Even earlier, the earth moving at a reservoir called Keuser came to a screeching halt when the team-and-scraper man discovered he was building the dam with gold-studded dirt.

If anything came of that gold, it wasn't enough to make the paper take notice again. The dams went on rising. Water, and what it would produce down in the valley fields, was more valuable.

Actually it isn't surprising to find gold-trace in so many places on and around Grand Mesa. That sheet of hot lava had roasted the strata it flowed over, in the process concentrating any gold it contained. And erosion chewing at the lava cliffs frees it to move on down the mountain by means of glacier, water and wind. There are immense deposits of these gold-bearing (slightly) gravels along Plateau Creek. On the south side of the mountain the deposits lie in great alluvial fans, one after another. They can be seen in cross-section in a few places such as Cory Grade on Highway 65.

Besides gold in and on Grand Mesa itself, the precious metal has been found in almost all the geography visible from the top. Gold was assayed in Escalante, Dominguez, Roubideau, and Cottonwood Canyon rock; in iron ore mined in Peach Valley; in sand dug from a Garnet Mesa basement. A gold boomtown at the confluence of the North Fork and Anthracite Creek was at least large enough to have one saloon, the Log Cabin Saloon, and long-lived enough to have one shooting — the Log Cabin faro dealer.

Gold has been found everywhere along the Gunnison River. During the Great Depression mechanized gold washing operations at the west base of Grand Mesa were powered by an old Star car. Gold "show" was so promising that the penniless firm (three out-of-work guys) hand-scraped a road down to it. Promise was all. Flour gold, it washed tauntingly down over the ribs of their flume like tiny creatures on fluttering gold wings.

The most noticeable piece of Grand Mesa geography — besides its black basalt cliffs — is the Eye. The Eye peers at western Colorado scenery from half way up the south side of the Mesa, two great jutting cliffs of white sandstone separated by a retracted dark pupil, and topped by a bulging red bluff like a swollen eyelid.

The Eye was the site of Grand Mesa's wildest and weirdest gold rush. (If you can't locate it from the above description, sight from the Delta rodeo grounds straight up past Devil's Thumb and you'll be looking at the Eye. But it won't be looking at you, it's focused over on the West Elks where the best of its coal burden is being mined.)

Because the formation is so prominent, geologists used it to tag the layer of coal that rides on it, running straight through Grand Mesa and all other coal fields in this part of the world. Rollins Sandstone they named it for Joseph Rollins who opened the first mine into its coal vein. Joe didn't discover the Rollins gold, he'd sold out by that time.

On June 20, 1913, the county newspaper reported: "Delta Has Gold Scare!

"Quietly for the past two months samples of the coal vein in the Rollins mine on Grand Mesa have been taken for gold assay. Samples from the delivery bin at the mine gave $9.50 gold. Ashes from the engine furnace were panned and a string of colors shown.

Bottom of the mountain. The lava cliff-rim is just above the last line of snow. Farms along Tongue Creek are backed by 'dobie badlands' and the mile-high stairway of climates. That pale triangle half way up is The Eye, site of the coal-mine gold rush.

"Mr. Earl Dugger, owner of the mine, claims to have carefully sampled the vein which is some twenty feet thick … and obtained average results as shown by certificates of assay …. This could be the biggest strike in the United States. The assay is double that of the Homestake in South Dakota.

"Many Deltans have caught gold fever and gone up to stake claims."

———

People who had never poked questions at a funny-looking rock or opened a book on geology began prowling and reading. Was gold hiding in other layers besides Rollins? Or other mineral treasures even more profitable than gold? What's this immense heap of rock made of, anyhow?

Prospecting fever heated up, fanned out: "People are staking claims in all directions. Old finds are being re-prospected.

"Joe Crabill is blocking out some ore in his Roubideau claims which rumor says is worth $100 a ton."

Another location in "some soft iron stuff panned a string of at least a thousand colors." On a quartz vein near Collbran 150 claims were staked out.

But the continuing big news was the Rollins coal-mine strike.

The Tudor family of Colorado Springs, absentee owners of the Kuhnley mine just over the ridge from Rollins, came to take samples of their coal for assay.

People began to calculate how much gold there was in a vein of coal slicing Grand Mesa from Rollins straight through to Cameo on the Colorado River. And not just from side to side — end to end: B. J. Smith affirmed, "The entire coal strata bears gold for the full length of Grand Mesa."

Reading about it people in Utah and New Mexico who lived in the vicinity of coal seams riding on top of that same Rollins Sandstone began poking around to see what treasures they might have been living with — or without.

The newspaper editor was cautious, especially about the Rollins discovery: "…big gold strike stories are not to be believed. If a man did strike it rich, he wouldn't talk about it till he had his ground secured, which takes time."

But shortly the editor himself was up there staking out claims, perhaps influenced by the fact that claims had been staked by two of the town's most influential men — J. Frank Sanders and Judge M. M. Welch. Sanders was already rich on gold from the Bachelor Mine he'd discovered near Ouray, so he ought to know. And Judge Welch was just about always right about

---

PREVIOUS LEFT: The up side: To the eyes, nothing could be more quietly serene than this pool on the rim of the Mesa. The ears tell another story…

.PREVIOUS RIGHT: The down side: Water, dropping as much as a thousand feet from that serene pool, shatters to spray and must regather to form a stream ranchers can lay dam to.

everything. He said, "We are now satisfied that the entire product of the mine will carry $5 to $12 per ton in gold. The problem is refining. The affinity of carbon for gold is said to be a strong flux resistant, and more heat is required, as well as longer heating period to do the work, than with ordinary quartz."

To this and to another dissenting opinion — that if gold was found in coal it was a freak — the paper responded: "Gold has been found in coal in Wyoming. The coal was treated for 28 cents a ton, gold averaged $4 a ton." Less than half what Rollins coal was assaying at the Pueblo Sampling Works and the School of Mines at Golden.

Two claim-stakers, E. T. Minney and Roy Smith, did some testing of their own — at home. Scooping up a couple of buckets of Rollins mine left-overs from the backyard ash pile, they did a little panning, and then roasted the leavings over a bonfire. They were rewarded with a tiny gold button at the bottom of the pot when it cooled.

Apparently Rollins gold came partially pre-roasted. Editor Anderson wrote, "At certain distances apart and immediately above the main coal strata are found evidences of volcanic heat. Ledges have been burned until their iron cappings were curled into cinders, which in places resemble slag. Beneath this cinder rock is a strata of pre-roasted rock which is a mixture of quartz and rock. As this great blanket floors directly on the coal vein, the heated period must have dated back a sufficient number of ages to have allowed the vegetable matter it compressed to become a solid carbon vein long before its time of cooking."

On August 8 two even richer strikes were reported in the vicinity of the Rollins Coal mine " . . . running high in gold, and on which returns have been secured showing $20, $40 and as high as $80 in gold per ton, coming from rock that can be treated by the panning process."

Rollins Mine owner Duggers, named his home claims for his woman: The little Mina Group — Little Mina Mines 1 through 4. Rapidly taking them from stake-out, to recording, to actual assessment work. Other gold-rushers were not far behind: " . . . the *Delta Independent* publisher, A. M. Anderson, was one of the first to hire teams and send up miners."

At this point Dugger and his associates — J. J. Randolph, a mining man, Guy Gilmore of Cory and A. E. Reynolds of Eckert — held a sort of "open house" at Rollins to display the progress of the brand new tunnel. Mrs. Dugger prepared dinner up there for the swarm of guests who climbed halfway up the mountain to crowd around tables set up on the narrow ledges outside the mine.

A week later Randolph was reporting that the tunnel had entered a five foot strata of phonolite. No assays had yet been made on the phonolite, but the paper noted that "The phonolite rock is similar to that at Cripple Creek, and is considered very favorable. Samples of porphyry and phonolite as well as nuggets with large percentage of platinum have been found elsewhere on Grand Mesa."

That was August 22, just sixty-three days after the first announcement of the strike. It is the last thing the papers have to say about the Great Rollins Gold Rush.

After that, nothing. No explanation, no follow-up. Nothing.

What happened? It doesn't appear to have been a scam. The gold was there as the assays certified. Did it play out? Was refining too expensive?

A dictionary of about the same vintage as the gold-strike describes "phonolite" as a group of green, gray, or brown volcanic rocks containing much alkali feldspar and nepheline.

They were apparently still working on the theory that volcanic action in or close to the formation had retorted the gold. But there is no evidence of volcanic activity in Grand Mesa anywhere near the strata level where that coal-gold was found.

What seems most likely is that in prehistoric times a coal seam above the existing coal veins at the Rollins site had caught fire from lightning-caused forest fires and burned back into the mountain as far as oxygen was available. The heat of the burning performed the roasting, concentrating process, that produced refined gold and the slag-like material the prospectors took for volcanic phonolite.

And incidentally produced that slag-red bulge of inflamed eyelid you see above The Eye.

When their exploring tunnel had gone beyond the reach of that prehistoric mine fire, it tapped only ordinary Grand Mesa alluvial stuff — almost any panful of which, according to some early prospectors, yields enough colors to keep a man eternally hopeful — and broke.

Within our time Rollins coal has caught fire several times in mining accidents, its tunnels sealed in hope of cutting off the oxygen. In vain. Right now Rollins coal is probably on fire somewhere inside the mountain. More than once in recent years the creeping heat has emerged through the cut of a gully wall setting fire to the juniper forest. Free at last, the flames race up the mountainside like a kid out of school, creating spectacular fireworks at night and ominous domes of smoke by day, before firefighters can put it out and bulldozers can push it back down where it came from.

Sometimes the inner fire burns near enough to the surface to create pits, according to Ray Toole, former Rollins owner. "You had to watch for deep pits where the gound had caved, some straight-sided and impossible to get out of if you fell in while alone. I used a stick to sound out the grund over hollow places that might cave under my weight." One of the Peterson boys found out the hard way when his horse stumbled down through soft earth-ash to red hot rock that scorched all four hooves before he could scramble out of the pit.

Westmoreland geologist Jim Roberts said there is no gold in North Fork coal, and was surprised it had been found in Rollins coal — or in coal at all. He theorizes that prehistoric floods deposited layers of gold-bearing clay in the decaying swamp vegetation, and that the process which turned peat to coal and turned clay to slate may have concentrated the gold in the crystallizing pyrites sometimes found in coal. This would explain why gold is found in Rollins seams and not in North Fork seams — coal seams at the west end of Grand Mesa contain more slate.

Red Davis, who knew Grand Mesa gold better than anybody, hadn't been born yet when that brief coal-fired Gold Rush struck. But he described what he had seen in mines elsewhere:

"When you find gold in coal it is tissue gold, thin leaves of pure gold between pure coal." ❧

13

The Seven Fat Years

The map of Grand Mesa is liberally spattered with Bull — Bull Creek, Bull Basin (two), Bull Basin Reservoir (two), Bull Creek Reservoir (five), Bull Creek Cowcamp, Bull Creek Schoolhouse, Bull Park, Bull Mountain, Bull and Brown Trail.... Most of these places are on the north side of the mountain, and most can trace their origin to one man, Milton Parker.

The next summer after the Utes left, Parker and his partner, Orson Adams, came West with the idea of establishing a big cattle outfit in the Plateau Valley. They selected a creek drainage between Spring Creek and Cottonwood Creek which until then had no name other than whatever the Indians had been calling it. Midway between its source under the rim of Grand Mesa and its mouth on Plateau Creek this stream slows down in a wide basin that in 1884 was unusually grassy. Competing vegetation — a stand of aspens described as "formerly too thick to ride a horse through" — had been burned away when lightning and disgruntled departing Utes took advantage of an especially dry year. Graze, taking advantage of the burnt-over, was by then stirrup-high.

Parker and Adams appropriated this high mountain valley by shipping in the start of their cattle spread — fifty head of purebred registered bulls.

Not one cow.

Parker came from Washington D.C. where he was connected with the Post Office Department. Adams was from New York City, not fresh and innocent out of the Garden of Eden as his name and the Parker-Adams enterprise induced Plateau Valley jokesters to jibe later. It isn't likely that these city dudes hadn't some grounding in the bovine version of the birds and bees, so naturally it could be supposed the Parker brought the bulls expecting to buy the heifer half of the equation when he got here. He would have needed quite a few. Depending on the age of these bulls — from adolescent two-year-olds capable of inducing ten calves a year to prime-time five-year-olds able to father forty — he would have needed between five hundred and two thousand cows just to make ends meet.

He found no cows for sale. Plateau Valley folk chose not to believe this, not even when Parker's unsuccessful efforts to buy cows ranged as far as Kanab, Utah. With glee and full innuendo they christened creek and basin for those bachelor bulls. The usual greeting from straight-faced cowboys riding into Bull Basin camp was "How's the calf crop?"

After two or three years Parker drove his bulls across the Dolores River to Sinbad Basin where the outlaw cattle rustlers and bank robbers who were holed up in that "robbers roost" either had herds of cows to make the bulls' lives more useful or their hardened ways had inured them to very tough steak.

Bull Basin is four square miles plus in extent, plus a few acres. The "plus" came about when a survey correction line and the forest boundary jostle each other in the Basin; two of the mile-square sections got bulldozed (sorry!) into including about a third more acreage than is normal for a square-mile section. Perhaps unhappy at having his mail addressed to a placename that was a community joke, Milton Parker moved east a couple of creeks to a wide place on Deacon Gulch which promptly became Parker Basin.

Separating Bull Basin and Parker Basin is the upper end of a long, fan-shaped stretch of relatively level land called Mormon Mesa. It is partially composed of a glacial deposit known as — what else! — Bull Lake. But this use of the word is an import, coming from Bull Lake, Wyoming, where that particular ice age glacier was first studied by scientists.

Just to show how mixed up things can get geologically, glacial depoists of Bull Lake ice age found down in Bull Basin are called Land's End Till because geologists first noted them in moraines way up on top in the flats east of Land's End cliff.

Moving mountains of ice grinding rocks against each other for millennia, manufacatured incredibly rich soil out of the strata that compose Grand Mesa. Over and over, in their oral and written memoirs, first settlers repeated what they saw when they first came: "Grass every where outside the forests was growing think and stirrup-high.

Stirrup-height was the usual measurement. But even down along the Stinking Desert below the west end of Grand Mesa grass was described by early-comers as "high enough to hide a baby calf at suck."

"The Whitewater drainage, now covered with sage, was then covered with bunch grass up to a horses eyes," Edgar Rider remembered.

In those days sagebrush was so scarce that a cowboy had to rummage through acres of tall grass to find a twig of it to make tea for bellyache or the diarrhea that kept yanking him out of the saddle.

Grass grew so tall, thick, and chemically rich that folks said cattle beefed up just looking at it. Not only rich, but self-perpetuating, no end to it. With lure like that, the cattle came pouring in from the East, from Texas, from New Mexico.

Ed January, writing his memories frugally on the backs of letters, recorded estimates of some of the early herds: "Marsh Huckolls brought in 2500, Jim Barnard had 1900 head, Botsford 800, Billie Balsh 600, Woods Bros. 1200, Henry Kohler of the Bar I outfit ran 2000, and Tom Lamb of the Figure 4 had about the same, Tom Mower 600, Bill Donley 200, King Bros 200... and others I don't remember."

Some of them came by chance.

J. F. Brink of Green River, Utah, was led to Grand Mesa by his cows — unwillingly. When 200 head turned up missing he tracked them into Colorado where he discovered they were being butchered to feed railroad construction crews camped below Whitewater, which was the point the Denver Rio Grande had then reached in its race to build a railroad across America before somebody else did. The cattle rustlers were there too, holed up at Whitewater. After Brink got Sheriff Rowan to deputize him, he shot one of them — the infamous horsethief George Howard.

In the process of recovering most of his stock Brink noted that the grass in the Whitewater drainage was "eye-high to a horse." About a hundred percent better than his over-grazed Utah range. That November (1882) he moved his herds (estimated by E. D. Stewart as between 2500 and 5000) up over the Hog Back and down into Plateau Valley. His home ranch included the Ute race tracks and the site where Chief Douglas had held the Meeker women captive.

Eastward on Grand Mesa, in Muddy and Divide Creek ranges, the influx of cattle outfits was perhaps even greater, but nobody was keeping tab on how many thousands of haunches bore which brand. One means of guessing the number of cows trailed in is to tally how many steers were shipped out: Ten trainloads bawled their way out of Hotchkiss in one fortnight.

The seven fat years, Alex Hawxhurst dubbed that era.

And those were only big stockmen. The number of cattle any one of them brought to Grand Mesa range didn't compare to the total of range stock pastured by homesteaders taking up land on all sides of the Mesa. Most of them raised cattle, from half a dozen to a couple of hundred head, taking advantage of the free range as a paying sideline to farming. With herds too small to be worth one cow-hand's pay ($30 per month plus grub), they formed pools of several hundred head each, hiring a rider to watch over the pool's cattle on the range — to ease them uphill as summer climbed the mountain, and ease them back down as winter pushed from behind, and in between times protect them from bear, mountain lion, cow thieves, and other predators.

Ed January's own family contributed to the cattle population, but on a small scale. Traveling in two prairie schooners, each with a trailer behind, the Januarys came in 1895 bringing not only a small herd of cattle but a number of exceptionally good horses.

They settled and put their animals to grass on upper Ward Creek. But they didn't join a pool; son Ed was big enough to ride herd. It seems to have been good for him. As Ed pointed out: Making the decisions you had to make alone on the open range, and knowing you'd have to live with the consequences, made a man of a boy mighty quick.

There was no control over how many head were put to graze or where. A man brought in a spread of cattle and the lands he grazed them on — in some cases the complete drainage of a certain stream from top to bottom — became "his." Often the stream or some feature in it took his name, as Buzzard Creek, Parker Basin or DeCamp Peak. Cows, of course, paid no attention to such restrictions, but roamed about, chewing where they chose. So every fall a big community roundup was necessary to get them sorted out according to the labels branded on their backs. Spring roundups were smaller and continuous, each cattle outfit gathering cows to brand calves with the company logo while still sucking the identifiable mother.

When the calf crop reached a certain stage the males were castrated to make them grow more tenderly marketable muscles. Until recently when "Rocky Mountain Oysters" became a far-out fad, these organs were left on the ground where they fell.

The Dude cattle outfit, under the management of Bill Kinney, did the same for its heifers, hoisting them up by windlass and performing ovarian section on their lower bellies. Alex Hawxhurst told about it in his memoirs, saying the operation was successful but never caught on. Alex didn't explain why the Dude outfit thought spayed heifers would increase in value enough to spend two months doing it. A heifer makes good eating as is; the surgery may have merely been a part of the then-current fad for unsexed meat such as the capon rooster.

———

Cattle, like buffalo, are wired to hit the trail just ahead of winter — drifting southward in the case of buffalo, and downward in the case of cattle grazing on mountains. One of the early cattle trails came down Doughspoon Creek to winter-graze along the Gunnison River.

None of the old timers remembers how Doughspoon got its name. Somebody lost one there? Or somebody found one there? But all of them know what a doughspoon is — a man-size cooking implement, about eighteen inches long, made of pewter-colored iron.

We saw one in action when brother Ira Edwards was a lad riding herd down on the Arizona Strip for ex-outlaw cattleman Bill Shanley.

Opening the top of the flour sack, Ira made a bowl-sized depression with that huge spoon, poured in water and canned milk (on the range not a cow in miles would stand still for milking), added a pinch of salt, three or four pinches of baking powder, and stirred until the mixture took up enough flour to be of biscuit consistency. From the lump he pinched off pieces and dropped them into the dutch oven on top of meat (beef, mutton, venison, rabbit — whatever was handy) that had been browning and making gravy of itself on campfire coals since breakfast. Filling the dutch oven lid with coals he put it in place, then squatted back on his heels and told cowboy stories for as long as it took the dough to bake. When the lid was lifted, there the doughspoon biscuits were, golden brown on top, gravied underneath. Heaven!

Where camp bread was leavened with sourdough starter instead of baking powder the big spoon got a workout in whipping enough air-born yeast into the start to make it ferment.

Cowboying wasn't all joy, however, especially during roundups in certain areas of Grand Mesa such as Salt Creek and Whitewater where drinking water was so alkaline it gave the men severe and sometimes chronic dysentery. There's the story Alex Hawxhurst told about one bunch of fellows who discarded their overalls and just wore chaps.

———

Mormon Mesa, the tableland between Bull and Parker Basins, got its name when a group of families left Utah for this part of Plateau Valley, the driving force being overpopulation and polygamy.

In the forty years since the Latter Day Saints had left Missouri and trekked across the plains, their herds of cattle and sheep had expanded far beyond

---

Ancient drift fence that once told cattle where they could and couldn't graze, now decorates the scene for campers and hikers.

Utah's range capacity to feed. The Saints began bringing large herds and flocks to harvest summer grass in western Colorado.

The state had run out of "people room" too — that is, the capacity to support people at the current stage of agriculture and industry. The "last pioneers" had to settle elsewhere. Facilitating the move, the Mexican Colonization and Agricultural Company was organized to promote Mormon colonies in Mexico and Colorado.

Twenty years before Grand Mesa was open for settlement, the Edmunds Act had made polygamy illegal in the United States. After more than a thousand polygamists had been imprisoned, the Church itself officially renounced the practice. This resulted in even more colonization as devoutly polygamous families sought out-of-the-way places where they could continue to practice their religion unobtrusively. At least one still exists, the sedately polygamous town of Colorado City (formerly Short Creek) on the Arizona-Utah line.

Old timers' memoirs, either from truth or tact, do not disclose whether Mormon Mesa was home to such a colony, but Helen Hawxhurst Young in *The Skin and Bones of Plateau Valley History* notes that settler Heber Young was a nephew of Brigham, that he and the Dame Brothers left Utah "because of the United Order," that "Lucinda Dame Young's was "a polygamist family," and that "Grandma Dame had been a plural wife, smoked a pipe, and was an herb doctor!

Lucinda's son-in-law, Delos Webb, came in with a lot of cattle and horses and a lot of family. He and his sons and their families flourished so well they eventually owned most of Mormon Mesa and all of Parker Basin. Not trusting banks, old Delos buried his money on the home ranch, and would dig into his savings (literally) only to buy more land. Some of the ranches he acquired were paid for with what was described as "mighty moldy gold." If Old Delos forgot where any of it was buried, it's still there. There have been no reports of finding minted treasure on Mormon Mesa — as yet.

Of the stockmen's many contrivances to hoist hay into tall stacks using only horsepower, the Mormon haystacker is one of the few still to be seen. It is elegant in its simplicity — a great log boom swiveling on a pyramid of four timbers. Your eager camera will find several Mormon haystackers in the Grand Mesa vicinity.

——— ———

Probably not polygamous, but definitely oversupplied with women (or undersupplied with men) was another wagon train that came over the mountain in 1884.

Mormon hay stacker. Boom swings in any direction; team-powered block and tackle lift hay into a tall stack. A few remain, but are rarely seen in action.

"A train of nine wagons drawn by oxen, from Arkansas passed thru town Monday," the Delta paper reported. "They were bound for Plateau Creek country and were going by the road over Grand Mesa."

Some of the ox drivers were girls; they were not riding, they were walking. On bare feet.

If you had walked barefoot all the way from Arkansas, across the plains and over the Continental Divide, you could take one more mountain in stride, literally, even though a mile high. And bad as it was the old Military Road up and across the top was better than the alternative — all the way around the west end of the Mesa and back over the roadless hump of the Hog Back. An ox train did pretty well to average six miles a day, not only because they were slow but because, unlike horses, they do not graze at night and must be allowed daylight time to feed. Any short-cut, however difficult, was preferable to tripling the mileage out around the Horn, and up over the Hog Back.

Among those barefoot ladies was Charley Atwell's wife who was to initiate Plateau Valley folks in the niceties of Arkansas etiquette:

"A woman don't sit at table with the men, you stands quiet, smoking your pipe, with a leafy branch in your hand for keeping the flies shooed away whiles the family and the hired hands eat. When they've et you eat."

Master of the wagon train was Joshua Barnes, a man of many talents one of which was witching for water. With a forked peach branch clamped in his fists, Joshua located most of the wells in Plateau Valley.

Joshua was also famous for the three sons he sired: Frank, Jesse, and Bill were celebrated far and wide for their fiddle playing and their capacity for — and staying sober while — ingesting quantities of hard liquor.

———

With all the larger ranches each requiring seventy-five to a hundred working saddle horses, and few of the other thousands of settlers getting by with less than four, horse-breaking was a needed and popular skill. Owners and hired hands broke their own ranch-bred colts. Entrepreneur bronc busters broke wild ones they caught by halter-trap on Grand Mesa, and some became so skillful they did nothing else, roving the country, breaking horses for hire or contract.

Not a few avoided bronc-busting altogether by stealing pre-broke equines, as the name of Horsethief Canyon attests.

Stealing horses was the major crime of the time, and not all of the horsethieves were swashbuckling men. One was a swashbuckling girl of twenty-two. At the time of her arrest for stealing Murray McGrew's horse and gear Leona Todd Smith of Surface Creek was described in the paper as "a daring and fearless 'cowgirl' who rides a bucking bronco as good as any cowpuncher on the range and carries a six-shooter strapped to her waist."

You can't break broncs riding side-saddle in long skirts, so one would wonder if Leona didn't come under suspicion because in 1906 she was wearing pants and riding astride, except that at the time of her arrest for horse stealing she was out on bond, charged with stealing calves that belonged to John Koppenhoffer.

Her defense, presented by her lawyer Judge Welch, was as wiley as that of the male horse thief who claimed he couldn't possibly have stolen any horse because he was in prayer meeting at the time — Leona maintained she was just holding the animals pending the arrival of the owner.

J.S. Rarey's classic, *The Modern Art of Taming Wild Horses* had been out for a quarter of a century but that Ohio trainer's ideas of taming horses by getting to understand their thinking, and never letting them catch on to just how

---

Comes to scattering hay bales, horse power is twice as efficient as tractor—no driver required. John Rozman runs his "engines" by remote control using four gear shift: Gee, Haw, Whoa, and Schicht, which last the horsepower translates into "Slow forward:". That dark hulk lurking in the trees is the Haunted House.

powerful they are, hadn't reached this far west. The prevalent method here was to jump onto the horse when he wasn't looking, spur him to do his dangdest, and stay on (if possible) until he gave up.

Even when it was only a corral chore, breaking a horse was always a show; rancher and neighbor, wife and kids perched on the fence cheering and booing. But even when rodeos became promoted events they were not entirely for the amusement of the people hunkered in the stands. They were performance opportunities where cowboys could demonstrate their skills in front of possible ranch employers. Staying on top of a bronc was a kind of informal resume, you might say. Chet McCarty made it more than that.

In the *Plateau Valley Story* McCarty is described as, "a pleasant, freckled-faced kid and pretty good rider," but nobody thought much about it as all the boys were pretty good riders. Chet attended Collbran grade school for a while — time not totally wasted because at least it gave him the mathematical know-how to figure his income tax which turned out to be quite a job. Chet won bronc-riding prizes all over the United States and Canada, and ended up with a national championship won at Madison Square Gardens."

The six pioneer ladies, whose memories make up that Plateau article, told about another cowboy, big-hearted, big-bodied Carmichael who after winning the roping contest celebrated with Prohibition liquor to the point where his singing out-decibelled the announcer.

The constable put him in the little jail and told Carm to lie down for a while, locked the outside door, and went back to the rodeo. Carm did not want to be alone, and he did not want to be in jail either. He bent the iron bars, kicked the pot-bellied stove into a corner, and kicked out the windows. But he went out the way he came in — through the door, which was nothing but firewood when he finished with it.

Once outside Carm tipped his hat to its usual jaunty angle, rolled a cigarette and sat down on the jail steps. There he remained until the constable returned in the evening. It took all his winnings to pay the fine, but he didn't mind, he had enjoyed himself immensely.

———— ————

As for those fiddling Barnes boys and their rough-riding peers, Alex Hawxhurst had this to say:

The "forging iron"—a horseshoe bent in a circle, heated in a fire and held in the grip of two green sticks, was used to forge your brand on somebody else's steer. Roy Bell demonstrates. Rusty Tyler says at one time Texas law shot people for owning one.

"The attitude toward women was a curious mixture of formal politeness and boisterous conduct, and while the pendulum sometimes swung to rowdyism, it was rowdyism without rudeness. It really showed up at dances.

"Each week there was a daylight to daylight dance (that is, from just before kaint see to just after kin see, because wagons and buggies didn't come equipped with headlights and Grand Mesa was nearly roadless.)

"One night at 3 a.m. the music went on strike. The old man laid down his fiddle. 'Boys,' he said, 'you'll have to go home in the dark. I quit.'

"There was a great protest, and the old man said, 'This is a hell of a lot of work for $1.75. Besides I ain't had a drink tonight.'

"The caller got after the boys for holding out on the old man. In the end almost another dollar was collected, and the drink that came hard at 3 a.m."

Most pioneer towns had one store built two stories high to house a hall upstairs where Saturday night dances were held, and traveling troupes put on plays such as *Uncle Tom's Cabin* and *Ten Nights in a Barroom*.

Alex Hawxhurst continued: "At one time there was a fad among the fellows to attend the dances with a Colt .45 stuck in the waistband of their pants. It was what Norman Croall would describe as a bit of swagger. Englehart and Parkinson had a large dance hall over their store and in the winter season there would be a Saturday night dance every week. After the dance the fellows on starting home would fire away whatever loads were in their guns, along with a lot of whooping and horse racing.

"One night at one of these dances Bill Barnes said, 'This is one helluva dance. I'm going home.'

"It being customary to fire away your shells on leaving, Bill just galloped around the dance hall and shot out the lights. When the broken glass began to fall, those who were out on the floor dropped down just in case of bad shooting. Milt Englehart went downstairs and got some new lamps out of the store, and when they were lighted Deafy Smith was found lying under one of the benches with his face to the wall. They went and pulled him out. Not being able to hear, he didn't know the shooting was over. Seeing the lights shot out and a lot of people dropping to the floor he thought they were killed."

Alex concluded, "There is a point I want to bring out in connection with this incident. Three lamps in five shots fired from a galloping horse is not the shooting of a drunk man."

14

Hog Back and Sheep Tea

"You chaps-wearing cow punchers had better buy a lot of sieves to strain your drinking water, or you'll be living on sheep tea in two years!"

When Frank Reid made that prophecy he was speaking to his cattlemen neighbors in Plateau Valley, but he was talking about the entire Mesa and, in fact, the whole western slope of Colorado, foretelling the huge bands of Utah sheep that would soon come pouring into Colorado, consuming its grass and trampling streams and lakes.

The seven fat years were over.

Three factors produced the seven lean years: A drought drastically reduced the amount of forage, a national depression forced people to stop buying beef, and the grass was playing out — there were already too many ruminant bellies on this mountain. The last thing ranchers needed was hordes of sheep competing for the thinning range.

Lowland range went first because cattle from all the surrounding mountains were trailed down to be wintered out on the limited valley range. By the second season there was almost nothing for them to eat along the bottomlands. Ranchers plowed and planted these newly-barren lands to hay, reassuring each other that fork-fed steers put on weight faster penned up than when roving the open range, especially if the critters were glaze-eyed happy on fermenting corn silage.

But then grass began to thin on the summer range — the wide benches of "climate" below the cliffs. From the first, those rim-cliffs had prevented cattle grazing the lusher grass up on top except on the more accessible east end. But as herds increased and grasses thinned, stockmen eyed the untouched heifer-high meadows up there, and began trying to figure out how to dig out rim-trails that could be negotiated by weavy-walk cows — not the most agile mountain climbers in the animal kingdom.

The Miller Trail was started up Whitewater Point (now Land's End) by Larry Miller, the Pickett brothers, and Edgar Rider in the fall of 1886. After a year and a half of wrestling boulders and blasting rimrock, they put the first cows up. Not all of them made it.

"Many cattle were lost in driving them up," recalled Forest Supervisor Ray Peck. "At one time thirty head of cattle went off the trail at Whitewater Point and were killed in the sliderock. When I came in 1922 those old trails were strewn with bones of cattle that had fallen on the rocks below."

A few cattlemen, foreseeing ruin with or without sheep, pulled their herds elsewhere or tried to organize range control among their fellow ranchers. One or two sidled toward government control; they weren't very popular with their neighbors. In fact some spreads greedily imported yet more cattle to cash in on the free grass while there still was some.

Frank Reid was no big-time sheepman, the 500 bucks he ran on the Hog Back weren't even his, so hardly anybody paid attention to his sheep-tea prophecy. Frank was always sounding off, they noted in their memoirs.

But later, when Nate Harrison said the same thing, they listened. Nate and the Dude Cattle Company had come into the Valley with 12,000 head of cattle.

"I have wide acquaintance in Utah from buying steers there, and I know there is going to be a wave of sheep hit this country. When they come it will be by the thousands; where they bed you'll have weeds instead of grass. In five years the last of you cattlemen will be gone from here."

Nate took his own advice and moved his outfit to the other side of the Continental Divide.

———————

Sheep raising in Utah was fostered by the early-day Deseret church-state as one of many means of furthering self-sufficiency — wool that was grown, woven, and worn without dependence on outside traders. In the quarter-century between the time Utah was settled and the western slope of Colorado opened to settlement, Deseret sheep got out of hand — and out of grub. They had overgrazed the land to the point that they were, as one Utah game warden put it, "eating so dadblamed close they leave teeth marks on the rocks."

Sheep, early cattlemen pointed out, nibble grass with their front teeth. They can bite off blades as close as an eighth of an inch from the ground if they have to. This leaves the plant almost no green chlorophyll to live and grow on. A cow, on the other hand, grabs a mouthfull of grass by swiping her tongue around it and pulling it toward her teeth. No way she can graze that close.

And sheep, whether by nature or from millennia of domestication, are psychotic. When scared or confused, they rush together for protection in numbers, even though some of them get crushed in the process. And anything can scare them, a clap of thunder or a sheepdog that forgets his training and chases a rabbit. Because of this flocking tendency (bunches of sheep are not called flocks for nothing) sheep are economical to raise. One trained herder and two trained dogs can handle a band of a thousand almost as easily as a hundred.

In the milling of panic, or preparing to bed down, the earth is hoof-chewed clean of every living plant. Visualize a thousand sheep huddled together, rib to rib, each with four hooves, each hoof cloven with four cutting blades along its edges. Sixteen thousand little knives hacking at the soil as they churn in panic or nervously hunker down for the night — each night in a different place. Nate Harrison was not alone in prophesying weeds where grass had been.

There were sheep on Grand Mesa from the start, in fact that "sooner" pioneer Enos Hotchkiss was the first sheepman on Grand Mesa. Enos got into the sheep business unintentionally, taking a small flock on a bad debt. It paid, so he stayed with it and by 1893 had sold his cattle and gone into sheep raising exclueively. Grand Mesa registered that switch for all time — the high glade on the Muddy that had been his cow camp became known as Sheep Park.

But most of the early sheep raising was merely a family ranch sideline. Like potatoes and pigs, wool supplemented main crops of corn and beef on the hoof.

"Sheep within reason was OK," one cowman later summed, "but sheep by the thousands? Sweeping across the range like an immense vacuum cleaner set on shag!"

They came. Like intermittent seas, like tides, the fluid flocks poured across the Utah state line and split under the prow of Grand Mesa. Some flocks turned south toward the San Juans or to access Grand Mesa grazing lands from the North Fork of the Gunnison. By the thousands they came pouring toward the Hog Back, aiming at Plateau Valley.

Settlers thought the Hog Back would keep the sheep out; it sure kept people from going to town!

———

The Hog Back rides like an empty saddle on the bucking country between the Rim of Grand Mesa and breaks down by the Colorado River. If you stand near the Airway Beacon on the northwest tip of Grand Mesa, Chalk Mountain is the white butte about halfway between you and the Colorado River (yes,

Permissive mother allows last-year's lamb to prolong babyhood into adolescence.

Grand Mesa has two Chalk Mountains, one at each end). The Hog Back is the ridge connecting the Mesa with that whitish mountain. From Highway 65 Chalk Mountain and the Hog Back dominate the western skyline all the way down the north side of Grand Mesa. You are looking at some of the wildest country on this mountain, more rawly eroded because the chalk only recently (in geological time scale) lost the protective lava that made it a part of Grand Mesa.

A true divide, the Hog Back cleaves the waters, not only water on the ground, separating Rapid Creek and Mesa Creek drainages, but water in the air — climate. Its hot west face pushes desert a little higher up the slopes; the weather-shadow of its east side permits the lush range to extend farther down the mountainside. It was the grassy range of the vast cup called the Plateau Creek drainage that Utah sheepman had their eyes on.

To get there they had to cross the Hog Back.

Just how rugged is the Hog Back? According to one report, loaded pack horses have tipped over backward, scrambling up its scarps. Another memoir has Chief Shavano leading the Meeker Massacre rescue party across the Hog Back by moonlight lest the white men glimpse what they were teetering across and lost their nerve.

Plateau Valley pioneers, who for ten years had no other way to get to their county seat, to the railroad, to a market for their produce except over this stony turbulence, penned letters and memoirs telling what the Hog Back was like.

Alex Hawxhurst wrote: "Picture a team toiling up Rapid Creek pulling a loaded wagon, the driver walking alongside to lighten the load; behind the wagon walked the largest boy carrying a rock to put back of the wheel when the team had to rest (which was every few yards); behind was another boy leading a cow, then the woman leading a child by the hand." And it wasn't a two-horse team because, as another pioneer describes, it took six: "By doubling up with Mr. Palmer, the mail carrier, the six horses carried our wagon to the top."

Another old-timer explains why the going was so rough: "I had supposed the Hog Back was one large mountain, as it appears from Grand Junction, but it is a succession of hogbacks one above another. You can get over only by climbing the gulches of Rapid Creek. And what a road! It is now up the mountainside, now down into a gulch or an abrupt curve into a creek and always full of rocks." This contributor to the early day newspaper concluded: "I thought, 'If I ever get there I'll never go back over that road!'"

That's why there was no distinguishable road up over the Hog Back, just wheel-scratches groping this way and that. Every man who wrangled it resolved never to take the same route back. Even the mailman and his horse got lost.

But Hog Back was all they had. Railroad and wagon road had not yet been wedged between river and cliff down there where the Colorado River bores through the Book Cliffs; and the Military Road up over Grand Mesa had deteriorated to its beginnings — when horses couldn't cope and it literally took an army to haul a wagon up.

The Army had abandoned it. With the Utes gone, the road was no longer an inter-tribal military facility. Fort Crawford continued at full complement, however, because keeping the troops there was cheaper than building duplicate facilities for them somewhere else. The soldiers still did their soldiering, sent off on long contrived treks, wrestling wagons down into and up out of various wilderness booby-traps, just to keep young men worn down to a properly obedient frazzle.

At the other end of the road, the new town of Delta saw opportunity in the Plateau Valley quandry. Even before the sagebrush was cleared off Main Street *The Delta Chief* was prodding county commissioners to fix up the Old Military Road.

"This road will be the best route to reach the Garfield Carbonate Camp... Residents of the White River county claim 300,000 head of cattle in that section. This estimate is probably high, but Delta is the nearest railroad shipping point and in summer it would bring all the travel from Plateau Creek directly to Delta."

In other words, it was easier to haul your wagon up to the top of Grand Mesa, all the way across and down the other side than to cross the Hog Back. Plateau settlers had the same idea. The only market for their increasing production of animals, fruit, grain, vegetables, eggs, and butter was Grand Junction. Because it took six horses to haul a wagon up the Hog Back, they had to travel in wagon trains in order to double up. This meant they arrived with vastly more produce than the new little town needed or could buy.

Patrick McCafferty described the problem. "Grand Junction never bought a full load of our grain or potatoes, or took more than ten of our hogs or more than a dozen chickens at one time. Two loads of produce would glut the market. If we happened to have five loads in a wagon train the surplus frightened those people nearly to death."

Tired of waiting on "the slowpokes of Mesa County to give them an outlet," Plateau Valley men went to work with shovel and scraper, aiming to put their wagons in Delta before July of that same summer. Delta County commissioners declared their end of it a county road which made it subject to poll tax maintenance — every voting man was required to put in so many hours on road maintenance or pay poll tax to have somebody else wield his shovel for him.

By October *The Delta Chief* noted incredulously, "The Grand Mesa Military Road is beginning to be a pleasure."

(In case you would like to trace such vestiges of this historic road as haven't been asphalted into Highway 65, *The Delta Chief* left directions: It forded the Gunnison at Baker's Crossing near the mouth of Forked Tongue Creek, went up Surface Creek, past Cedaredge, crossed to the west side of Milk Creek, around Bald Hill, and skirted the south end of Trickle Park. Passing east of Leon Peak it went down Park Creek to nearly its mouth thence across Plateau Creek, Buzzard Creek, and Divide Creek to the Grand River [the Colorado] almost 12 miles below the mouth of Roaring Fork. You may find tokens of its early use despite a hundred years of overgrowth — a rider for the Brown cattle outfit, found an ox yoke somewhat to the east of this ghost road.)

Of course the Military Road was only a summer road; teams and wagons couldn't cope with eight-foot snow. But because it had the potential of carrying Plateau Valley's produce for the entire growing season the Mesa County commissioners were prodded into action. Eventually a wagon road and rails were squeezed between the Bookcliffs down along the Colorado River.

———

The Hog Back became a battle front when Utah sheep began flooding toward Plateau Valley.

The war began small; Utah sheepmen first broached the Hog Back with herds of a few hundred to test the resistance, or they got local friends like Frank Reid to do it for them.

"A band of 500 bucks, owned by Utah men had wintered at the Frank Reid Ranch in Plateau Valley," Forest Supervisor Bill Kreutzer remembered, "One night a group of men surrounded the band at a sheep camp on the Hog Back, a divide between the valley and the desert range." The masked men killed the rams and sent the herders back with word to keep all sheep away from the Plateau Valley if they didn't want further trouble."

"Frank was a local man," Alex Hawxhurst remembered, "but his attitude was so aggressive he couldn't be ignored. Reid repeatedly said he would welcome the chance to kill some of those cattle lovers. Well, he got his sheep killed and came near breaking the record as a long distance runner."

Overnight a line-of-site string of rock cairns appeared along the ridge of the Hog Back, each accompanied by a sheep carcass to make the meaning clear.

Bucks, 200 of them, were also involved in the next skirmish. Billy Grant was sitting by his Hog Back campfire cooking his beans and bacon, when he had company — two cowmen who chanced to ride by for what the paper called a "fireside chat" concerning the advisability of what he was up to. Billy affectionately patted the two brand new guns he was wearing, one on each hip, and said, "These'll see to the protection of the bucks."

"Next morning," the account concluded, "the two six-shooters lay on the table of one of the cowpunchers. The bleaching bones of those bucks had messages for encroaching Utah sheepherders for the next decade. They didn't pay much attention.

"Despite the warning, within a short time the sheepmen attempted to drive in a band of 800 ewes. They crossed the Hog Back in the daytime, but that precaution availed them no security. One hundred masked men met them on the Plateau side. Seventy-five stood guard while the remainder killed the animals with guns and clubs."

———

A Forest Service Supervisor wrote, "In 1888, a Fruita sheepman brought 10,000 head of sheep from Utah... and in 1890 the Mormon Church sent an outfit into the Valley with 40,000 sheep and about 40 men to guard them. A portion of these sheep were rounded up and killed by Plateau men, the herders were badly scared and warned not to return. The next spring, another Mormon was headed back into the valley presumably as a feeler, with 1700 sheep. He was met on the Hog Back with a volley of 45's and every sheep in the outfit was killed; a herder was wounded and a ranchman killed."

None of these masked killers was indicted, much less convicted. Leading suspects, men in whose area a raid occurred, had absolute alibis. Plateau Valley cattlemen were visibly at home or at prayer meeting when sheep were killed on the Hog Back. The same for the North Fork ranchers who would be conspicuously kicking up their heels at a hoedown when masked Plateau Valley riders slipped over the mountain to return the favor.

Not even famous lawman Doc Shores could run them down.

Pete and Nels Swanson were bringing several thousand sheep up through Kannah Creek in 1907. With them was Grover Cornett, riding the range preparatory to bringing in flocks of his own from Cisco, Utah. Suddenly from over a rim ten or twelve cowboys blocked the way. They drew their guns, and in the course of shooting sheep shot Pete Swanson. Nels and Cornett took Pete to the Paunchford Ranch on Indian Creek, and called the law and a doctor.

Both were unsuccessful at their jobs — the doctor lost Pete, he died that night, and United States Marshal Doc Shores never did find out who those gun-slinging cowboys were.

Doc had better success with train robbers. In the fall of 1887 four robbers held up the passenger train at Whitewater and took off into the wilds. Doc Shores, in addition to the D&RG's Pinkerton men, traipsed all over Western Colorado and Eastern Utah, and from one end of November to the other (and through twenty pages of Doc's memoirs) before he got the last of the robbers in Price, Utah, by "kidnapping" him from the authorities there and taking him into his own jurisdiction. Lawing was rather informal in those days.

———

The Hog Back whitened with bones. Sheepmen began bypassing it. Two thousand sheep slipped in by way of the Book Cliffs, were driven over the oil shale cliffs at Parachute by two hundred masked men.

When the owner of those sheep came from Utah to view the scene of destruction, he is said to have remarked, "I have seen the market go up and go down, but this is the biggest drop I have ever seen sheep take."

The battle line of rock cairns was extended north across the Colorado River and south on barranca-tops toward Delta. One, at least, still stands, visible from Highway 50. Sheep were shot, clubbed to death, and otherwise discouraged on the North Fork and Dry Creek. A band was driven over a

---

Three sheep-herders drive a flock up Cory Grade turn-off. The one in the middle works twelve hours a day for bed, bowl, and an occasional bone.

Gunnison River cliff above Pleasure Forks. A band was dynamited on Buzzard Creek.

On the heights above Kannah Creek cattlemen posted lookouts with spy-glasses turned toward Utah. Upon sighting sheep-raised dust clouds in the distance they set off charges of dynamite to signal ranchers to ride to the Hog Back and head them off.

Sheepmen fought back. With a herd of old ewes as bait, gunmen set up an ambush on the Hog Back. Unsuspecting Valley ranchers rallied at the Beehive, preparatory to attack. But a gully-washer storm kept them from riding to the Hog Back and falling into the trap.

Frank Reid's forecast about "sheep tea" came true. In May of 1894 the *Grand Junction News* complained that the water of the Grand Canal, main source of domestic water, was noticeably contaminated.

Meeting secretly, cattlemen organized the Western Slope Protective Association. Even their wives knew nothing about it except not to ask questions. Decades later somebody revealed the Association's oath of secrecy to a forest ranger who, apparently, was afraid to tell who told him; and Forester Peck, in writing about it did not identify even the ranger by name:

"I, _____, in the presence of Almighty God and the members of the Western Slope Protective Association here assembled, do promise and swear that I will keep inviolate and not divulge to any person or persons whomsoever any secrets or activities or names of members of the association, that I will do my utmost at all times to protect the ranges of northwestern Colorado against invasion by sheep. All this I promise and swear with a firm and steadfast resolution to perform the same without any mental reservation whatsoever, binding myself under no less a penalty than that of being shot to death should I ever in the least violate this my voluntary obligation."

One man talked too much and paid. He was Sylvester McCarty, miner and road overseer who was known for having a big mouth and who happened to be pasturing 300 sheep for a Grand Junction sheepman.

Sylvester and Betsy McCarty came in 1881 from New York to Aspen where he worked in the mines. After they moved to the Plateau Valley he worked in New Castle mines then at various ranches, moving about, raising field crops, a few head of cattle, and a lot of babies. When McCarty became road overseer it may have been the most prestigious job he ever had. At any rate he felt important enough to sound off to cattlemen.

"McCarty was a man who said whatever he wanted to — to anybody he wanted to," Alex Hawxhurst remembered. "So everybody knew where he stood regarding sheep."

Just for sheep. This swingy, cable-hung, loose-board bridge across the Gunnison River daunts all human feet except those of the sheep herder and intrepid small boys. When the herd had crossed, enough of the boards are removed at each end to defeat intrepidity.

Two men, Bart Johnston and Reuben Pitts, recalled the event that happened when they were boys. "It was in the early 1890s when the sheep and cattle war raged. Cattlemen met secretly and planned their strategy, and delegated the part each man was to play. Sylvester McCarty attended these meetings and was quite vocal, in and out of meetings.

"One morning as overseer he was working a strip of road on the south side of the creek. He was alone, and someone on the hill above shot him. The

cowmen blamed it on the sheepmen, but many thought it was done by the cowmen because dead men carry no tales.

"McCarty was brought to the Pitts cabin by the mailman who had found him crawling along the road, badly wounded. He stayed with mother until father got home. McCarty was restless, and wanted to get out of bed and get even. He lived until evening, shortly after his wife Betsy got there.

"The funeral was conducted by an itinerant minister, Rev. Davis, at the Pitts place. It was outside because the homemade coffin wouldn't go through the door. The coffin had rope handles, and rested on two chairs. It was the first funeral I ever attended, and I saw nothing strange in a lack of music or flowers. But a bunch of men riding with their hats off was something else."

"Fifty cattlemen rode in the funeral procession. Many had revolvers or guns in their scabbards. He was buried in the Collbran cemetery which was a pretty primitive place covered with sagebrush.

"The County Coroner heard he was buried without an inquest, and rode to Collbran and ordered the body disinterred. The Coroners jury reached a verdict that McCarty was slain by a bullet by an unknown assassin.

"Betsy was left with eight children, and she no bigger than a whiffet, the youngest six weeks old. The cowboys banded together to pay off the mortgage on the home.

"Several years later, John McKee and I were grubbing sagebrush out of the Cemetery when John's mattock struck iron. It was a loaded revolver, rusted. Others gathered around and all agreed it was likely hidden or lost at McCarty's funeral."

The sheep and cattle wars dwindled away with the passage of grazing laws. Terrors of crossing the Hog Back faded into history when it was by-passed by road and railroad down along the Colorado River. But some of those groping trails across it still survive, though faintly.

The Old Ute Trail, for one. After coming up around the bulge of the mountainside from Kannah Creek, it went up Sink Creek to the Bench, then northeast around the Big Blowout above what was the Vincent Ranch. Utes marked the trail by up-turning rocks at intervals, making sign-boards of their mineral-white undersides. Some of those rocks still mark that trail. Though you won't find the tipis Elgar Rider noted near Middlemist Ranch, who knows what fascinating trash their residents might

One of Grand Mesa's fascinations is how frequently patterns on the earth are repeated in the sky.

have left in the dust for you to discover? Someone did find an old cap-and-ball pistol in the buck brush here, Rider wrote in his memoirs.

"A branch of buck brush growing up through the trigger guard was an inch in diameter, demonstrating how long the weapon had lain there unnoticed."

Big Blowout, by the way, is not a blowout but a huge slide — as near as Grand Mesa comes to having a glacier cirque.

You can cross the Hog Back on wheels now — jeep wheels. But Dale Bittle of the Forest Service warned that the trail in places crosses private land through locked gates, requiring permission.

The easiest way to climb the Hog Back is the way the pioneers wagoned toward town, from east to west, up the relatively gentle slopes of the eastern side. The trail (at first a road) leaves Mesa Creek at the old Brink Ranch with its historic Meeker Tree.

Following the Tate Creek drainage, the trail loops around Barney Hill, and climbs to the top of the Hog Back.

The "crest" of the Hog Back is so mixed up it's hard to know when you are on it. But if you grope, like those wagoneers did, the view will tell you when you've found it. Beyond a swelter of Rapid Creek's squirming side-canyons, Grand Valley swings leftward from your feet; on your right Plateau Valley circles vastly beneath the distant skyline of Battlement and Mesa rims. From the rim-rock wall behind you the Mesa itself breaks off in a surf of forested benches and hidden lakes. The 600-foot bump in front of you is Chalk Mountain. The 800-foot chasm the trail rims out on is the head of Big Wash.

Who owns this turbulent wilderness? You do.

In 1892 your government took it over in your name, saving it from ravenous range bellies, devastating loggers, and water-greedy irrigators that altogether unchecked would have made this heaven a barren, eroding hump on the skyline. ❧

15

Government Edges In

"Next thing you know they'll put a pen in the clove of a cow's hoof and demand the cow sign her own permit to eat grass on Grand Mesa!"

That was the saying going around in the late 1880s when it was rumored the federal government planned to make Grand Mesa into a Forest Reserve requiring permits to put cows on public lands they had always grazed with no restrictions.

Colorado was the first state in the Union to assert rights concerning mountain woodlands — forestry being part of the 1876 Colorado constitution when Territory became State. Colorado didn't invent legal forest restrictions, it was prevalent in Europe; Plymouth Fathers brought it over, passing an ordinance in 1626 prohibiting timber cutting on colony land without official consent. The Fathers couldn't make it stick, nor get it on the books when the colonies became the United States — there was so much virgin timber on this continent that passing restricted cutting laws seemed ridiculous. Colorado couldn't enforce conservation either; miners, loggers, farmers, hunters, and stockmen went right on doing what they'd always done — grabbing.

If you had a big round saw blade and a wood-burning steam engine, you could pack it in and set up a sawmill wherever the timber stand looked profitable. You started digging for gold or oil wherever you glimpsed a glint or a leak. You grazed your cattle herds where you pleased, and as many as you could trail in. You set fires, burning off heavy timber to open up areas to the sun and provide more grass. If you discovered a nice stream of water above your homestead you hitched team to scraper and created an earthen dam; the water you diverted belonged to you though you didn't own an inch of the land the ditch traversed or the resulting lake submerged. You shipped fish by the carload if you could dynamite that much, and as many deer hides as you had bullets and marksmanship to bag.

Then government began withdrawing certain western lands from homesteading and unrestricted private use. President Harrison's administration sent Colonel Edgar T. Ensign this way to lay out the boundaries of what they named Battlement Mesa Reserve. Battlement Mesa is a similar, but much smaller, lava-crowned flat-top mountain to the northeast that once was probably a continuation of the same lava outflow that created Grand Mesa. Erosion cut them in two, and now they stand staring at each other across the great bowl of Plateau Valley. Why the Harrison administration chose to name the Reserve for the smaller mountain nobody knows.

Surveying the area, Colonel Ensign charted reserve boundaries just below the lava rim-cliffs, to take in only fir and spruce forest. Earlier that year a group called the Western Slope Congress recommended confining the forest reserve to the rim itself. They sent Congress their recommendation in June, Ensign didn't get his off until sometime in December.

United States lawmakers ignored that Western Slope Congress and didn't wait for Ensign's report to arrive. It was Christmas week; members were rushing legislation through in order to get home to the family. So, on December 23, 1892, sitting in Washington, D. C., looking at a map of Colorado, they drew the reserve boundaries.

Those borders extended almost down to the Colorado River on the north, and halfway down the south and west slopes, taking in established farms, orchards, ranches, and mines. Within them thousands of acres of potential farmland were closed off to homesteading.

Protest letters and newspaper blasts were so hot they scorched the paper they were written on — at least that's how the yellowed, century-old pages look now. A few ranchers, aware that overgrazing was destroying the range, knew some kind of control had to be established; but most protesters raged at the federal usurpation of all minerals in the ground, all growth on top of it, and the very water that fell from the sky.

Blamed by everybody, Colonel Ensign defended himself in print, citing the much smaller Reserve his report had mapped, but the government didn't back him up. Instead, it tacitly saddled him with the blame by easing him elsewhere. Protests had effect, however; eventually the Reserve was whittled down from 866,400 acres of mountains and valleys to 665,400 acres of mountaintop.

The move that put Grand Mesa under Federal lock and key coincided with the most belligerent period in Grand Mesa history. By shootings and by running sheep-bands over cliffs cattlemen were in process of establishing their right to keep sheep off the mountain. By charging a fee to fish in the Mesa's biggest group of lakes, fish hatchers were setting the stage for a fifty-year fatal feud. And every farmer, rancher, and peach grower whose holdings had been included in that original reserve was trigger-set to fight further encroachments.

In view of all this the government came in on tip-toe that first year. Cattlemen were lords. The United States, in the form of the newly created Forest Reserve, didn't dare tackle them face on. Instead, forest rangers eased into control by first suggesting that cattlemen drop by the office if they felt like it and indicate how many cows they had, offering to issue free permits to range that many on Grand Mesa.

Ranchers weren't fooled, they knew the permits were a one-way gate, that ultimately the government would assess fees and set limits on the numbers grazing the reserve. The smartest of them knew government had to act to save the range because nobody else would. Two or three of them had even suggested it.

The first chain of forest supervisors were political appointees who operated the reserve on the spoils system, staking out claims for themselves in the names of kinfolk, and accepting kickbacks for favoring certain stockmen — according to a later supervisor, Lewis Shoemaker. In his book, *Saga of a Forest Ranger,* Shoemaker said those first appointees knew nothing about forestry, and a lot about "the grab-and-git system." Three were ex-army colonels, two were doctors, and one was both. The doctors were told to quit practicing medicine while drawing government salaries. They paid no attention but went right on profitably looking into throats and prescribing the usual opium to soothe colicky babies.

Getting rid of those first unscrupulous supervisors was accomplished nationwide when forestry was transferred to the Department of Agriculture in 1905, but according to Peck one young ranger was already cleaning up Grand Mesa.

The kid's name was William Kreutzer. He took his job seriously. Early on, when advised by an official to get himself a dictionary so his reports would read better he had bought a "flexible covered Webster's, and a book of 100,000 Synonyms and Antonyms both of which he studied earnestly and faithfully," as he later told Shoemaker. Of course he also had *Rules and Regulations Governing Forest Reserves* described as his guidebook and bible. "Bill Kreutzer saw that those rules and regulations were enforced. It was as if he had been molded alongside a straightedge and could not therefore do it otherwise."

Kreutzer's father and grandfather had been foresters in Germany. When Bill — who grew up on a cattle ranch over on the Eastern Slope — heard that federal forest reserves were being set up in the United States he went to Denver and applied for a job. He was still so young he almost didn't get it, but they took a chance on him. According to historian Abbott Fay, young William Kreutzer was America's first forest ranger.

Stationed at Sedalia, he hewed so strictly to the rules of how a forest reserve should operate that the fat cat officials there couldn't stand it. They got him transferred to what was then being called "Battlement Mesa Reserve" with more meanings than intended.

The doctor-army officer who was currently Battlement Forest Reserve supervisor was having a hard time getting past Kreutzer's uprightness to award pieces of public lands to the politicians who had helped him get the job. He first tried to push Kreutzer out of his way by promoting him elsewhere, as the Sedalia Reserve had done. When that didn't work, he tried unsuccessfully to trap him into an error that would get him fired from the service. Then, counting on Kreutzer's stubborn bravery, he set a trap to get him killed by telling a squatter that if a ranger asked to examine his claim he had the right to order him off with loaded gun. The supervisor knew Kreutzer wouldn't budge. He didn't, the squatter did.

(This is the same Kreutzer who when investigating those illegally cut telephone poles — remember? — worked all day under old Otto Peterson's randomly pointing gun, just waiting until he could get hands on it and remove the bullets. A powerful man. It's no wonder young Ott — watching this happen that day — had a change of heart, from poacher to warden.)

Strong, brave, but not bull-headed. When Kreutzer found cattlemen working at cross purposes with each other, with the range capacity, and with the reserve he got them organized into a working group with an elected committee of five to keep Forest officials advised on range conditions on all parts of the reserve.

In 1905 the supervisor did manage to rid himself of Ranger Kreutzer by getting him transferred to the brand new Gunnison Forest Reserve that President Roosevelt created along with thirty-six others that year.

Teddy Roosevelt shifted the Forest Reserves from the General Land Office to the Department of Agriculture because, the President yelled in print, "Forestry IS agriculture, the growing of trees!"

Roosevelt's administration cleaned up the Reserves (renamed National Forests), firing all personnel suspected of turning public assets to private profit. Heads fell right and left, Lewis Shoemaker wrote. But not Bill's.

William Kreutzer survived that political housecleaning, and before long was supervisor of Gunnison National Forest. He retired as supervisor of Colorado

National Forest after serving forty-one years with the Service, longer than anyone else in its history.

Courage and the rules were about all those early forest rangers had to work with, almost none of the federal money went for equipment. Kreutzer named eleven rangers assigned to the Mesa that first year — and totaled the government-issue tools the eleven were given to work with:

Six shovels and six axes.

Each of those first rangers holed up in a tent (if he had one) until he could cut logs, build cabin, and fence coral for his horse and packhorse (if he had one); using in turn one of those six axes and six shovels (unless he'd brought one).

What were their duties as rangers? Pioneer Ed January listed them in his memoir: To preserve the water-supply, to regulate timbering, to control grazing, and to oversee people-use.

Regulating grazing was by no means first on the list then or now, but the belligerent cattlemen put it there.

The ranger was expected to tally every cow, calf and bull, to issue permits, and collect cash. Even after that first free year, the cash was slow in coming in because rancher Fred Light opened a test case to see if grazing fees could legally be collected, and until it was settled in court a number of ranchers refused to pay. (Fred lost.) And anyhow many cattlemen were skilled in dodging the full count, having long practice in fooling the county tax collector about how many cows they actually did have.

It was not until John Lowell was supervisor in 1924 that cattlemen fully realized the benefits of government controlled grazing. A cattleman from the range along Muddy Creek moved west, putting his herds (steers alone numbered a thousand) to winter-graze a great swath of country that included Peach Valley, Rogers Mesa, and slopes under the Point (near the size of the state of Delaware), and aiming to summer-graze his stock on the Grand Mesa range above those lands. It would have wiped out the original ranchers. Supervisor Lowell served notice that if he saw one steer wearing that brand on the forest in the Point District he would cancel the outfit's grazing permit on the Muddy. The outfit backed down. From that time cattlemen were on government's side regarding control of public lands.

Grazing permits are not put up to the highest bidder, but are attached to the land owned by the original permittee, a kind of homestead right that passes on down through the generations. If you buy one of the many cattle ranches ringing a National Forest, part of what you pay for is that ranch's permits to graze a regulated number of cattle up in the forest meadows. How early in spring you may put them up there and how soon in the fall you must bring them down is determined by range conservationists trained to read the seasons.

It was (and is) the summer job of the rangers to constantly assess range conditions and see that cattle are shifted from overgrazed sections onto valleys and parks where the grass is untouched. The first big moves were from the chewed-bare slopes under the west rims onto the east Muddy range where grass was still, according to one ranging ranger, "up to my horse's eyes."

Cows have a built-in homing instinct. Moved from grazed-to-the-ground Sink Creek over onto to tit-deep grass below Crater View, they still have a yen to meander back home to Sink. One tricky way to coax them to graze where decreed is to put the salt-lick block there. But salt doesn't always do it. To effectively handle the range great long drift fences began to snake their way through the forests, across the meadows and down the mountainside, dividing the Reserve into sections. At first they were brush fences, made the easiest way possible by cutting down whole trees and tilt-piling them to form a branchy rick. A few of these may still be seen, but if they were made
o   f
everlasting cedarwood it's hard to tell whether they were built by early foresters or by earlier Utes as guide fences to ease game to where hidden hunter was waiting. Later drift fences were built of aspen — "quaker" pole worm fences — zig-zagging off into infinity. Where worm fences cross regular deer trails, space is left below the bottom log so the fawn can wriggle under the fence his mom has just jumped over.

Nowadays drift fences are often barbed wire strung on metal posts driven into the ground. You can tell when you are driving from one range-section into another by the noisy cattle guard across the highway. Cows have the right-of-way up here. If you come onto a cow who has hunkered down on the nice warm tarmac to chew her cud, drive out around her carefully. She won't sue you if you hit her, but her owner can.

By the way, unless you happen on the Peninsula road on the right day, you are not likely to see cowboys trailing herds of cattle down the Mountainside come fall. Nowadays cows commute in trucks. Oh, they kick up a fuss about it, milling around and bawling, but at roundup time (yes, that hasn't changed) they dutifully board. The ones with window seats (crowded against the semi's slats) may even watch the scenery and tongue their noses at passing motorists.

———— ————

Though they have greatly improved under strict Forest Service supervision, grasses on and around Grand Mesa have not come back to anything like the lushness pioneers described over and over – verbally and not to the press, lest they attract competing stampedes of ruminant bellies.

Many ranchers today think it never was that lush. They pooh-pooh old-timers' descriptions of stirrup-high grasses. Just try to tell anybody that 'dobie benches – such as the barren miles between Crawford and Paonia – were once lush with eighteen-inch bluestem and curly grass, as Laura Clock's published collection of old-timers' memoirs describes them!

Pioneers' descriptions are too frequent, too various and too consistent to be disregarded. The grass *was* thick and tall.

All attempts to bring the lower benches and valley range, such as the Stinking Desert, back to anything like that grassy productivity have failed, including the valiant effort of the Girl Scouts to reseed Uncompahgre benchlands, and widespread seeding via helicopter.

Will anything bring that lushness back? Nothing less than another ice age, some experts state. Those grasses, they maintain, got their start when rainfall was something like 400 inches a year. As post-glacial climate turned drier the grasses learned to root deep, tapping moisture several feet down. Larger root systems required taller green-growth above to produce chlorophyll nutrients. When the chlorophyl factory was grazed to the ground, and the eons-old protective much trampled away, the plant went out of business. For good. And without mujch to hold moisture between rare rains it can't reseed itself.

Grasses are long-lived perennials. Nobody knows how old a natural grass plant is because it lacks the redwood's "tree ring" means of measuring, but some rangeland scientists believe the individual grass plants making up the ranges that lured cattlemen and sheepmen westward had put down first root at least as far back as the wet conditions following the last ice age. Something to think about-this one little clump of blue-stem you are fingering may be older than the redwoods, older than the bristle-cone pine, breathing in oxcygen and breathing out carbon dioxide for some 25,000 years. We knew range grass was a perennial, but we didn't think it was that perennial!

Growth taking the place of grazed-away grass was desert herbage such as sagebrush, cactus, and shadscale that can sprout and put down root in the flick of time after a shower that happens at just the right moment; plants having the capacity to shut down between infrequent rains; plants that have invented protective devices such as thorns, bitter taste, and dirty-colored leafage. The kind of plants that grazing animals don't like to eat.

Cowboys who need sage tea to stop the trots don't have to hunt through a mile of tall grass to find some now.

–––– ––––

Ed January's list of forest rangers' responsibilities failed to include two very important ones: To build trails and roads, and to keep track of game populations.

At first there were just two roads, the Old Military Road and the Nuckoll Trail, both antagonistic to wheels. Indian trails threaded inconspicuously through the woods, and cow trails wriggled off toward grass and water. The Forest Service laid out new trails, using a one-wheeled odometer pulled by a horse to measure distances in the forest.

The Old Military Road and its groping detours made the Alexander group of lakes accessible to vehicles from the first. By wagon or buggy it took two days, with a camp-over at Ginter's Grove above Cedaredge.

The first autos could make it in one day, but not easily. As late as 1950 the road was so steep, crooked, and washboardy the Carpenter's Model A Ford, using all its power and jouncing like a shook rug, would spin on one switchback until it got enough tire-grip on the gravel-grid to forge up to the next.

On the other side of the mountain, the resort group called Mesa Lakes was accessible only by horseback and packmule until the new Forest Service wrangled something like a road. That's when Bill Stroud started his twice-a-week stage run. To get out of sweltering Grand Junction you took the train upriver to DeBeque. Boarded the stage coach and jounced and twisted up the mountain, cooling as you climbed until you came out on the flower-fringed, ice-cold lakes and the cabins those New York ladies built.

In 1957 the state took over both roads, eventually changing them from rutty spirals that let themselves be pushed around by every bluff and creek, into paved Highway 65 that slashes its way up the mountainside and down the other side "ir-regardless" of anything geography shoves at it — including reprisal mud slides.

Many of the roads and trails were created by CCC and WPA workers during the Great Depression, among them Land's End road, Trickle Park road, and the Crag Crest Trail.

People had been squirming along the double-sided precipices of two-and-a-half mile Crag Crest even before there was a trail — females somehow making it in long skirts and petticoats.

John Wettrich holds a curved rock showing how Grand Mesa basalt tends to shell off rather than blow up when dynamited.

During the Depression, the Forest Service decided to improve the trail. Not too much. Not enough to take away the adventure. Just enough to make it a little easier on shins, elbows, and on the nerves of mothers whose sons are up there leaping from rock to rock over pure nothingness.

That was in 1937. The Service allotted $1800, one summer, and unlimited dynamite to get the job done. John Wetterich of Cedaredge headed the crew of seven men.

Not long ago we had the honor of being guided the length of Crag Crest Trail by the man who created it — the first time John himself had hiked the trail since he built it.

"You wouldn't believe the amount of dynamite it took to make a foot trail the length of this ridge. Couldn't use heavy equipment because that would destroy what we were put there to make accessible — the natural beauty of the surroundings. So every rock to be moved had to be blasted down to a size we could hassle by hand.

"Some of this lava seems to have cooled while rolling, and when you blast that kind, it just pops off a shell like an onion, and you have to repeat the process till it's down to size. We'd lay dynamite sticks on or under the rock, pack wet clay over the charge to contain the explosive force, and then set it off. Lucky if it shattered off a few inches at a time. Ten or fifteen sticks to one big rock was about normal. Every morning five of the crew would each carry 40 pounds of dynamite in a pack."

In the deep gaps between the "vertebrae" of the spine, rocks had to be piled up to make fills that were wide enough to accommodate a footpath, and then enough earth carried up to create the path itself.

In the 1970s the trail was improved to make it eligible for the National Recreation Trails system. Forest Service engineer Charles Miller vowed not to "improve it to death."

"We have decided against suggestions to gravel the whole thing, blacktop the whole thing, put guard rails in the narrow places, steps in the steep places, and other 'conveniences' that would take away some of the challenge and excitement that are so much a part of hiking the crest."

Our second trip along the Crest was horseback — which for safety reasons is no longer allowed on the Trail. In squeezing around one of those towering "vertebras," our horse walks out on the very lip of the path to avoid bumping our leg against the cliff wall. Not that he gives a whoop about our leg, but the bump might teeter him over the edge. This horse is a rental vehicle,

Crag Crest Trail and John Wettrich, the man who created the path along this narrow spine of the "beast that is swallowing Kannah Creek".

How to take bad pictures even on Crag Crest Trail–riding scared and shooting between the ears of an out-of-focus horse.

---

been here before, knows what he's doing; so we might as well relax, hook our arm through the reins, and point the camera at a piece of the immensity below.

Forest management is a balancing act. How many cows can graze up here before the elks starve out, how many deer can browse before brush becomes too thin to protect the soil from erosion. How many board feet of timber can be cut before....Money is part of the balancing act. Permits, licenses, and fees help finance the construction of roads and buildings, buy materials, and pay the salaries of people who ride the range, host tourists, and clean up after picnickers.

Presumably before man arrived with his weapons and wants, the wild creatures struck a population balance of their own. By feeding on fawns the coyotes and wolves and bears kept deer and elk to graze-sustainable numbers. Eagles and such took care of excess beavers and whelps, whelps of chipmunks, and so on down to the infinitesimal. This balance was apparently not disturbed by Indians hunting with bows and arrows.

But weapons powered with gunpowder rather than arm muscle changed all that. To stem the slaughter State and Forest Service imposed rules — how much game you can kill, where, and in which weeks of the year. At first the number was zero for all three — to give game a chance to come back.

During that time one resident was so incensed that anybody claimed the right to tell him when and where he could hunt, that he flaunted his scorn by spreading deer hair up and down Cedaredge's Main Street including a wad of it on the post office steps.

The state's first female game warden turned him in. She was Freda Bourne, a Cedaredge resident who had helped Ranger Bill Kreutzer on another occasion by alerting him to five illegal deer carcasses hanging on the back of Ott Peterson's cabin.

Today deer are so plentiful on Grand Mesa that you're likely to see some every time you prowl it, especially if you linger into twilight when they come out into the glades to browse. (By the way, if you find a tiny fawn, nestled in a camouflage of foliage, staring you eye-to-eye, leave it alone. The mother has placed it there, told it to stay put while she feeds, and will return to give it suck as soon as you are out of sight. If you think the poor little thing is abandoned and "rescue" it by taking it home to bottle-feed you will have ruined its life.)

Elk, being grazers prefer the pinyon-juniper climate band. There, among scattered trees they find both grass to eat and tree-cover to duck into.

———

As for the predators, they came and went with the food supply. After early-day hunters wiped out deer and elk for their hides and teeth, the coyote population fell to near zero. Nothing to eat. But when cattle and sheep (mainly females) surged onto the range by the tens of thousands this mountain table became a vast banquet of tender lamb, veal, and colt. The coyote population exploded. Alex Hawxhurst tells us:

"As a female coyote raises from six to eight pups a year (and if all goes well the bitch pups can have pups next year) they increase pretty fast."

That little Alex Hawxhurst, whose severed finger was saved by the natural cleansing of worms eating away rotten flesh, had grown up to be a man having instinctive rapport with the thinking of wild creatures.

Animals, Alex wrote, are not supposed to have a reasoning mind. When the situation calls for a decision, there is no time for reason. When man is forced to act in a flash and survives he calls it luck, not giving himself credit for having that other kind of mind.

"To make clear my contention that all animals have a means of making themselves understood among one another I'll be obliged to deal extensively with the coyote."

During that coyote population explosion ranchers and rangers were killing them by any means possible — poison, traps, guns. One man got thirty in a week by using strychnine. Government sent in Biological Survey men equipped with traps and poisons, planning complete extermination. Scores of fur-buyers scented profit and came trooping in. Sheep men paid bounties.

Alex Hawxhurst was in the middle of it, not only did he trap coyotes, he raised them and by using chocolate taught one friendly coyote pup to fetch sticks. He concluded there are two kinds — the dumb, that would do anything for chocolate, and the smart, "never to be tamed to the least degree. And they don't interbreed."

"The coyote was an easy mark to start with, but he got wise very rapidly. I started trapping in the days when anyone could catch a coyote, but as I gained in experience they also gained in the matter of self preservation."

By taking advantage of environmentalism, ingenious coyotes have multiplied from near extinction to the point where their appetite for lamb is devastating flocks. Sheepmen now have limited permission to use poisons.

––––––––

To help people have a good time on the Mesa and yet keep their numbers from harming it, is a growing share of Forest Service duties. Housekeeping, you might call it, hosting visitors, providing camping sites, picnic tables, information centers, collecting trash, and enforcing rules about usage and fees. This phase of forestry, which scarcely existed in Kreutzer's time, is expanding as the population swells, as its leisure time increases and its pleasure in outdoor beauty deepens.

CCC boys and WPA men built the first public camping and picnic sites at selected lake-side scenic spots, or snuggled deep in the woods. Using materials around them they constructed wooden tables, stone campfire pits, and backhouses. Then all summer long each Monday after the weekend surge of visitors, the campsites were (and are) inspected and cleaned.

Road and trail signs — telling you where you are, what you are looking at, and what not to do — were placed, and replaced…and replaced….

"Hunters shoot signs full of holes, cows rub them down, and porcupines chew them up," John Wetterich pointed out on that Crag Crest hike. "Porcs especially like signs made of plywood. Evidently to them the glue is like the goodie in an oreo cookie."

––––––––

But National Forests were set up to save the trees, as President Roosevelt emphasized; anything else a ranger busies himself at is a sideline.

––

At one time the "in thing" for the Bureau of Land Management was chaining off pinyon and juniper to make room for more grass for more cows and more deer.

Preserving the Mesa forests by preventing fires and by controlling lumbering is a form of water control, every bit as crucial as building control dams. Because that's what the Grand Mesa forest is, a great flat deep-freeze dam.

Those miles and miles of towering dark green shadow hold the water up here in the form of snow, letting it melt away slowly come summer, rather than in the great destructive, unusable floods that would sweep down the mountain if the flat ground up here were naked to June-July heat.

One city, twelve towns, and a hundred thousand acres of farmland depend on holding that water up there until needed.

For that reason Grand Mesa's trees are more valuable than any minerals in it, than any stock that grazes on it, any gas, oil, coal, or vacationers spending money to have fun up here. And, more to the point, vastly more valuable than any profits by clear-cut lumbering.

Yet lumbering was essential to the development of the west — and the lands around Grand Mesa. Every homesteader had to make a roof for himself, he didn't get it with the land. Every town lot was bare until the owner erected something on it. Shipping lumber in was too expensive, even after the railroad came, and unnecessary with that mountaintop of forest overhead.

Earliest sawmills were "saw pits" where two men wielding a long straight saw blade — one on top and one in the pit — yanked back and forth until they had made boards of the log lying between them. Steam-powered circle-saws came in on wagons and were set up under the Mesa rim.

Because the conifers on Grand Mesa are Engleman spruce and fir (subalpine and Douglas) with little if any loggable pine, this has not been one of the big timbering watersheds in western Colorado. But the Mesa was close to unlimited market on all four sides, and tree-cutting was totally unrestricted — unlike today when every potential board foot is accounted for and trees marked off before harvest.

A sawyer could set up a mill where he liked, cut as much as he wanted.

At first the product was rough timber — railroad ties, studs, rafters, and barnboards. But as area industry began to diversify some mills specialized, turning out plane-smoothed siding, barrel staves, apple crates, and even delicate cigar boxes for locally grown tobacco. Biggest use now is aspen wood flaked and pasted together to make particle board.

Sawmills were the cause of some forest fires. Of necessity the mills operated up where the trees are, even in winter, because it was too expensive to wagon-haul all the waste — chips, slab, bark, and sawdust — in the form of whole logs down to a sawmill in the valley. Instead, they set up the mill near the logging spot and used the resultant waste to power the saw. It's easy to visualize how those early sawmills caused forest fires — the flaming maw of a steam engine licking out at the sawdust and chips being shoveled into it from mounds heaped all around.

But sawmills were not the first nor the worst when it came to starting forest fires.

At the time the government took over it was estimated that 168,000 of the Reserve's 640,000 acres had been burnt over in fires started variously — by God in the form of lightning, by Utes for easier hunting and in revenge at being driven from their country, and by settlers for personal reasons such as: to provide more acreage for grass to grow on and make it easier to round up cattle; to put a rival sawmill out of business; and — as in the case of Frank Mahaney — to get a job putting it out. One fire was started by kids smoking out a rabbit. Some fires, of course, blazed up where the butt of a hand-rolled Durham got out of hand. God's role in the fires was minor since He usually accompanied the incendiary lightning with its own fire extinguisher, rain.

——— ———

Snow being the Mesa's greatest asset it behooves forest rangers to keep track of how much there is in the bank, so to speak. Recorded data — amount and moisture content — is made available to farmers trying to guess what kind of crop to plant come spring.

Grand Mesa snow depths range from six to ten feet. The higher figure tells a farmer under the system that he can plant just about any water-greedy crop he likes; the lower one indicates he had better let the cornfield lie fallow this year in order to keep the orchard trees alive.

The earliest water-data computing machine was a long stick driven into the ground, penciled in feet and inches. These instruments were placed at strategic places miles apart in each ranger's district, and accessed by surfing between them on skis.

Not as much fun as it sounds. In making the rounds there was exactly as much uphill as downhill, and no lifts. You worked alone, if you got into trouble, you got yourself out of it or else. It wasn't much easier if you had help at hand.

Forest Ranger Gordon Harp had finished his measuring route and with six friends was enjoying some shortcut downhills just for fun. No cleared runs, either, in those days.

"Zipping down a particularly steep incline he fell and crashed into a tree with sufficient force to break his leg in eight places," the weekly paper reported.

No rescue helicopters, of course.

On a toboggan made of two skis strapped together the six pulled Ranger Harp down to the town of Mesa. The trip took five hours, most of it in pitch dark. ❧

To build roads so people can get in, to build drift fences so cattle will stay put, to keep forests occupied with snagging irrigating water in the form of snow, are only three of the jobs your Forest Service does for you.

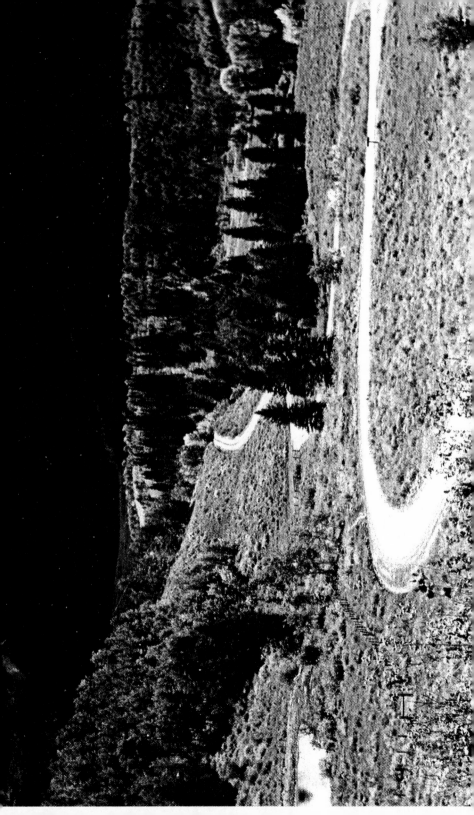

16

Damming the Waters

Considering that water is Grand Mesa's most valuable asset, it is surprising that so little about the difficulties and drama of harnessing and using water appears in the memories and publications of those times.

In our office-study it requires seven feet of bookshelf, two file drawers, and umpteen kilobytes of computer hard-drive to contain gathered data, articles, and memoirs about Grand Mesa. Among them are less than a dozen pages concerning the actual damming, ditching and distribution of that water.

Oh, there were some incidents — Two men armed with irrigating shovels were standing at a ditch-head arguing about whose turn it was to draw its water. They were yelling, and standing so close the spit of their cussing wet each other's faces. One emphasized his point by ramming his shovel into the ground, incidentally chopping off his neighbor's toes. Another irate rancher silenced an opponent by plunging a pitchfork through his larynx. J. Keiser got shot in the head (non-fatally) at a ditch company meeting. And Old Otto Peterson shot William Besgrove in the arm for opening a head gate out of turn. But there was never anything to compare with gun-toting masked men running two thousand sheep over a cliff.

However, if we tried to squeeze into our study files the court records of water-litigation in the five counties that border each other on Grand Mesa our walls would burst.

Less than seven years after the Utes left, the Delta newspaper was griping about the rash of lawsuits over water rights that, though mainly unwinnable for lack of criminal evidence, were a continual drain on county funds. The situation didn't get any better.

District Judge George Kempf said that the Grand Mesa water system was the most complicated area of litigation in the state, and he doubted that any one legal brain could sort it out except possibly that of A. Allen Brown. Brown's son Bob (who is himself now district judge) remembers that his father took several Surface Creek cases all the way to the Supreme Court, thereby creating law.

How could this be?

Most irrigation systems stem from one body of water behind one dam, with one main canal-outlet branching off into ever smaller ditches to reach the last acre.

Nothing could be farther from the situation on Grand Mesa. Some 300 lakes and potential lakes lie scattered all over the immense top and down the sides, draining in all directions of the compass. Each had to be dammed separately, its outlet ditch squeezed down through one of the creek-bed breaks in the rim or through rifts in the Toreva-block slump-walls below the rim.

You could file on a lake, hitch teams to scrapers, and build a dam on it. No problem, just hard work. But then how did you get the water down to your farm in the valley when the nearest gap in the rim was already flowing with somebody else's ditch water? As more and more dams were built it is tempting to visualize ditches stacked one above the other squeezing along creek-cut sags in the rim. That didn't happen.

One solution was group development of dams allowing multiple users of outlet canals — with paid permission of course.

You took a reading from the wier on your dam's locked outlet box (water was at least as precious as gold in your locked safe deposit box) then you tallied how many acre-feet you put into the stream from your lake on top against how many you took out at the ranch below. But can you prove it was really your water if somebody else says it's his? Hard to put a brand on water. Multiply this situation by several hundred, and by deals in which somebody sells his water rights but not his ditch-rights, or sells land that has been stripped of its water rights.

Lawsuits loom.

One was Big Time. The Whitewater Land Company — one of several water scams in this part of the opening West — concerned Grand Mesa water but only in theory. The company sold several hundred thousand dollars worth of shares in their irrigation-land company (to Easterners, sight unseen) without bothering to acquire anything to put into the ditches that they never built on land that they hadn't bothered to own. They were convicted of using the mails to defraud.

Biggest group-development of irrigating water was the Surface Creek Ditch and Reservoir Company that eventually raised the levels of, and linked together with ditches, a chain of twenty-six lakes known as "Alexander Lakes" or the "Grand Mesa Lakes Group," on the headwaters of the Surface Creek and Tongue Creek drainages.

Those early dams were built with scrapers — horse-drawn scoops with a johnny bar control that allowed you to tip the scoop and spread the load of dirt evenly. There was no compaction other than hoof and boot plodding back and forth as the inches of earth built up.

Smaller dams — rocks piled in log framework — on streams and canals raised the water level enough to shunt some of the flow into ditches that wriggled off across the mountainside to irrigate fields and meadows on remote benches. A popular tool for getting the correct gradient in laying out ditches across turbulent country was a long hose full of water. It was open at both ends, if the water was kissing the rim at both ends it was level no matter how it twisted and sagged between. You measured down from the far end to set the next gradient stake, enough fall to keep the water moving, not so much it would wash out.

—— ——

Washing out was what those team-and-scraper dams and ditches did almost without exception — and frequently. Before dam construction using modern heavy equipment, terrible floods swept down-mountain toward the Colorado and Gunnison Rivers. More than once Plateau Creek bottomlands were scoured free of everything manmade.

On the other side of the Mesa half a town was washed out.

Austin was a thriving town with a National Bank of its own, and all the industries and businesses it takes to support one. It sits on Gunnison flat-lands where Alfalfa Run slots down through the river bluffs. Residents were used to having to mop out their basements when a freshet made the lower Alfalfa run too fast and deep. They didn't worry about Alfalfa Run's vast upper drainage because Fruitgrowers Reservoir held it back — until a day in 1937.

That day a slippage ninety feet long appeared on the outer face of the earth fill. Men worked feverishly to strengthen the dam but the slippage lengthened. Heavy equipment was unable to cross the structure to strengthen the weakened place. Realizing that if the dam broke the 3400 acre-feet of water (an acre-foot is the amount of water it takes to cover an acre one foot deep) would not only wash out Austin completely, but a good part of Delta and most of the river-shore ranches as far away as Grand Junction. Working frantically against time the men made a detour channel for that water. Even so, it came down in a twenty-foot wall, rolling over itself in a tumbling crest armed with uprooted trees, brush and timbers that had been houses and barns. The entire population of Austin stood on the cliff-bluffs, like spectators on the top row of a grandstand, and watched it come. Incredibly slow for such power. And watched it go, taking the east half of town with it.

––––– –––––

Grand Mesa lakes and springs provide domestic water for one very populous city (Grand Junction) and a much bigger city with hardly any people at all (Orchard City), and seven small towns.

Orchard City, perhaps unique in the United States, was formed just to bring Grand Mesa spring water into farm kitchens — and the toilet in from the backyard.

By 1911 all the towns on and around the Mesa had domestic water pipe lines. Everyone else who didn't live beside a spring or mountain creek hauled water in barrels. Oh, of course there was the water in those irrigation ditches reaching every farm, but they were turned off in winter and anyhow they were too often the flushing systems for backhouses built over them and cow corrals built across them.

Farmers and ranchers on Surface Creek Mesa decided to become a city so they could have domestic water. Incorporating Orchard City in 1912, they began laying pipe lines from crystal-pure springs on the mountaintop, and out to the city limits miles and miles of farms away.

Each year, as the mayors of Colorado towns and cities gathered for their annual meeting in Denver the favorite moment was when the Orchard City mayor rose and introduced himself: "As mayor of the largest city in Colorado, I ..." the roar of laughter invariably drowned him out. Orchard City mayor, we hear, can no longer make this brag because Denver got jealous and enlarged itself.

A garage-size town hall, domestic water, and pieces of water-related equipment are about all Orchard City has in the way of public facilities. No schools, no post office, though its boundaries enclose several of each. And, although Californians (including the Carpenter and family) discovered it and are presently clotting things up with subdivisions, Orchard City is still largely farmland.

The water is pure — presently being bottled for shipment to more contaminated places on the continent — and there was always plenty of it. You could use all you wanted paying a flat rate of $25 for three month's use. But those first pipes weren't very big; to keep from reducing your neighbor's pressure, you were assigned certain lawn-watering times, morning or afternoon, every-other-day, etc.

Guy Dixon's job was to drift around and see that no one was selfishly watering out of turn. Guy was very impressive about it, at least he impressed one pre-schooler. During a sudden shower that occurred most reprehensibly outside the Austin family's assigned hours, little Corky Austin came tearing into the house yelling "Mommy! Does Guy Dixon know God is watering?"

All of these water uses concern Grand Mesa water after it has come down off the mountain. Up on top the Mesa's water is primarily used as something to catch fish in.

The most famous, the most written-about shooting on Grand Mesa was not cowboy gunning sheepherder, or armed battle over who can take irrigation water from what lake. The Fifty-Year Feud, involving mob violence and arson, was triggered by nothing more than one man defending his right to cast fishline where he pleased.

W.A. Womack may have been stubborned into throwing that forbidden line by two dirty tricks that were played on him by white men in Indian territory while he was crossing the plains to get here.

People who moved to Grand Mesa brought their stories with them, layered them into the mountain's history just as prehistoric seas receiving grains of matter from elsewhere, layered clays and sands into stone strata-record of what they were made of and whence they came. One of the Mesa's history-strata lay in the brain of Womack's daughter who was celebrating her hundredth birthday when we last talked with her.

Minnie Womack sits before the birthday cake that cannot hold so many candles, stroking the handle of the churn she used crossing the prairies, and remembering...

She doesn't have to try very hard, because in 1938 her mother, Eliza Womack, had the forethought to write her memories on paper — history in situ, as archeologists might say, fixing them to their strata-place in time. That hand-written account is the treasure of her grand and great-grandchildren.

"It took us four months to get here from east Texas." Eliza wrote. "But first we winter-fattened the cattle on grass and hay put up over in Indian territory (now Oklahoma) so those 200 cows would come though the trip in good shape." Mr. Womack was a man to think ahead.

Eliza herself was exceptional, contributing to Womack's corn and cattle income by working "outside the home" before its time. "Raising cotton was my business. With the help of the children we managed to save a little money. But corn and cotton prices got so low that we decided to go West.

Turning that first furrow on unbroken land is hard labor for man and mule.

"On April 1, 1889 we set out — a party of twenty-four people, the J.E. Coles and their five boys, the English Coles and their three girls, my sister and her husband, the Morris Kings and their son, my husband and me and our seven children.

"The older folks and the small children rode in the wagons and the larger boys rode horseback and drove the combined herds of 310 cattle. There were three covered wagons, one being hauled by ox team, and a fourth wagon that carried the new calves that made their advent into the world while we were on the journey. The baby calves rode till they got strong enough to keep up with their mother on the trail.

"In order to save the cattle and ourselves, we didn't rush, traveling from six to ten miles a day, and always resting on Sunday. I personally drove a team all the way and feel that I know from the hardships endured, the true meaning of the word 'Pioneer'.

"We traveled first through the Chactaw Territory, then into the Chickasha Territory, and from there into the Kiowa Territory.

"We had the entire route planned, but just before we left the Kiowa Territory, a white man came to our camp and advised us to change our plans and go through the Comanche Territory, assuring us that that was the safest way and that we would be safe from attacks of Indians. So we traveled that way.

"That night we camped on the prettiest creek I ever saw. The boys drove the cattle onto a little hill somewhat like Garnet Mesa over there, and tried to bed them down. This process was always interesting. The boys would ride all around the cattle, singing and whistling, and singing and whistling, till they all bedded down.

"While they were doing this they noticed an Indian who kept riding back and forth on the hill above the cattle. Then English Cole came riding to the wagon and said: 'Give me the gun; there's an Indian up there and I'm going to shoot him.' And I said: 'You won't do any such thing. Don't shoot at any Indian, because they would scalp every one of us.'

"Next morning we prepared to leave. The boys started the cattle ahead of the wagons and we went over a little hill at this creek, and when we got to the other side, the Comanche Indians came pouring in there and ran into our herd and shot one down.

"And before the skin was off it, they had eaten that cow up, blood raw! They actually ate the entrails! I had heard of that before, but now I saw it with my

A small part–the most populated part–of Orchard City, the "biggest city in the state of Colorado." That squiggle of trees to the right is a piece of Surface Creek, home of the belligerent anglers who stood off the U.S. Forest Service, and were prepared to take on the British Empire.

own eyes. A child would hold the end of the intestine in his teeth and an older one would skin off the outside from the dung, then cut off small pieces and feed it to the children.

"The Indians refused to let us go, so that night the men placed the wagons in a circle and stood their guns up against them; and we camped right at the end of the wagon . . . We'd brought a big tent and plenty of everything — meat and food of all kinds, and we milked the cows, set the milk to rise cream, and had a big wooden churn in which we made butter as we went along."

This is the churn her daughter Minnie is fingering at the centenarian birthday table. At 13, Minnie's duty — among many others — was to see that the family never lacked butter for campfire biscuits.

"While we were waiting," Eliza's account continues, "the squaws rode around the wagons and raised the wagon covers to see what we had in the wagons. They took a ham and other articles of food, but we didn't dare do a thing to prevent them.

"I have no idea how many Indians there were in the neighborhood, but fifteen or twenty remained around the wagons constantly and we didn't dare cook a thing during the day, for we couldn't possibly have fed them. The boys tended the cattle all day and that night. At midnight we dug a small hole in the ground and made coffee and cooked meat and eggs. Then we had the boys come in one or two at a time, and eat.

"My husband and Mr. Cole went and hunted up Chief Quanah of the Comanches, and when they reached his headquarters, there was that white man who had advised us to come that way. He had deliberately trapped us.

"When they found the chief he said: 'Me rich, but my boys hungry. Give the boys two cattle in the morning and they won't bother you.'

"Well, we gave them the two cows, and were so glad to escape that we didn't wait to see whether they ate them blood-raw or not. (The three cows they lost to the Indians were the only livestock lost on the entire trip — and one of those they assumed went to the white man who had tricked them into the Indians' hands.)

"We got away as rapidly as we could, and all along the way for a mile and a half or two miles we saw Indians sitting beside the trail with their guns

Minnie Womack Smith and her churn both survived the covered wagon trip across the plains to Grand Mesa, in spite of two raids by redmen and two scams by whitemen. Minnie is here celebrating her hundredth birthday.

across their knees. It looked as though they were just waiting for a sign to attack, but their chief wouldn't let them.

"One night soon after that we stopped to camp, and the boys herded the cattle and got them bedded down just above us. The Indians came down and shook sacks and things and frightened the cows. We had gone to bed, and here came those cattle roaring down there — stampeding. If they had hit us, they would have killed everyone of us. The boys got their horses and bedded the cattle down, and these Indians tried to scare them again, but the five boys wouldn't let them.

"We reached the Red River and as there was no ford there, we drove the wagons up the river thirty miles to a ford, and then returned to the other side. There we met the boys, who with the aid of a black-and-white shepherd dog, Ol' Dan, had got the cattle across.

"Dan was a wonderful dog. They would cut out about twenty cows and say: 'Dan, take them across,' and he would swim across and come right back and take another twenty, continuing until they had all been taken over. We brought Ol' Dan all the way and kept him until he died of old age.

"Sometimes when we camped, there was no wood or other fuel anywhere around, so we would dig holes in the ground, make fire in it, and cook with cow chips.

"In one of the wagons we carried a barrel of water for cooking, depending on streams along the way for stock water. But on one stretch the cattle had no water for three days. They were nearly exhausted. When, suddenly coming over a hill, the cattle scented the water in a stream, they broke into a mad run down to the stream and drank their fill.

"At one time we ran out of cooking and drinking water, but the men dug down a few feet in the bed of a sandy creek and got enough water to last until we could get more.

"The first place we reached in Colorado was Trinidad. There we met a man named Ralph Barnard, who assured us that Colorado had no grass and that the whole place was adobe hills. So we decided we had better sell all our cattle except a few. We sold him all but twenty-four head which were divided equally between Mr. Cole and my husband.

"This man paid us the pitiful sum of $8 a head for cattle my husband had paid $30 for. In the bunch was one of the oxen with horns measuring seven and a half feet from tip to tip. We afterwards learned that those horns, mounted had sold for a thousand dollars."

On edge after those two dirty tricks, Womack was picky about where he chose to settle. As they crossed the state he rejected site after site — Trinidad,

Cimarron, Uncompahgre Valley — finally choosing land on the south slope of Grand Mesa west of Eckert.

W. A. Womack prospered. During the Seven Lean Years when drought and over-grazing drove one cattle-rancher after another to leave the country, he acquired more cattle and land — and the water rights that came with the land. Joined by Dick Forrest and four other neighbors he formed an irrigation company to store water on the Mesa above their ranches. They dammed sloughs and ponds in Kennicott Park to create a series of five connected lakes called the Womack System. Some of these reservoirs still bear Womack's name.

A little over a decade after he came, W.A. Womack had parlayed those twelve cows into a herd so big he needed a bunkhouse full of cowhands to handle them. And he had acquired enough land that, even after subtracting Eliza's half-share in his estate, each of his eight children would inherit enough to establish a ranch-farm of his own.

In the process W.A. hadn't softened a whit. When Surface Creek Ditch and Reservoir Company (of which he was a charter member) accused him of taking water wrongfully he went to court and won. And when the Ott Petersons, father and son, were caught in the act of illegally dynamiting fish in Grand Mesa Lakes, Womack was a member of the jury that belligerently came in with a verdict of not guilty.

Eliza Womack's written memories, skipping all the hard work and hard planning that went into Womack's success, end bitterly:

"Little did we suspect what a price we would pay for that investment, for on July 14, 1901, Frank Mahaney, a half-breed Indian, shot and killed my husband. This was done at the insistence of William Radcliffe, an Englishman who had purchased property there and had boating and fishing rights." ❧

17

King of the Lakes

William Radcliffe was a British barrister who got his law degree at Oxford. Whether or not he was a descendant of the John Radcliffe who endowed Oxford Library and was physician to kings and queens is unknown but he acted like it.

Radcliffe was aristocratic, influential, and known for the elegantly tailored tweeds and cheviots he wore at his homes in London and Somersetshire, and in Paris which was the center of his social life in Europe, and at the Denver Club, center of his social life in Colorado. His sartorial concession to the raw frontier of the 1890s on Grand Mesa was to don hunting garb — beak hat, scarlet jacket with tails, cravat, and whipcord trousers in tall, polished boots.

In 1896 Radcliffe bought title to the Alexander Lakes group situated in public lands — Grand Mesa's choicest public lands. And along with the title his money bought exclusive fishing and boating rights in those lakes. He posted wardens to see that his rights were enforced, and was accused of starting the battle over lake-shore privileges known as the "Grand Mesa Fifty-year Feud."

How could anybody, especially a foreigner, buy government land along with the armed right to keep everybody else off?

It wasn't government land.

Each person in the United States who is twenty-one or older has the right to stake out and prove up on one homestead in his lifetime. If he can find one. (The Carpenter found one on the Arizona Strip as late as 1933. The last "open land" we heard of was in Alaska).

Early settlers in the Grand Mesa area didn't waste this precious right on land so high in the sky that the summer growing season was only a matter of weeks — much too short for corn and peaches. Instead they homesteaded down in the valleys and then, to irrigate their fields, they filed a different kind of claim, an easement, on the overflow water in one of the lakes or possible reservoir sites up on top, never actually owning the land around and under the water.

But three men chose to stake out regular homesteads up on top — William Alexander, S. L. Cockreham, and R. E. Eggleston. It wasn't considered a smart move. Grand Mesa isn't farmland, the season between frost and frost is too short for any crops except meat-crops with legs — or fins. What people didn't know, and never did accept, was that these homesteaders planned to harvest — not corn and peaches — but fish. Filing claims the very summer after the Utes left, their total 480 homesteaded acreage included or shored on most of the major lakes that then made up the upper Surface Creek drainage waters known as the "Grand Mesa Lakes."

The government, seeing what might happen to all such lakes, quickly passed laws forbidding private homestead usurpation of bodies of water on public lands. That was too late for the Grand Mesa Lakes, they were already privately owned and parts of them still are.

When homesteader (lakesteader?) Eggleston discovered that the lake he had staked claim to was barren, he set up the Mesa's first fish hatchery.

"With a great deal of enterprise he succeeded in getting spawn and stocked it," the paper recounted. "This he did for several summers until now (1901) the lake amply swarms with fish."

R. E. Eggleston was a hunter-trapper, a river-rover, who lived by harvesting beaver pelts along the whole of the Upper Colorado. He wrote clever letter-articles for the paper — signing them "The Trapper" — that recounted his adventures, including the discovery of the mummified body of an Indian maiden that he found in a cave below the west end of the Mesa. But no single piece of water could hold The Trapper for long; he camped on his lakeside homestead just enough summers to prove up on it and then, tired of trying to defend his "artificial" fish from poachers, he sold out.

The lakes that Cochran and Alexander filed on were just naturally full of fish, the trouble was that they didn't stay that way. Fishing was commercial and massive. As early as the second summer after the first settlers arrived the brand new *Delta Chief* was reporting that the fishing equipment being used on Grand Mesa was dynamite. "William Follet came to town with 250 pounds of fish," and he turned around and went back to haul in another wagonload.

S. L. Cockreham, with frontage on three lakes — Baron, Eggleston, and Alexander — held out longer, all the time complaining about the poachers that made his holdings less than profitable.

Lake homesteader William Alexander was an easygoing fellow with a friendly and slightly odd grin. His front teeth looked double, as if he had never shed his baby teeth. This was a big factor in trying to identify skeletons when he turned up missing.

Alexander's 160-acre homestead included part of the lake that bears his name and all of Twin Lakes. On Alexander Lake he constructed rowboats and rented them to the summering people who rented the little log cabins he built along the shore. He doubled his land holdings — and multiplied his lake holdings — by buying the 160 acres that Trapper Eggleston homesteaded, including Big and Little Eggleston Lakes. Alexander's way of coping with the poacher problem was to try to keep ahead of them by creating more fish in the little hatchery he built. The increased fish population merely drew more fishermen.

Perhaps recognizing that he was too easygoing to run a profitable enterprise alone, William Alexander took a tougher man, Richard Forrest, into partnership.

Dick Forrest, for whom Forrest Lake is named, was an Irishman who had formerly worked as a spy on the Indian Reservation. An entrepreneur, he acquired stock in several irrigation companies and more pieces of land than he could keep track of — at least that's the impression you get from seeing his name so often on the delinquent tax notice. Or perhaps he was one of those early-day entrepreneurs who made a "business" of letting their land taxes lapse and then, at the last moment, bargaining the county into a reduction to save bookwork and sheriff-sale expenses. Sometimes he got overextended; A. W. Lanning bought a piece of Forrest farm property for $49 at one sheriff sale.

To make fishing in their lakes worth the fee — and to grow "crop fish" for shipping to mining camps — the partners enlarged the hatchery, "milking" lady trout by the thousands on the assumption that these rancher-poachers would no more think of robbing a lake of its farm-hatched fish than of sneaking baby chicks from a neighbor's henhouse.

Fish aren't chickens. People went right on doing what they'd always done. Alexander and Forrest might own shorelines and lake bottoms, the Surface Creek Ditch & Reservoir Co. might own the water that flowed out of them, but the fish swimming around in there belonged to everyone — like wild deer, like wild rabbits.

The Radcliffe Lodge on Alexander Lake in 1894, a part of the Englisher's "baronial estate." When his warden shot a Surface Creek poacher, a mob of 100 men burned this building and everything else Radcliffe owned. (Photo courtesy of the Delta County Historical Society.)

To enforce his "Positively No Fishing Except by Permit" signs Dick Forrest posted armed guards, a move which is what actually started the Fifty-year Feud that Radcliffe is credited with. It didn't do much good; cases against poachers were invariably dismissed because judge or juror had committed the same "crime" himself — perhaps only yesterday afternoon.

To counter Forrest's takeover of the lakes, fifteen Delta professional and businessmen put together enough money to buy Sam Cochreham's 160 acres, acquiring shorelines on Baron, Eggleston, and Alexander Lakes. The group's idea was to ensure themselves a place for fishing and summer recreation in unsettled times when everything seemed up for grabs — the government just the year before had taken over the entire Mesa by making it a National Reserve, regulating where cows couldn't graze and sawmills couldn't cut timber. Now Alexander and Forrest were claiming legal right to tell the public where it couldn't fish.

The fifteen organized themselves as the Grand Mesa Resort Company in 1893, surveyed lakeside lots, built cabins with paths leading down to little boat docks, and began fishing.

It wasn't that simple, as the paper reported:

"Mr. Forrest and his friends seem to be prepared to uphold what they claim are their rights, and the men who want to fish are preparing to go ahead and fish when they please. It looks as if there's going to be as much fun over the privilege and rights to fish as there is in catching fish."

What Mr. Forrest said in reply was prophetic: "The bad feeling stirred up through trying to protect my fishing rights on the lakes is getting so bad somebody's liable to get bumped off."

The hatchery partners played another card.

They had owned stock in the Surface Creek Ditch & Reservoir Company ever since it was organized — overflow from their cluster of lakes was a large part of that company's assets. Now, the partners traded their shares for a written agreement giving them "exclusive fish cultural rights and boating privileges on all the lakes." And then to keep the company pushing for their side they verbally conceded fishing rights to all SCD&R company stockholders. Money from that sale of shares enabled the irrigating company to raise existing dams, greatly enlarging lakes — one by as much as fifty feet — and build new dams creating new lakes in the cluster known as Grand Mesa Lakes which eventually numbered twenty-six.

This was the situation when Englishman William Radcliffe heard about those privately owned lakes through friends — probably at the Denver Club.

Rich people were scattered thinly through the world's population, but they almost always knew each other and mingled at certain places where hunting of one kind or another is good — such as Paris in France and the Denver Club in Colorado. That club was Radcliffe's operating base when he was doing trophy-collecting hunts in the Rocky Mountains and not on the Kilimanjaro in steepest Africa.

Among Denver Club habitues who might have told him about the lakes were lawyer friends Judge A. R. King of Delta and Judge Beaman of Carbondale, and coal-iron mogul John Osgood who was creating a Swiss village for his miners and a forty-room castle for himself on Crystal River just east of Grand Mesa.

Or perhaps Radcliffe learned of the lakes through two other Deltans whose background was more like the Englishman's own. Nicholas and Thomas Mostyn were sons of Sir Pyers and Lady Mostyn and cousins of the Duke of York. Remittance men, they came to the Western Slope in 1886, fell in love with it and acquired a cattle ranch on Ash Mesa south of Grand Mesa. (The remaining part of the stone house the Mostyn brothers built on Ash Mesa still has a bit of the baronial air.) To the menage they added a winter home in Delta and a summer home in Ouray. Remittance men were an important factor in the settlement of the West. Paid rich allowances by their families to stay out of England — thus avoiding conflicts with the landed inheritance of the firstborn — they came to America bent on becoming "landed" on their own. Both Nick and Tom Mostyn frequented the Denver Club, according to the press.

Radcliffe knew what he was looking at when he saw the Alexander-Forrest setup. A once-in-a-lifetime opportunity. With his barrister background he realized what few of the settlers seemed to understand, that these were the only lakes on the Mesa that would ever be privately owned. Recent laws prevented filing on such bodies of water, here or on any other forested mountain in the U.S. The establishment of the National Reserve would keep it that way.

That the setup included a fish hatchery was pure serendipitous velvet. Because fish — the catching of, the history of, and making money by — was Radcliffe's big thing; as his obituary would point out.

Radcliffe named a good price. The partners turned him down.

He went off to get organized. Even before he acquired the lakes Radcliffe and what the paper called "a group of Eastern capitalists" had formed the precursor of Grand Mesa Lakes and Parks Co. Radcliffe didn't head his company — right from the start he showed more interest in fish than in the money to be made by them. Instead he made an American friend, D .C. Beaman of Carbondale, the company president. Beaman, a lawyer-judge and

legal representative for Colorado Fuel and Iron, was described in print as a "wiley wire-puller." (In those pre-libel-suit days a newspaper could call anybody anything in blackest lead type and get away with it.)

Armed with more money, Radcliffe came back with a bigger offer. It too was turned down by the Alexander-Forrest partnership.

But the next time Radcliffe raised the price Dick Forrest accepted. By then Forrest was sole owner of the valuable homesteaded lake property.

His partner had disappeared.

————

Old-timer Gregory Smith recalled the story of that disappearance for the *Surface Creek Champion*:

"Alexander and Forrest had several men employed at the lakes and each summer would ship a lot of fish from the depot at Delta. Alexander did most of the hauling, as I remember. On one of these trips he had shipped his load and had started back to the lakes. He never arrived. The next day the team and wagon (one of the old style express wagons with low front wheels and the seat in the front of the body) were found between what is now North Delta and Tongue Creek, but Alexander had disappeared."

The wagon was intact, no sign of runaway, accident, or problem of any kind. The team was quietly munching on graze as best they could with the bits still in their mouths.

Some years later a skeleton was found under a tumble of branchy logs near Slaughter Grade in a position that the law opined indicated an "assisted" accident. It was tentatively identified as William Alexander by its odd front teeth. But a doctor disagreed, pronouncing the man an Indian, his teeth worn down from a gritty lifetime of eating *aturi* made of cornmeal ground on sandstone metates. So the mystery remained.

For several weeks that skull was displayed in the *Delta County Independent* window, as if hoping some passerby would recognize a friend by his bones.

Coincidental with discovery of the skeleton, suspiciously so, one of Alexander's former employees came up from New Mexico and declared those couldn't possibly be Alexander's bones because he had recently seen him down there. The sheriff wanted to hold the informer until he got at the truth of things, but County Commissioners declined to pay for his keep. He too disappeared.

The right to fish. To dream. Perhaps catch something...Half a century before this lad was born, men laid their lives on the line for nothing less than that right.

Was Alexander the first victim of the Fifty-year Feud? Speculation at the time included the possibility that Alexander's body lay at the bottom of one of the "bottomless" lakes. Subsequent conjecture has implicated both Radcliffe and Forrest. Did Radcliffe want those lakes so bad he had Alexander put out of the way because he refused to sell? Or did Forrest want to sell so bad he killed his stubborn partner to free the deal?

Meantime, in the spring of 1895, Dick Forrest went to court and won a default judgment against the missing Alexander, acquiring all of his partner's interest in the property for $3025.

Soon afterward he accepted Radcliffe's third offer.

——— ———

Once he owned the lands bordering those lakes Radcliffe set out to create what the *Denver Post* would describe as "a baronial estate."

This Englishman had already acquired a hunting lodge and a thousand acres in the highlands of Scotland, but obviously he liked Grand Mesa better. Bringing in architects and construction men he erected a large, rustic-elegant lodge on the lake shore in which to entertain friends from England, Paris, and other parts of the world. Along the shores he built cottages for summer guests. Clustered in the woods were workshops, stables and tack rooms for his fine horses and elegant English saddles and harness, as well as dwellings for the staff that such an establishment required. Many of these were loyal "retainers" imported from his overseas estates.

How Radcliffe centered his life on Grand Mesa is evidenced by the furnishings he brought to his private lodge — antiques, objects d'art, family heirlooms. The library included a priceless collection of first editions. Wall-mounted hunting trophies demonstrated how much of the world this man had roved before settling on Grand Mesa as his ultimate home. Heart of the decor was a large painting, the portrait of a beautiful woman whose significance was never explained but which so impressed those who saw it that the painting of the Lovely Lady is mentioned in every account of the Grand Mesa feud.

That the portrait had a special meaning for Radcliffe no one ever doubted, but the Lovely Lady was not his wife. This tall, fair-haired man just under forty, was unmarried.

Mountain luxury aside, Radcliffe was chiefly concerned with the fish hatchery and the unique rights that went with it. Adding to the Alexander-Forrest structure, he built a $15,000 hatchery capable of producing trout by the millions, and a large ice house to store a winter's harvest of lake ice for use in keeping the fish fresh during the hot summertime haul down the mountain to the Delta depot. He was soon shipping fish by the iced-carload as far east as the Atlantic seaboard.

Britisher Radcliffe was so happy with the Grand Mesa setup, and with America, that he went down to the Delta county seat and filled out an application to become a United States citizen.

When reporters from newspapers on both sides of the mountain rode up and tied their horses at the hatchery gate, Radcliffe himself graciously showed them around. They toured a series of ponds where "pre-school" fish were fed and moved into larger pools as they grew, until big and rambunctious in their fish-teens they "graduated" to Alexander or another of the natural lakes.

The fish population of the lakes, he told them, had been greatly diminished when he took charge. His plan was to build it up to be the finest in the state. To do it he had to stop all that poaching.

First he indicated who couldn't fish in his private lakes by establishing who could. He prepared rod-and-line fishing permits which he magnanimously offered free to any Delta County resident who came up to the lodge and asked for one — implying what the newspaper said in print: "Those found fishing without permits will be looked after by the deputy game warden."

That didn't work. It simply miffed folks into fishing more than ever.

He posted guards — wardens, he called them — authorized by the Bureau of Fishing and Hunting. Later Radcliff swore he had not armed his men, but it seems unlikely that an unarmed guard could have persuaded a rancher-cowboy type to go with him down to the sheriff's office and be charged with fishing where he hadn't oughta.

Not one of the trespassing charges stuck. Judge Welch was on the side of the poachers; people had been free to fish those lakes ever since the Indians went out. Besides, fishing at that time was not mere sport but a necessary source of food and income for many families.

On a mountain shimmering with lakes why would fishermen pick on the only ones posted with "No fishing" signs? It wasn't just belligerence, those were the only lakes with any fish to speak of.

As Judge Welch said, when dismissing (as usual) the case against a poacher — Ott Peterson by name, "There are fish to spare in the Alexander group of lakes. More than in all the other hundred lakes put together."

How could such a thing be?

In the ten years since whites replaced Indians summering on this mountain all the other lakes had been fished out — the old and the new ones as fast as they were dam-created. Waters once dimple-patterned by leaping fish, quickly turned mirror smooth and dead.

Many of the lakes — the Toreva pocket lakes — never had had fish because their only inlet was by rain and snowmelt, and their only outlet was underground to springs below. If some of these pocket-lakes had been stocked by nature, it was by sheerest accident — Eagle, doing flyovers, losing his grip on his catch a couple of times — one male and one female.

Not crediting the "artificial" hatchery with changing anything, the judicial law and the people thought it was just natural that some of the lakes were barren and others just naturally became that way. The Alexander lakes just naturally had fish.

There was good reason why that group of lakes had more fish. Starting with Trapper Eggleston they had been consistently restocked and guarded to reduce the amount of commercial fishing. The real lake-depleters were the men who fished for profit, seining or setting off a charge of dynamite under water to reap the drifts of stunned but unmangled trout that floated to the surface. Even a poacher with a fishing pole could bring in half a bushel basketful in a single afternoon.

———

Finding that nothing came of taking offenders to court in a judicial system that apparently was composed of poachers, Radcliff sought the advice of two lawyer friends, A. R. King of Delta and D. C. Beamon of Carbondale. Their loyalty was assured by owning stock in his resort-hatchery.

Just how fraternal Radcliffe was with Beamon, lawyer for CF&I Coal, is unknown, but he was a houseguest in the Kings' Garnethurst home at least once — and without "his man" to care for his personal needs — as King's daughter Eula King Fairfield recalled in her biography, *Pioneer Lawyer.*

"An Englishman accustomed to servants, was something of a novelty in Delta, and one time, when he was an overnight guest in our home, he placed his shoes outside the bedroom door to be cleaned. Seeing them, I ran down to the kitchen to report. Father laughed. 'Well, we can't do a thing about it. Only a trained servant can polish an Englishman's boots.'"

The three lawyers joined skills and wrote a bill called a Class A License. Wily wire-puller Beaman got the Colorado state legislature to pass it. "Railroaded it through" is the term used by the newspaper.

Class A gave the owners of private land complete control over fish and fishing in lakes where even an inch of the shoreline was privately owned, though it wasn't worded quite that way. "...that has been or may be hereafter be

Radcliffe Lodge was built of logs, all-American rustic at least on the outside. If he had built it English-style of cut stone, it might be standing today. (Photo courtesy of the Delta County HIstorical Society.)

acquired under the laws of the state or the United States" is a sample of the lawyer phraseology.

It was good for ten years. It could be renewed every ten years to the end of time.

The license agreement made the United States government a partner in the project. Men from the U. S. Bureau of Fisheries were to work Radcliffe's hatchery and lakes for him, stocking them with trout and giving him 25% of the harvest — which in the very first season totaled almost two million eggs. Now the "wardens" who guarded his fish would be government agents of one kind or another, by-passing local lawmen-poachers.

Until that "Class A License" hit the press Surface Creek Ditch and Reservoir shareholders weren't aware that their board of directors had used company shares and members' fishing rights as collateral in securing more irrigation water in Grand Mesa Lakes. The fishing arrangement was verbal and applied only to the water. That is, without a Radcliffe permit they were allowed to fish in their own lakeful of irrigation water only if they could somehow manage to get out onto it without touching shore anywhere.

Instead of counting themselves special because they were the sole outsiders who could fish Radcliffe lakes, they were outraged that they had to get a permit to do so — humbly and in person apply for permission to do what they'd always been doing. Like raising your hand in school and holding up two fingers.

Feeling betrayed by their directors, they hit the ceiling literally, forging to the top of the world to fish those lakes whether they needed fish or not, just to show they damn well could.

———

One of the most righteously indignant shareholders was W. A. Womack.

On Sunday afternoon in July of 1901, he and four of his range riders — Frank Hinchman, Frank Trickel and Dan and John Gipe — went on a fishing jaunt, riding over from the Womack family's summer cattle camp on the Mesa top.

They were pulling in trout from a Radcliffe lake when one of the Englishman's wardens, F. A. Mahaney, came riding up and ordered them to get the heck out — or stronger words to that effect.

A bulky belligerent man, Mahaney has been described as a half-breed — half Irish, half Indian. He came to Radcliffe well recommended by the Forest Service which had called on him several times to fight forest fires.

What everybody but Radcliffe and the Forest Service knew for darn-near sure was that Mahaney had set some of the fires himself to get the job of putting them out.

Mahaney was armed and authorized — he wore a government badge.

Eyeing Mahaney's holstered gun, Womack signaled his men. The five of them silently reeled lines, and packed gear to leave.

———————

Homestead section lines are straight, lakes on Grand Mesa are any rambling shape, curving in and out of the artificial lines surveyors draw on their maps. Unless a lake is totally within your section lines, how can you "own" it? With a Class A License you can.

It boiled down to: Can you stand on government land — public land — and fish in a lake a part of which is the private property of people who hatched and "own" the fish you are casting a hook at? The fish don't know enough to stay over there, and nobody has built an underwater fence along the invisible property line to keep them over there. You really aren't breaking the law, are you? Yes, with Class A, you are.

Nor was it merely this one group of lakes. Conceivably anybody with enough power, resources, and ingenuity to wriggle a Class A License through the legislature could find some legal way to take over all of the lakes. The entire mountaintop could become one vast English barony, off limits to anybody not in the Britisher's retinue.

Setting their jaws, Womack and his men mounted and rode on up to another piece of property Radcliffe claimed — Island Lake.

Mahaney had anticipated them. He watched as they rode down the bluff to the lakeshore, and again ordered them off if they couldn't show him a Radcliffe permit.

Their horses' feet, fetlock deep in golden buttercups, were planted on government land, the far spruce-dark shore belonged to Radcliffe, the water in between belonged to the Surface Creek Irrigation Company.

"I've got a permit, but I won't show it," Womack has been quoted as saying. "As one of the original Surface Creek stockholders I can fish here whenever I please. If you don't think so, arrest me. Let the courts decide."

Hot words from both sides echoed off the spruces. Mahaney started to ride off, then turned and fired a shot in Womack's direction. It missed, but made Womack pile off the saddle to put the horse between him and that gun. Mahaney's next shot got Hinchman in the leg.

That was when Womack's horse, spooked by the gunfire, turned to face the shooter leaving Womack exposed.

Less than twenty feet from Womack, according to the report, Mahaney got off several shots at him, one struck him in the leg knocking him to the ground, another bullet left his body motionless.

Mahaney gun-waved the others off the lakeshore, threatening to kill them all. Even as they fled — four unarmed men crouching over their saddles, followed by a horse without a rider — Mahaney kept on firing. Then as if he'd come to himself and half realized what he had done, Mahaney yelled after them to come back and bury their dead.

Three of them raced away to inform authorities and rouse the people. Frank Hinchman, in spite of his wounded leg, rode to the Womack camp to tell Mrs. Womack what had happened. Eliza Womack, accompanied by one of her sons, reached her husband on the shore of Island Lake before he died.

———

The south side of the mountain was alive with riders that Sunday night, rushing inflammatory word of the shooting to ranches and towns, racing to get medical help for Womack and guarding the two doctors' long rescue ride, but mainly armed men searching the black woods and shadowy glades to find where Mahaney was hiding and kill him.

He wasn't hiding. He and the other wardens had gathered outside his cabin above Island Lake where they stoked a blazing fire and stood guard all night, armed with six shooters and rifles. They couldn't consult the boss — Radcliffe was over in Carbondale. Nor consult anybody else — Radcliffe had been talking about running a telephone line from Cedaredge up to his lodge but he hadn't done it yet.

About three in the morning a scouting warden brought back word that Womack had died. Faced with murder charges, Mahaney started down the dark mountain to turn himself in. He would plead self-defense, that he thought Womack dismounted in order to shoot at him from behind the horse's body.

It took Mahaney four hours to ride the forty miles to Delta because he had to travel off-trail and under cover to stay clear of men he knew were scouring the country for Womack's killer. Womack was a highly regarded cattleman, admired for his courage and savvy. Everybody liked Womack.

Sheriff George Smith didn't put Mahaney in jail, but hid him in the empty jury room, fearing the gathering crowd would overcome the three or four law officers at his disposal. Then later, when court was in session, Smith's deputy sneaked him down the stairs with the other citizens and out to the alley where a team was waiting. They drove to the county line where the Smith ranch provided shelter for hunted prisoners — and even housed court trials in those early days when the real law had to hide out from the saddle law.

All day long riders crowded into town, not hitching stoically to the horse racks, but riding restlessly up and down the dirt streets of the new little town, whirling and kicking up spurts of dust.

When court let out, at shortly after one o'clock and everyone had left, they struck. A mob of 125 men attacked the courthouse jail, breaking down every door and raging through every room. Not finding Mahaney they turned on the town itself. They broke into and searched the sheriff's home, the deputies' homes, lawyers and councilmen's dwellings. Any place they thought likely the sheriff might have concealed the killer.

He was nowhere in town. By that time a deputy had slipped him onto a train and escorted him into another jurisdiction at Gunnison.

Frustrated at not getting their hands on Mahaney, the mob focused on his boss.

Get Radcliffe! Radcliffe was the real culprit!

Denying peoples' rights! Hiring armed guards to enforce his greedy rules!

The thunder and dust of their hooves swept across the 'dobie trail, up Surface Creek, through Cedaredge, up the mountainside. Their rage and numbers grew as they took on converts as they went. It was dark when they arrived.

One account, not contemporary, says the riders who beat on Radcliffe's lodge door were masked, but that seems unlikely. These men were too sure the right was on their side to be other than boastful of their participation in enforcing it.

Radcliffe's caretaker, Jeff Smith, answered the stomping of their boots on the wooden veranda floor, their pounding on the door.

"Mr. Radcliffe isn't here. He's in Carbondale, visiting his friend Judge Beaman."

They didn't believe him. Pushing past they ranged through the lodge looking for its owner. Not finding him, their rage flipped out of control. Somebody attacked the painting of the Lovely Lady, known to be Radcliffe's chief treasure, they tore it to shreds. That set them off, they broke priceless crystal and porcelain, shattered sculptures and hunting trophies, ripped tapestries, trashed irreplaceable leather-bound first editions in the library.

Somebody yelled, "Burn the whole damn thing down!" And they did.

It has been written that Jeff Smith stood there, tears running down his face, watching the lodge and its treasures burn to the ground.

Still not sated into sanity, they set fire to everything else Radcliffe owned — the hotel, the cottages, stables, tackroom, workshops and the employees' cabins. Where buildings were occupied they held off until Radcliffe's people had time to collect personal belongings and leave.

Newspaper articles pictured those people trailing off the other side of the mountain, too scared to take the shorter Surface Creek road.

The mob, torches in hand, was bearing down on the last Radcliffe structure, his fish hatchery, when the manager there desperately ran up the American flag to imply that the hatchery was government property. At sight of the flag, it has been written, the mob stopped in their tracks, pulled off their hats and stood looking up reverently. Hard to believe, unless insane mob-rage in these men had peaked out leaving them limp and helpless as children. Quietly, not talking, hardly looking at each other, they got back on their horses and rode off.

That soft mood didn't last. With grim purpose they stationed armed guards on every Grand Mesa access route and waited for Radcliffe to come home.

––––– –––––

Who made up this mob?

They have been described as Surface Creek ranchers, farmers, cowboys; people who would have shot the pants off anybody who off-branded a calf hatched by one of their cows on public range, but who felt sublimely impelled to defend to the death their right to catch a fish somebody else had hatched inside his own posted private property. Fish aren't calves.

Their identities remain secret. Not one of the people who have written letters, memoirs, articles, and chapters about the action that highlighted the Fifty-year Feud has mentioned a name. The actual people who made up the mob of a hundred or so that burned Radcliffe's holdings, and waited for him at the depot armed with guns and lasso-lynch ropes, are as secret as membership in the Cattlemen's Association in the sheep war. Though they were masked during the more violent episodes, they were barefaced while waiting for him at the depot. And masks don't hide much when hat, ears, and way of forking the saddle belong to a man you have built fence with all summer. Down to the third generation, nobody is talking. There is no indication that the law ever tried to find out who they were or bring them in. Sympathies were not with the "King of the Lakes."

As one local said in exaggerated cowboyese, "To that Britisher we're all jist a bunch of nose-pickin' yokels. Well hell, yes, I picks mah nose. Being's I ain't no English cow, I cain't git mah tongue up there."

Radcliffe had gone to Carbondale to consult lawyer Beaman about poaching problems. Then he took the Midland up the Roaring Fork and Crystal Creek to Redstone to visit friend Osgood in his sumptuous "castle."

Osgood was waiting for him with a Denver newspaper headlined "Delta County Tragedy — Deputy Game Warden Shoots to Kill". That's all. Nothing about the burning of his lodge and other property, it hadn't happened yet when that paper was printed. News traveling by railroad mail car could be a couple of days late.

Radcliffe's decision was instant — get back there. Get a lawyer for Mahaney, but make it clear that Mahaney had been carrying a gun on his own — consequence of a personal quarrel, and not on Radcliffe's orders. Get things straightened out. Quick! The lives of five million baby fish depended on it.

Osgood lent him a steam engine hooked onto a private parlor car, and ordered all signals wide open ahead of it to get his friend there quick.

Quick is relative. No matter how rich you were in those days before jeeps and choppers, there was no quick way to transport your body from Redstone to Grand Mesa Lakes, though the two places are so close you could have seen one from the other through a pair of good binoculars if there weren't so many peaks between.

If only Osgood's Midland Railroad short cut from Redstone over McClure Pass wasn't still just ink on draft paper!

(Incidentally, if Osgood had completed that track over those thirty crow-fly miles from Redstone to Somerset, the Grand Mesa island of a mountain, including its shoulders to the east, would have been completely encircled by railroad track.)

———— ————

In the Delta depot Radcliffe's overseer, Jeff Smith, was desperately trying to telegraph his employer with word of the shooting, the burning of his lodge, and the mob waiting for him with lynch ropes.

Radcliffe didn't get the message, he had already left Redstone.

Breathing over the shoulder of the key-clicking telegrapher, Jeff Smith sent the same Morse-code message to stop after stop along the route Radcliffe was presumed to be taking. Each time too late; the one-car train was traveling faster than normal schedules, and on a through track. (There was no quicker way to send a message than by telegraph. Most towns had local telephones by that time, but no system interlocking them had been wedged into the Rockies.)

Finally at a section-house water-stop, the semaphore signal brought the engine to a halt, the agent ran out with a fluttering piece of paper.

A lynching? Him? Radcliffe wasn't scared, he was furious. What about those millions of tiny fish! Who was taking care of them? Get there! Get it straightened out! He waved the engineer on.

It isn't clear whether Osgood had the power to clear the track of a rival railroad company for his private car (he probably did, since he controlled

Colorado's best coalfields at that time including those serviced by D&RG) or whether Radcliffe changed from Osgood's Midland parlor car to a D&RG passenger train. From Fairfield's account it is certain that he didn't take the shortcut running along the north base of Grand Mesa between Rifle and Grand Junction. Perhaps landslip or washout had interrupted traffic on track still new enough to be unstable. Instead Radcliffe took the long way round — hundreds of miles in a huge oval through the Rocky Mountains to get just over the hump to Delta.

After leaving Glenwood Springs the wheels under him clacked east up to Minturn, south along the bulge of the Rockies down to Salida and over Monarch Pass, then west to Gunnison before heading back north toward Delta where he would still be a day's horseback ride from his holdings on Grand Mesa.

Even if Radcliffe was still on Osgood's one-car train, with everything sidetracked ahead of him, the engineer couldn't really lay on the steam because of raw new track conditions.

Railroad companies, vying to beat each other to the lowest passes and the levelest canyon bottoms, laid rail so hastily they skimped on support ballast, and threw up temporary bridges, planning to come back later and shore things up. Roads were subject to rock falls from overhangs that hadn't yet adjusted to losing their talus support. A train had to go slow enough to stop fast. And there were steep grades to chug laboriously over, frequent stops to take on water and coal.

Even so Radcliffe was traveling too fast to receive final warning of the lynch-mob waiting at the depot.

At the Montrose station — only twenty more miles to go — the train stopped to water up. Radcliffe was pacing the platform when A. R. King, returning from a business trip to Denver, looked out the car window and saw him.

According to Ula King Fairfield's biography of her father, the coincidence of that meeting saved Radcliffe's life. King piled out of the train, but managed to keep his voice cool and level as he advised: "Leave! Get away from this place as fast as the next train can take you!"

Radcliffe learned the details of the shooting, the burning of the lodge, destruction of everything he owned up there, the mob that this moment was waiting for his train to pull in, primed to string him up to the nearest tree.

The hatchery! Had they burned the hatchery? If not, who was feeding the hatchlings?

In the many write-ups of the Fifty-year Feud Radcliffe always comes out the villain, the overbearing, lordly tyrant. But his concern for millions of baby fish shows us another kind of man.

No, King told him. They still think the hatchery is government property.

So the hatchlings — the plant itself could still be saved — if he didn't show up and trigger things off.

Radcliffe took the next train for Denver to carry on the war from there. ❦

18

War With England Over Fishing?

At the state capitol Radcliffe and his American lawyers asked the governor to provide protection and enforce the rights that the State of Colorado had given Radcliffe when it issued that Class A License.

The governor hemmed and hawed politely, but was adamant: the way Delta County citizens felt about the Englishman and his outfit it would take a small army of state troops to ease him safely back onto his holdings, and a permanent army camp to keep him safe there. More importantly, with the Forest Reserve now in control of the mountain, that little state militia would be islanded, completely surrounded by United States forces under some service name or other. He didn't aim to take on the federal government.

Mahaney from his jail in Gunnison was also petitioning the governor. The State Game and Fish Department sent Charles Harris to Delta County to investigate what had happened. The citizens ordered him out, but in the process learned they had been tricked when the American flag was run up to keep them from burning the hatchery. That Englisher owned the hatchery too! Thirty masked men went up and burned the hatchery down. Now everything Radcliffe owned up there was ashes except the ice house, it refused to catch fire.

Luckily for those five million baby trout, in the interval between the two arsons Fish Bureau men had had time to finish out the hatch, and get the frylings far enough along to survive in open lakes.

Radcliffe gave up on Denver and went to Washington, but not before contacting Delta officials to cancel his application for United States Citizenship. As an English citizen he could put the fight on international level.

The newspaper saw that original application for American citizenship in a new light. Writing five days after the murder, the *Independent* said: "Radcliffe applied to the county court some time ago for his first papers, which were to be used as a blind in working his leasing scheme through the legislature (that Class A license). He never intended to take out his second papers."

Radcliffe "enjoyed" a bad press all over the western slope, but the *Ouray Herald* was nastiest describing him as "a snob lounged in indolent ease on his native English heath;" his loss as " a few spawn and a shack he calls a hotel," and his arming of Mahaney as "ample proof that the feudal system is in full operation right here on the western slope of Colorado." The *Herald* called Radcliffe a man without a country, who had renounced citizenship in Britain, and then canceled his application in the United States. And who hoped thereby to put his little fracas on an international basis.

At the nation's capitol he did just that. Working through the British vice-consul, Radcliffe filed a two-hundred and fifty thousand dollar claim against the United States for the damage done to his property. (In today's money, gauging by the price of a loaf of bread then and now, that would be close to nine million dollars.) Then he leased his Grand Mesa land and lake holdings to the Bureau of Fisheries for one dollar per year just to have watchmen on his property.

Radcliffe went home to England. There he was elegantly married to his fiance, a New York girl he had met while she was visiting his lodge on Grand Mesa. Was she the Lovely Lady? Nobody knows.

That was in 1902. By 1904 when he hadn't received a cent from the U.S. not even that Bureau of Fisheries dollar — he publicly threatened to use his influence to bring war between England and the United States.

This stirred up President Roosevelt no end. What! The Boston Tea Party all over again? Not in his administration!

He put pressure on Congress and they quickly voted to pay the Britisher the twenty-five thousand dollars he had finally agreed he would settle for.

The day Radcliffe took ship for England should have ended the Grand Mesa Feud, and returned public access to those lakes. It didn't. He still owned them and that Class A License, and still had every intention of returning. As a worldwide game aficionado, he knew better than anyone that the Mesa's chief asset was its lakes.

By remote control, through the Grand Mesa Lake and Park Co., he leased his holdings to the Federal Bureau of Fisheries, not for profit — he was to be paid one dollar a year — but to keep that precious Class A from lapsing for lack of use until things quieted down and he could return. Actually, things never quieted down in his lifetime. And he never got that dollar.

The bureau's first manager, A.E. Tullian, had scarcely pitched pine-bough shelter for the replacement hatchery when a band of armed night riders surrounded the place and told him to get the hell out. He did.

The next manager, a man named Hall, got the same treatment from night riders. Hall hunkered down in his tent, after signaling the Forest Reserve to send U.S. rangers to the rescue. After all, creation of the Reserve put the whole Mesa under Federal jurisdiction.

U.S. Forest Rangers chickened out; most notably Colonel DeBeque, whose war experiences evidently hadn't prepared him for anything like those belligerent Surface Creekers. After the Mahaney-Womack shooting, Supervisor Craig (who wouldn't go near the place himself) assigned DeBeque to that area. DeBeque refused to go, saying the people of the Cedaredge country told him they had declared open season on rangers, and he believed them. Other rangers found sudden crisis they just had to take care of over on the westend or back on the eastend.

Forest regulation came to a shivering halt.

So who eventually ended up in charge of the turbulent south section? That young sprout forest ranger, William Kreutzer. Bill took the job cheerfully, resolved to bring peace to that side of the mountain if it had to be at gun-point, which it was right off the bat.

On his way to Alexander Lakes Kreutzer was nooning when two young man calling themselves a committee from Cedaredge rode up and ordered the ranger off their side of the mountain. They said because Womack was killed by a government agent, the people of Cedaredge had decided to keep all wardens and rangers off the area.

They gave Kreutzer thirty minutes to leave.

The men were armed. Kreutzer's .45 was out of reach over where his coat was. So what did he do? He came at them with a grin and outstretched hand as if to shake on the deal and grabbed the gun from the nearest man's holster. After shooting in the air to show he meant business, he disarmed the other "committeeman," removed the bullets, and handed the guns back to their owners.

At the hatchery Kreutzer found Hall in his tent packed to leave. Bill tried to talk some courage into him and, failing, watched him take off across the Mesa with rifle at the ready. That very night a dozen or so riders circled the

---

Providing lures for Grand Mesa fishermen is an on-going industry. Dave Rowe's fingers learned the required dexterity while disarming bombs and mines in World War II. More recently Thomas Whiting heads a company that raises fancy chickens to grow those bright feathers.

hatchery, yelling threats at Hall. Kreutzer dropped to the ground — a canvas tent isn't much protection against bullets — and yelled back:

"I'm Bill Kreutzer, the forest ranger. Hall isn't here. You've run him off the Mesa; and I'm telling you, that's a serious offense. He is a government agent, and you'll have to account to Uncle Sam for your actions. I advise you to go home."

"After some discussion among themselves," Ranger Peck wrote, "the riders did just that."

The next hatchery manager, W. T. Thompson had a couple of brilliant ideas. First he hired Dick Forrest as off-season caretaker and fish hauler. Though Forrest started it all by posting "No Fishing" signs when he himself owned the lakes, he was "one of the boys," being a Surface Creeker with a ranch down there.

When Thompson called a meeting of the two judges on opposite sides of the fish question — Judge Welch who never convicted a fish poacher, and Judge A. R. King who was Radcliffe's friend and a stockholder in the company. And he persuaded the judges to call in all the people who had been charged with poaching but never convicted. There were a lot of them because any poaching case that Welch couldn't dismiss he just tabled indefinitely.

Promising to run the hatchery "on the sole interests of the sportsmen of the county, state, and nation," Thompson offered to drop charges against any poacher who would sign an agreement acknowledging the government's right to fish-culture privileges. He must have been some talker! Everybody signed. Even Ott Peterson, at that time the area's biggest and most pugnacious poacher.

The hatch that season was eleven million fish. Under the new arrangement the frylings grew to catching size uncaught allowing Thompson to stock Eggeston Lake with brook trout and Ward Lake with rainbow. He fared so well that a Denver Commercial firm noticed, contacted Radcliffe, and made an offer to lease those Class A fish hatching rights.

Radcliffe was keeping a finger in the Grand Mesa fishing pie. In fact it is possible he and his American wife might have been in Delta for the wedding of Judge King's daughter Ula if the invitation hadn't reached his Beech Court home too late for him to catch the steamship Imperator — steam being the fastest way to cross the Atlantic in those days.

He gave the Denver firm a short-term lease.

Private ownership again! Big money telling folks where they could and couldn't fish! Fishermen — and that was just about everybody — went wild.

A member of the Denver firm warned his company, "If you leave a man in charge, don't be surprised that by morning you may receive a telegram that he was mislaid."

About this time President Theodore Roosevelt changed the name of the government's holdings here from Battlement Mesa Reserve to Battlement Mesa Forest.

Since Grand Mesa is several times larger than that mere butte, Battlement Mesa, this would seem to have been the time to acknowledge that fact by renaming it Grand Mesa Forest. But perhaps the original name was so deliciously apt — a wild-west fight over fishing! — that Washingtonians couldn't resist leaving the Battlement label on the mountain. After all, President Teddy Roosevelt, knew the whole story from the first, having done his Grand Mesa bear hunting and campfire tales-listening during those feud years.

———— ————

After Radcliffe's lawyers got Womack's killer out of jail — they managed to reduce Mahaney's voluntary manslaughter sentence from eight years to two — nothing is heard of the Englishman until 1911 when his precious Class A License was up for renewal. Apparently he had given up on America. He sold it.

The buyer was the Grand Mesa Resort Co. Under the management of prominent Delta merchants and professional men, operating as a non-profit, non-dividend-paying corporation, the resort was doing well.

That company didn't invent the resort as a refuge from the heat, pests, and diseases that could make hell of summering in the valley before air conditioning and waste disposal laws. The Mesa was used that way from the very first.

For cattle-ranch families "moving top-side" was a delightfully necessary part of the work year. When cows and cowhands were trailed to the top in the spring you took the kitchen where the crew was, setting up tent with a metal-framed hole for the cookstove flue pipe.

For town families with small children, summering on Grand Mesa could be a matter of life and death. Temperatures in the valleys range in the nineties. Homes were trapped in a squared-off grid of alleys lined with privies, henhouses, and barns for buggy teams and milk cows. Excrement from these had to be put someplace, usually a temporary heap in the alley. Fly heaven. The dehydrating diarrhea called summer complaint killed so many infants that some families didn't decide on a name for the newcomer until Baby had survived his first summer.

Transporting the family gear up there from either side was an ordeal that any horse who ever did it never forgot. One mile straight up, twenty odd miles of anything but straight ahead. Ruts. Rocks. And dragging from the collar a lumber wagon loaded with beds and bedding, stove and kettles, chests and boxes packed

with a summers worth of families needs. On being reined in that direction some horses tried balking, smart ones faked a limp. To spare the team, adults walked much of the way alongside bossy, the portable milk supply.

But once there it was paradise, even for the horses. Cool, flowery camp-bliss beside lake or brook.

To enjoy that paradise, without the ordeal of what amounted to moving twice a year, more and more Delta people bought Resort Company stock and built a cabin on the lot that came with membership. Having a cabin waiting for you, furnished with elegance or egg crates, you and your kin could come up on horseback or by stage (later Durant or Ford), and find everything you needed already there from last year. Other needs could be filled at the store which was one of the concessions the Resort Company leased out along with lodge, restaurant, and boat rentals.

The Company fish hatchery, as before, was manned by U.S. Bureau of Fisheries personnel who stocked the lakes and paid the company $300 to $700 for taking spawn.

"The U.S. Government paid for the privilege of keeping the resort company's property valuable," Maude Karger summed up in the *Delta County Independent*.

This wasn't big-money, absentee ownership, this was neighbor folks. The ball was in home park — you wouldn't poach fish that belonged to your grocer, your doctor, or your son's teacher, would you?

You would. Fish-poaching went on unfazed.

The fifty-year Feud turned from guns to briefcases, court hearings and legal manipulations. The Isaac Walton League was invoked to swing its power against fishing restrictions. Expenses for the Resort Company began to exceed income.

Sensing a crevice of possibility, the town of Delta set out to acquire the Resort holdings and establish the Delta City Park in those lakes, and they almost succeeded. The bill they introduced in congress was in its second hearing when it was defeated by furious protests from Grand Junction and neighboring towns.

When it came time to renew that Class A in 1929 the Forest Service terminated its agreement with the Resort Company, then the Service reneged on the termination, not sure they had legal grounds for it. Then they got a bill passed that forbade granting Class A's except where all water involved is on private land. Then they proposed a bill canceling all current Class A Licenses, then they canceled the canceling....

Fish dive for deep water, fishermen seek shelter, but flowers stand up to the low-scudding storm.

Part of their difficulty may have been that Senator Hillman was a member of the Resort Company.

Somewhere in there the U.S. Government got around to recognizing how big the Mesa is by changing its name to the Grand Mesa National Forest. This was in the administration of the non-boat-rocking president, Calvin Coolidge, best known for his terse summation: "The American people didn't want anything done, and that's exactly what I did."

The Resort Company was going broke fighting for ownership of a fish hatchery that was mainly profiting poachers. Seine in hand, folks brushed past the "Fishing by Permit Only" signs with no fear of the law. By this time that super-poacher Ott Peterson had seen the light and been converted into a super-zealous game warden arresting people, it was growled, for even thinking about game poaching. But even Ott refused to arrest anybody for fishing in Grand Mesa Lakes.

Getting sanction from a local court, the Resort Company posted pink paper "No Trespassing" signs every two or three feet around their holdings. Not just along the shorelines that the company actually owned, but all the way around all five of the lakes its fishing easement encompassed. Every two or three feet! It says so right here in the Forest Service annals Mary Cameron gathered into manuscript form back in the early sixties.

The lakes must have looked like they were going to a wedding.

Those fluttering pink No Trespassing signs — most of them on Federal Property — gave the Forest Service the evidence it needed to go to court and assert public ownership of fishing rights without risk of losing the case and thereby establishing a state or federal precedent that could "cause irreparable harm in the future."

The suit was dropped when the Resort Company, deeply in debt and threatened with foreclosure, sold its Class A License fishing rights to the state for $5,000.

The Fifty-year Feud was over.

With weird coincidence William Radcliffe died that same year. Eula King Fairfield's biography carries a paragraph from the announcement in a British newspaper:

William Radcliffe, noted fisherman, who once operated hatcheries on the old Ute Reservation in Colorado, died today at his home, Beach Court, Upper Deal, Kent. He was 81, and had traveled extensively to study the past and present methods and folklore of fishing. ❧

Fantastic sculpture creates a roadside art show where spring sun carves winter marble that snow-plows piled up while opening access to Resort Company cabins.

19

Just Made For Joy

Grand Mesa Resort Company is alive and thriving, in a carefully unobtrusive way. Shareholder members have lifetime leases on the lake-side plots, which they never own but may sell by selling their shares. To protect the scenery from garish architectural fads, the kind of structure a member may build on his lot is subject to a board of directors. From the start most have been cabin-style with a steep roof to shed heavy snow, a big veranda for lake-watching, and space inside for lots of beds because, as Esther Stephens says, "You never know how many friends you have until you build a Grand Mesa Resort cabin."

Today Grand Mesa's 300 lakes, its myriad streams and brooks are open to the lures and bait of anybody with state fishing license in pocket. Limits can vary from season to season depending on the interdependent populations of fish and fisherman.

Colorado Division of Wildlife hatcheries keep the lakes stocked with half a dozen kinds of trout — rainbow, brook, cutthroat, grayling, and splake, as well as unprotected sculpin, dace, and suckers.

The deep waters of Island Lake have allowed splake (a cross between brook and speckled trout) to live to a ripe and massive age. Time after time splake pulled from this "bottomless" lake have broken state and world — and their own records for size. Some fishermen think that these record catches may be survivors of the same long-ago spawn-planting and that, shielded from bait temptation by the depth of water, just continue to get bigger and bigger down there. The splake that the Carpenter's son-in-law, Paul Patton, caught in Island Lake held the record for only a few years.

———

Playing with water in one form or another is the chief recreation on Grand Mesa's 300 lakes. (By the way, 300 has been the official count for several years, the number depends on how big a sheet of water must be before you call it a lake, and who is doing the calling. One ranger estimates there are nearly a thousand.)

In summer the sport is fishing and boating or a combination of both. After winter-cold has solidified the water, it is skiing and snow-mobiling. No swimming; in that brief summer at ten thousand feet, deep waters stay so cold that if your boat capsizes you may have only minutes to get to shore before chill begins to immobilize your body.

When skis first skidded on Grand Mesa snow it wasn't for fun. It was a rancher or his cowhand hunting a lost cow that failed to catch the autumn trail-trek down off the mountain. She'd be holed up in a brushy pocket or islanded in an exposed point where she would die of starvation unless rescued. Bovine brains, unlike the elk's, aren't wired to paw at snow to get at the grass beneath. Norwegian snowshoes, those early ranchers called the skis they planed and polished out of boards. Also work-vehicles were the skis used by forest rangers to take readings from snow-depth poles set up at various points throughout the Mesa tablelands.

The first just-for-fun skis on Grand Mesa were school-made. In their manual training classes Grand Junction high school boys made skis for themselves and to sell. Montrose boys began even younger. According to Stephen B. Johnson Jr. eighth grade boys fashioned skies out of one-by-four pine boards. Soaked and tip-bent, with only a leather toe strap nailed across the middle for emergency ejection.

Those ranchers and school boys were not bringing anything new to Grand Mesa. The oldest ski in the world, discovered in a Swedish bog, is thought to have been lost there 4500 years ago, and a rock carving depicting a pre-Norwegian skier had been dated about 200 B.C.

Even skiing for fun is hard work if you have to "herringbone" your way to the top in order to slide down. An easier way to get up there in pre-lift days was by car — you picked a slope with a loop of road crossing both ends, inveigled a friend who didn't like skiing to drive you to the top and then be there at the bottom to pick you up — as many times as you could talk him into.

Rope tow-lifts were strung on Grand Mesa slopes in the 1930s, one above Cedaredge and another near Mesa Lakes. Those were the Great Depression days with little money for food much less for getting yourself pulled uphill so you could fall back down. In building their tow, the Grand Mesa Ski Club ingeniously used the motor from an old truck for power, setting it up at the top of the run because — as Stephen Johnson points out, "it's much easier to pull a rope than to push it." Power was transferred from motor to rope by looping it in the groove between dual tires at top and bottom of the slope. You grabbed the rope at the bottom, pointed your skis uphill and slid all the way to the top.

The present, modern Powderhorn Ski Lift was started in 1967 by the Colorado Grand Mesa Ski Corp. It has survived many financial crises and a few seasons when weather reneged on supplying enough snow — after all, this mountain sits on the edge of desert. Powderhorn has some big advantages over many other ski lifts, however. It is closer to a major airport than other Colorado runs, it is lower in altitude making it a little warmer, and it crests on the edge of a vast tableland rather than a mountain peak as all other ski lifts do. That tableland is a utopia of cross-country skiing and snowmobiling.

Cross-country skiing was what those cowhands and forest rangers were doing, but they called it work and, because they were traveling alone, avoided the thrill of untried slopes. When Forest Ranger Gordon Harp took the slope that ended in a tree it was "after hours" and he had enough friends along to rescue him when he got in trouble.

Grand Mesa presently has nine miles of groomed cross country ski trails, well marked, and free to the public. Volunteers of the Grand Mesa Nordic Council groom these miles after every snow storm. They point out that a groomed run — allowing for diversity of technique, rhythm, speed and equipment — is the safest and easiest place to learn to ski. Each season the organization sponsors the Nordic Ski Race and skyway Nordic Ski Center at the top of the mountain.

Cross-country ski trails are marked for your convenience, not constriction. There's nothing to keep you from striking off anywhere across the glittering white levels and gentle slopes. Unlike exploratory cross-country skiing in other mountain areas, there is almost no danger of causing or experiencing an avalanche on this great tableland. You are advised, however, to have a topographic map and a compass to keep you aware of where you are. This is a very big surface in the sky with features that have a fascinating, but deceiving, trick of almost mirroring each other.

———— ————

Like cross-country skiers, snowmobilers are not limited to marked trails. They can zoom off anywhere, even out along the narrow thread of Mesa-top to Indian Point. But they don't go it alone — they know that nobody is more helpless than a snowmobiler alone on a the edge of the world with a dead motor.

There are a lot of them; so many in fact that it is chiefly because of snowmobiles — which must be trucked to snow depths where they can take off — that the Mesa has been opened to year-around access for everybody via Highway 65 from both sides. Before the advent of these little vehicles, the highway was cleared only when snow-plows were not needed elsewhere. Between times, wire gates swung across the tarmac to keep people from driving their cars up into trouble.

Members of snowcruiser clubs maintain trails threading the tablelands. A favorite, according to club official Lee Wise, is the trail that connects Powderhorn Ski Lift with Sunlight lift above Glenwood Springs. Lee advises: "Give yourself time, it takes all day to get back to where you left your truck," and he adds an aside:

"Powderhorn will skoot you down the lift and pull you back up if you indicate you intend to eat at their restaurant."

Ski lodge restaurants have few problems — just about everyone who buys a ticket is going to eat there. But running a restaurant on the top of Grand Mesa is a sometime thing — owners come and go. New management, entranced by this wonderful place, buy out old management that has been forced to sell because four summer months of patronage hasn't paid for eight winter months with hardly a hungry mouth in sight. Some of the come-and-go cuisines have been exceptional — Chinese, Italian, Bavarian. Imagine coming in from a twenty-mile hike up to the Lily Ponds, dumping your pack on the floor, and being offered *Truite en papillote a l'aneth et au citron!* But you are unlikely to find the same proprietor — if any! — in that same lake-front café next year. Julie Wise explains, "It's hard for them even in summer. Too many people bring their own food for picnicking, too many bring their own kitchens in camp-trailers."

There are many campgrounds on Grand Mesa, but you are not restricted to them. Whether fishing, hunting, or as a base for exploring, you can set up tent almost anywhere on Grand Mesa (an exception, of course, the private property owned by the Grand Mesa Resort Company). Just be sure to leave the spot as clean and lovely as you found it or this privilege may have to be taken away from you and all of us. If you want the convenience of water tap, trash disposal, and toilet you'll be happy to pay the small fee at the maintained campgrounds.

———

The Mesa is not a one-act play like a false lake dammed in by desert where the wife can be captive to a powerboat whether she likes ripping around on water or not. There are as many different things to do and see up here as there are people to discover them.

The Carpenter heads toward the mountain in his '59 shortbed, off to ponder the inner depths of things while watching fishlure floating in deep waters. We stow our camera equipment in the sleepy-ole '60 Chevy and follow him up, off to capture the outside of things for the paper.

Then lunch together at Alexander Lake Lodge, watching chipmunks sit up pretty for us on the log veranda rail.

Then, after the long, long summer afternoon, our two separate days come together on the Rim over cups of thermos coffee. Gazing at immensity far-walled by three mountain ranges, we try to spot the gleam of sunset on a window of our house one mile down and seventeen miles over. We never do. The Carpenter built it cuddled into the bluff. Cozy and efficient as the inside of a decked sailing craft, two levels making a single roof.

––––––

Increasingly the Mesa is a place to explore the past, the visitors' center stocks several books and booklets on what has happened there, and at least one place exemplifies it.

The old Raber cow-camp on Land's End Road had been singled out for preservation. It is now a restored historic site, made possible by Winifred Raber's memories of thirty summers of cooking and riding there; by Sally Crum's ability to raise federal grant money to finance the restoration; and Billy Bailey's ability to do the restoring.

All three are experts in their lines.

Bailey created Fort Uncompahgre in Delta from the ground up, modeling it on the scant descriptive fragments left by fur buyer Antoine Robidoux.

Sally Crum, archeologist with the Grand Mesa-Uncompahgre National Forest, is the author of a book on even older outdoor life-style, that of the Ute-Indian — *People of the Red Earth.*

As for Winifred, a short time after she married Bill Raber, he and his brother John bought a large cattle outfit, and she found herself cooking, cleaning, and riding herd up there.

"My husband helped build the reservoirs and maintained the range," She recalled. "Bill always said summer camps are all right, it's nice to have a bed in the kitchen. It was a tough life, but I liked it. I did my cooking and ironing at night so I could ride in the daytime."

Come fall, the Raber cattle trailed down Kannah Creek and over to the rails at Whitewater, one of the biggest cattle-shipping points in the area.

These days the restored cabin is posted with the facts of life — its own.

Writing in sky and on lake, jets and snowmobiles leave temporary messages in frozen water.

Fishing is relaxing (at least until that Big One gulps the hook), horseback riding is exhilarating, down-hill skiing shoots the capillaries full of adrenaline, but exploring the Mesa on foot enriches all of you — body , mind, and spirit.

The body swings along miles of paths through forests, beside lakes, across blossoming grasslands — even more miles where there's no sign that foot ever trod before your own. The muscles test themselves on interposing cliffs to climb, brooks to leap, or stream-bridging fallen logs to teeter-walk across.

And all the while the mind is doing its workout, exploring the enigmas that lie everywhere up here like petals lifted to the sun. What are these strange wriggley ropes of dried mud, interlacing and knotting as they crawl down the hillside? What caused this queer bowl-sloped depression in the forest, big as an Iowa barn turned upside down?

The answer to the first question is pocket gophers, but that only makes you wonder: How? Well, by packing mud behind them as they burrowed under deep snow. But why? All that labor, when they could as easily have stored summer-food as chipmunks do. Who knows why? The proposed answer to the second is ice, a huge lump of buried ice-age ice that left holes in the earth when it melted. But how did the ice get down there underground? And why isn't this hole a pond or lake like the other depressions on the mountain? Who knows?

Perhaps there is no better sign of eternity than that every time science comes up with a good first explanation it leads to a deeper mystery. Quantum theory to Continental drift, every answer ends in a question mark.

So be it, as you walk the Mesa the peace and the beauty stretch your soul. *Thigunawat*, Home of Departed Spirits, Utes named this mountain.

Throughout this chapter we have been talking about recreation — ways to have fun. Put a hyphen in that word and you have a different meaning re-creation.

Both Indians and settlers tuned to the power of this lofty stillness for the life-direction of their young. The white man's organized use of Grand Mesa's wonders to make better, happier kids began in 1920.

By that year Dr. Egerton, district superintendent of the Methodist Church, tackled the Forest Service and secured all-time rights to land on the south shore of Baron Lake and set up an Epworth League camp.

Members of the snow-mobiling Frasier family line up to zoon off.

After other denominations joined in, sharing the summer weeks among themselves, the camp was renamed the Youth Institute. Its unstated purpose: to make goodness fun, to provide an apex experience, to induce motive and focus for the random adrenaline forces of teen transition. Youth leaders recognized that adolescence required the altered internal chemistry produced by emotional transition rites. If the "tribe" doesn't provide it as a cultural step, the teens invent it for themselves through chemical thrill of risk, crime, violence, drugs, or peer worship.

Working together the churches built canvas-sided bunk-cabins, a happily echoing mess hall, and a beautiful tent-shaped chapel, its timbers held aloft by force of anchors in the ground.

By day the young folks hike to Lily ponds, or along Crag Crest Trail, go boating, work together at learning crafts, attend supportive classes, or explore the Mesa wilderness alone — you need to walk only ten minutes from any spot on this immense mountain to be utterly alone, open to the touch of stillness and beauty.

It isn't all sweetness and light, however. The adolescent shenanigans of that Ute tribal rascal Coyote, are not absent from whiteman's youth camp. For instance:

One summer evening, while we were filling in as camp nurse, and busy soothing an office full of sunburns and scratches, a tall kid filched a bottle of turpentine from the medicine cupboard overhead (don't ask us why the camp infirmary kept turpentine). He sneaked in and swabbed it under the tail of the superintendent's wife's cat. The wife went almost as berserk as the cat.

But such incidents are rare and do not disrupt the flow and purpose of camp life: After a jolly supper in the mess hall there is an evening of campfire jokes and heartfelt singing followed by a thoughtful goodnight message ending: If you feel called, rise early and go out into the forest alone... to meditate and seek.

Those who feel called waken at dawn and slip silently away, each finding a lone place — on a log by the shore, under a sweep of pine branches, beside a clump of monkshood, to feel, to contemplate. Some kneel with lifted face.

A sailboat glides through the dark forest shadow of the far shore, a moving miracle in the windless silence; the reflection of its white sail stretches across the water, singly to each, like a pointing finger.

Sun touching the tops of pines is signal. One by one the teenagers gather and sit on pew-logs for Morning Chapel. The purity of their young singing goes out across the water. Finished, they leave with a different walk, a facing walk.

Not new on this mountain. Young people had been using this high place as a God-approach for some time, as the Ute name for it reveals, and in rituals not too different:

There is the tribal evening around the pine-scented fire. Singing. Joking. The Old Ones telling funny stories, most subtly educating about the inadvisable pranks of Coyote. Finally a touching message from *puwa-vu*, the Wise One.

Then at dawn the Indian teenager begins his journey into the forest, alone and without food or weapon, to a place of lone thinking, of seeking the Dream, the Vision that will tell him who he is, what he shall do with his life, and by what symbol-name he shall thenceforth be called. ❧

20

Viewing the World from Land's End

Land's End? Or Land's Beginning?

In few places on this globe will you see so much of it as here on the jutting cliff called Land's End. You are looking at a horizon of five mountain ranges beyond an immensity of valleys that range wide and ram close — a mile below your planted feet.

First let the vastness shimmer along your nerves, then get to know the idiosyncrasies of what you're looking at.

A few decades ago you would have seen pedestal here with a cut-metal map and moving pointer to tell you the names of what you're seeing. But people or weather vandalized it away. Using this book as guide — either in the spot or from your easy chair — here are some of the wonders the pedestaled arrow would have pointed out:

To your far left, just around Shirt-tail Point are glimpses of the West Elk mountain range notable for its upthrust volcano throats called needles. To the south the glacier-carved San Juan Range — nicknamed the American Alps — knife a jagged skyline just this side of New Mexico. To the southeast, on a clear day, you can see Lone Cone, center of what is perhaps the realist old-time cowboying left anywhere. To the west, milky blue as a watercolor, is the jutting outline of the La Sal mountains in Utah. The La Sals are laccoliths, all that is left of an immense underground squeeze-lake of lava that never made it to the top until the ground above it was eroded away by wind and water. La Sal has a mate to the south, Sleeping Ute Mountain. Because of the curvature of the earth you can't see the jut of Sleeping Ute's chin and nose even from up here, but that stack of cumulus clouds shows he's snoring.

The reflection of a white sail points directly to the eyes that see it.

The long dark skyline stretching from south to north in front of you as the Uncompahgre Plateau, part of a strip of geography (reaching from northern Utah to New Mexico) that keeps moving up and down. The Uncompahgre Uplift, geologists call it because in our time it is in the "up" phase of what is perhaps its third push-up. The Dakota Sandstone that at present caps the mile-high Uncompahgre Plateau is the bottom layer of the mile-high mountain you are standing on.

If you are looking through binoculars — of course you did bring binoculars! — you see that the whole back-slope of the Uncompahgre Plateau is threaded with canyons wending down normally from ridge to bottom like inverted ribs branching from a spine. But one canyon is abnormal, cutting down through the mountain all the way from base to base. Unaweep Canyon.

Several geological explanations have been proposed for the Unaweep mystery — the floor of Unaweep Canyon is a watershed with streams flowing east and west from the middle of the slot. In how many canyons does a creek flow both ways? One theory is that ice-age glaciers reamed out canyons down both sides of the mountain. But, according to presently accepted theory river water cut that canyon. The geological studies Scott Sinnock completed to earn his doctorate theorize that Unaweep Canyon was created by five different river bulldozings: The Uncompahgre, the Gunnison, and the North Fork of the Gunnison in that order, and the Colorado River twice. At each low phase of the Uncompahgre Uplift one of those rivers flowed through that slot, then when the uplift resumed, pushing up stone strata faster than river could cut through, the water was dammed up and the stream shunted to another route. In the Uplift's next millennial low phase, according to Sinnock's theory, the Colorado River will take that short cut again, by-passing most of the Grand Valley, the town of Fruita and the little fishing docks at Riverside Park (or the archeological remains of them). Don't hold your breath.

North up Unaweep your binoculars will show that the Uplift's long, forested slope has turned into a red strata wall that abruptly curves into a dip — the Uncompahgre Plateau going underground temporarily. Here all slow-motion hell broke loose, geologically speaking. Faults, strata-bendings, over-lappings created the red-rock and cream-cliff maze of beauty the government set aside as the Colorado National Monument.

Forming the northern horizon of this Land's End view are the Roan Mountains, darkly cliffing and canyoning their way to Wyoming. Below the Roans, framing the farmlands of Grand Valley and the city-sprawl of Grand

Junction, are the Bookcliffs. Tilted at near forty-five degrees the Books stagger off to Utah starting with Mount Garfield down there beside the Colorado.

That little pup-tent squiggle of a tilt is the towering Mount Garfield that every Grand Valley view is anchored to?

Yes. Everything in sight from up here is arrested motion except the mountain under your feet. The real weirdo is Grand Mesa. How did it manage to stay level in such turbulence?

Actually, Land's End does include a view of about the only kind of geological motion that Grand Mesa has experienced — Toreva Block slumping. Shirt-tail Point, next point south of Land's End, is an instance of Toreva slumping caught in the act. The lava layer has split all the way down, and the whole point has slipped a little. Not to worry; people have been jumping their horses, dragging their wagons, driving their cars down into the slump and up onto the hump for over a hundred years. Toreva is a slow process, or needs ten times the present rainfall. Who named it Shirt-tail is lost to history, but why is obvious — it does look like it needs tucking in.

———   ———

Something is moving down there where U.S. Highway 50 crosses the Stinking Desert curving around the bottom of Grand Mesa. A semi-truck, so far below that even in your binoculars it looks like a gnat tight-walking a spider tread. That semi is traveling on pure history — the Old Slave Trail.

As soon as Indians got over being terrified of the saddlehorse that could come apart — the two pieces walking away from each other when the top half dismounted — as soon as they found out how exciting it is to ride one, how much easier it is to pack your belongings on a horse than to tote them on your back, how much more meat you can bag from horseback than on foot, how much fun it is to bet your bottom bead on racing one, they just had to have some. For Utes in this area, the best way to get the horse was to trek that trail down there south to the Spanish pueblos along the Rio Grande and appropriate them in honorable war raids. But since the pueblos were well armed, it became customary to trade for them.

The most valuable trade article Indians could lay their hands on was another Indian — a breathing commodity the Spanish used to till their fields, mine their gold, cook, and clean house. Gosute Indians were the most available currency because life on their desert range was so starvation-hard (roasted grasshoppers being the main entree) they may have been almost glad to be yanked from it and sold into well-fed servitude. The feeling was not limited to Gosutes, witness some Ute Indians who wedged their own children into pueblo life, such as the parents of the pre-teenager who became Chief Ouray.

Can we understand the philosophy of all this? Of course not. Even when they speak the same verbal language Caucasian and Indian can't comprehend each other — the basic verb of the white man is do, the basic verb of the redman is be.

————

According to some historians Antoine Robidoux was the first to put wheels to the Slave Trail. In the early 1800s his carts crept across the scene down there, hauling baled beaver hides from his trading posts to shipping points along the Rio Grande. A little later this became known as the Salt Lake Wagon Trail when some of the immigrant Mormons chose this route to reach Brigham Young's new colony, the nation of Deseret now called the State of Utah.

The cliff-rimmed west end of Grand Mesa was so inaccessible that pioneers ignored it for almost a decade. Farmlands were laid out, towns popped up, and so many cattle poured into the country that rangelands, including the other half of Grand Mesa, were seriously overgrazed. Stockmen, eyeing the vast expanse of heifer-high grass on the west end of the Mesa, began trying to figure out how to build a trail up those cliffs that cows could safely negotiate.

Edgar Rider led the way. He rode by way of Kannah Creek and made it up the final steep cliffside notches by hanging onto his horse's tail the way Chief Shavano did in leading the Meeker Massacre rescue party six years earlier. The following year he and Larry Miller and the Pickett brothers started the Miller Trail. They "finished" it after a year and a half of wrestling boulders and blasting rimrock at Whitewater Point (the old name for what is now Land's End).

Not all the cows could make it.

"Many cattle were lost in driving them up." Forester Peck wrote. "In one drive thirty head of cattle went off the trail at Whitewater Point and were killed in the sliderock. When I came in 1922 those old trails were strewn with bones of cattle that had fallen on the rocks below."

Supervisor Peck was taking a good look at the trail, because the Forest Service contemplated turning it into a road.

A road hanging down off the west end of Grand Mesa would cost $141,000 estimated John Burgess. (Translate that 1920s estimate into 1990s money and you are talking millions.) That stopped the project dead for more than a decade.

A tiny slot of the vast view from Land's End. Mt. Garfield is the tilted pimple in the middle distance. The white slides are called "21" by the whiteman because that's what they look like to him. In Ute mythology they are Eagle droppings.

But it didn't stop the use of the west end of the Mesa. Evidently enough cattle were making it alive up the Miller Trail to chew the withers-high grass down to lawn-height, because in the summer of 1929 a group of gentlemen in cars and plus-four pants came on over the top from the east and laid out the Land's End golf course.

The *Delta County Independent* headlined:

"Grand Mesa Golf Club to be highest in the World."

"More than 10,000 feet above sea level. Site is near the Grand Junction municipal cabin two and a half miles off the Skyway."

"Natural turf covers the ground over which the nine hole golf course will be laid out by the golfers who carried their clubs along with them Sunday to aid in locating each hole, and put markers up. U.S. Forest Service permission has been secured."

That was in June. In October the stock market crashed and the Great Depression began. Not one more word about a Grand Mesa golf course.

Paradoxically a lot of things too expensive to do in good times became feasible in the Great Depression — the Land's End Road for one. The reason was cheap labor, WPA and CCC men worked literally for board and room (grub and tent cot), their work clothes (Army surplus), plus $5 spending money (that's 17 cents a day!), and $25 a month sent to folks at home.

Forester C. J. Stall, standing on the rim at Land's End, picked the road site for its favorable situation, choosing the steep chute of North Kannah Creek because snow would melt early on its sun-facing slopes. The name he gave it — Truck Trail — didn't stick, probably because the unavoidable tight switchbacks wouldn't accommodate a truck's long wheelbase without a lot of geeing and hawing.

The engineer was J. P. Reddick of Denver who at the time was ramrodding another Forest service project — the Divide Road running the hundred mile length of the Uncompahgre Plateau. In the summer of 1933 he left his crew on the Uncompahgre and came over to survey and locate the Land's End Road.

When Reddick was eighty-six he wrote us a long letter detailing the problems in laying out the Land's End Road. He said that even after forty-two years every one of the nineteen switchbacks were still etched in his memory.

From the rim the road looks as loose and random as a strand of ravel-kinked knitting yarn snagged down the mountainside, but it fits the available space as tight as dominoes in a box. In engineering terms, Reddick calls the sides of the box "Control Points."

Control Point No. 1, a gap in the rimrock.

"The only break in the rimrock bordering the Mesa for several miles here is just south of the point where the concession building now stands. A ways down the cliff toward the right I found a small nook in the cliff that if enlarged would be suitable for a 30-foot radius switchback curve to the left (this is the first switch back you come to on the way down). From this I would have continued the slant down along the face of the cliff but I came to rocks as big as barns, too expensive to move — so another switchback.

The first two miles of this road contained not one culvert, though it takes runoff from the entire face of the cliff and all the seasonal streams that pour over the rim. No culverts were needed, the water simply flowed under the roadbed through the loose jumble of slide rock. Eventually the slide rock silted up, as Reddick knew it would, and culverts were placed.

Control Point No. 2, Kannah Creek to the south.

"We had orders to stay out of the Kannah Creek drainage because that is where Grand Junction gets its City water. So we were limited to the North Fork of Kannah."

Control Point No. 3 was that immense mud slide you see to the north.

"At the first overlook to the west, a mile or so down form the rim, a tremendous mud slide exists. This starts at the very top of a lateral north-south ridge and extends westerly a long distance down the mountain. It's a quarter mile wide, and makes a vertical drop of several hundred feet. The surface is so fluid and unstable that constructing and maintaining a road across it would be impossible."

The result of the confining control points is what you see now — a road that shimmies back and forth across the two sides of its box — the forbidden water-supply creek, and the forbidding land slip. And all within the restrictions of a seven percent grade and switchbacks roomy enough to let a car swing around without backing up and trying again. At least one switchback wasn't that wide unless you were driving a buggy-short Model T Ford.

Control Point No. 4, though Reddick doesn't call it that, was money.

The Forest Service had $5000 a mile limit on road costs. Those first two miles down off rimrock cost better than $7000 each, but Reddick made it up on some of the easier stretches below. Also that first stretch exceeded the stipulated gradient, being seven percent. "The remainder is five-and-one-half per cent, rather low for a Forest road," he noted.

Reddick and helper Kenneth Bulick surveyed the road with an Abney hand level in the summer of 1933, placing little red and yellow flags, and cutting brush to get line-of-sight. "Very difficult because of thick growth of cedar and serviceberry impossible to see through. I walked. Never did have a horse. In the evenings I did the paper work by Coleman lantern in the tent. I lived half my life in tents," Reddick mused in the middle of his eighth decade.

Completing the project design that winter, Reddick and his crew of about thirty men came back in the spring to begin the actual work.

"In addition to my crew we had a hundred CCC boys. Not boys, men. World War I veterans thirty-three to fifty-five years old. An Army officer, Captain Feinter, was in charge of the camp. Tom Graham was liaison with the Forest Service.

Some of the work camps that were strung out four or five miles apart down the mountainside were dry, requiring that water be hauled, but others were supplied from "spigots" on top.

"Anderson would turn water out of a reservoir, and let it spill in a waterfall down over the rim to where we were camped.

"We finished the road that same summer, mostly hand labor — pick and shovel. Built the whole road, blasting and all, without injuries. Nobody in the hospital. Well, the camp cook ran off the road on his way back from celebrating Labor Day in town."

All CCC camps were under the control of Army officers who, as they found out to their astonishment, had limited authority. The Carpenter witnessed an instance while directing a down-timber clearing project in the Kaibab Forest. In those dour days CCC camp rations consisted of whatever there was a lot of and no sale for — in this case rice.

"After the CCC boys got fed up with chewing rice three times a day they conferred and one morning rose as a body and quietly walked out of the mess tent leaving their tin plates untouched. The officer just stood gape-mouthed. Mutiny! Nothing like this had ever happened to him in his whole military career."

And there wasn't a thing he could do about it — CCC stands for Civilian Conservation Corps.

The lantern-glow of CCC tents spangled the mountain for several summersful of evenings. Clearing space and building split-log picnic tables, those fellows made most of the campgrounds you visit now, including two down Land's End road — through Wild Rose and Steamboat Rock Campgrounds.

Working in different teams at different times the CCC, WPA, and Vets cleared and shovel-smoothed access roads across the Mesa, among them the skyway from Grand Mesa Lakes to Land's End. Chief attraction of that north rim road is Crater View, named when early settlers believed a volcano created Grand Mesa. Actually the vast hole framed by the encircling walls of Grand

Mesa and Chalk Mountain demonstrates where hills once stood, deflecting the lava flowing in from the east. Lacking that hard protective crust those soft-strata hills eroded into this "crater."

Though still negotiable, the original Skyway access to Land's End has been supplanted by a graveled road along the south rim above Kannah Creek canyon.

———————

Ever since the first baby buggy-shaped automobile made it to the top of Pikes Peak in 1901, it was sports drivers who ramrodded the brunt of automotive development (unintentionally and all in the name of fun) by demanding more and more power, speed, and maneuverability from metal and rubber. In searching the world for higher, steeper, twistier roads to test courage and car, these daredevils eventually found the Land's End Road.

By 1940 Louis Unser (relative of the Indy-winning Unser brothers) had won the Pike's Peak Climb so many times he was bored by it. From another racing buff — Wayne Sankey of Delta — he'd heard of Land's End, so he came over to give a road test run to learn its kinks. He pronounced them tougher than Pike's; then proved himself right when he smashed his car on an "S" curve and lost the 1940 race to a buddy, Al Rogers, also of Colorado Springs.

That first Land's End Hill climb was organized by the Grand Junction Camber of Commerce under AAA regulations. Mayor Ab Jenkins of Salt Lake City, himself an ex-racer, started the sixteen entries at five-minute intervals from Anderson Ranch down on Kannah Creek.

The Land's End course is unique in the world of Hill Climb Races because it is visible from start to finish by the spectators up in the "bleachers" — the lava rim.

When the second Land's End Hill Climb Race was held July 4, 1941, an estimated 2500 cars were parked on Land's End flats, and 12,000 spectators lined the cliff-top. Among the entries were several local boys — Bob Baughman, Henry Snook, and Wayne Sankey. Sankey, driving a car he built himself out of eight assorted wrecks, came in eighth. Al Rogers, winner of the 1940 race, missed a switchback, zoomed out into space and down a fifty-foot drop to slide rock and a fractured pelvis. Louis Unser, first man on top, ran the 14.5 mile, 5,000 foot climb in 17 minutes and 11.5 seconds.

That was the last Land's End Hill Climb Race for forty years. Five months later Pearl Harbor was bombed, and World War II clamped down every non-essential activity — even the manufacture of cars, much less the racing of them. In fact war had already changed things in 1941 — two of the racers, a couple of Frenchmen, only entered the Land's End race as a kind of consolation for having missed the Indy because their cars had been held up by British blockade. Incidentally, their fabulous French cars didn't do well, being too long to make any of the nineteen switchbacks in one swing.

In 1982 the Colorado Hill Climb Association applied to the Forest Service for permission to reinstitute the race. It was granted, and for a time the race was again an annual event. As this goes into print there is talk about resuming the Lands End Climb race.

––––– –––––

The stone building that stands lone and mysterious as a castle on the rim of the world at Land's End has been called Observatory, Shelter House, and Concession House as uses changed during its sixty years.

It was built in 1936-37 with WPA labor under the direction of rock-mason Ingal of Collbran. That the men had fun building this house is evident by the way they chose and matched odd shapes in big black lava rocks — fitting concave to convex curves, acute angles to obtuse bulges in forming the walls. A true work of art, with the added zing of tongue in cheek.

As an Observatory there was that mountain-pointing arrow swiveling around on a pedestal set up between building and cliff. As Shelter House, the main room was designed with view-facing windows on three sides and a big stone fireplace for warming the backsides of people doing the viewing. As a Concession House one room was provided with counter and a wall of shelves made of antique-dark wood that nowadays are stocked with mainly little bags of sunflower seed to coax cliff-dwelling chipmunks to scurry up and feed from your fingers.

From your parked car the stone path to the cliff-rim house threads a naturally tiled flower garden. Winds and the feet of visitors have bared and smoothed the lava sheet that cold has broken into uniform blocks. In the crevices, asters, larkspur, columbine, and nameless others bloom all the more furiously for being pinched for space.

––––– –––––

One of the first couples who "manned" the Land's End concession castle were Roger Blouch and his bride Bessie. It wasn't their honeymoon, they'd been married more than a year, but it seemed like honeymooning — two people in the only dwelling in this heaven-high Eden of a place. The Blouchs',

World's biggest grandstand? All seventeen twisty miles of the Land's End Trail Climb were visible to the 12,000 people who lined the rim to watch cars race up in 1941. There are plans to resume the annual climb.

who celebrated their fiftieth not long ago, still speak of that summer as their honeymoon.

Roger was a forestry student, paying his way by working. His jobs included marking beetle-damaged timber for lumbering, keeping the crank-type telephone operating by tracing trouble to where some aspen had crashed across the line, and cleaning the campground at Wildrose and Steamboat every Monday morning.

Bessie kept house in the private part of the Land's End building — wood cookstove, no plumbing. Minded the store — they made enough from candy, pop, and souvenirs that summer to buy their first brand-new car. And, between tasks, stood on the cliff-edge reveling in the scenery.

"It's fantastic to see a thunder storm gather beneath you. To look down at clouds. To watch lightning crack below you."

And she watched for Roger coming in from work, or coming up from town. Every week Roger went down the Land's End road to Grand Junction to buy supplies for themselves and the "concession." The last thing he loaded was a week's worth of ice.

"We had a fifty-pound icebox. By getting 75 pounds Roger arrived home with exactly fifty pounds of ice.

"I'd have kindling laid in the big old range, and would stand on the rim of the cliff watching for a plume of dust down in the valley. Then when I'd see Roger rounding a certain curve way down there in the Land's End road, I'd run in and set fire to the paper and kindling. There would be exactly the right amount of time to have dinner ready for the table when he pulled in."

Only two things marred the Blouchs' idyllic summer:

Cleaning Campgrounds, the only part of his job Roger didn't like — "People thought they were doing the right thing putting their coffee grounds and stuff in the fire-pits, but I just had to shovel it all out every Monday morning."

And seeing dogs get killed.

"Oh, we lost so many dogs!" Bessie's voice is tearful at the memory even yet.

"That's why the leash sign was put up at the parking place, but not everybody paid attention to it. A dog on the loose or looking out a car window, would spot a chipmunk, go chasing after it, and sail right over the wall. Hundreds of feet down the sheer drop! A few people were so affected they climbed down the ledges to retrieve the little body."

PREVIOUS LEFT: Land's End Castle, some call it standing alone on a great flower-threaded sheet of lava that ends in cliffs on three sides. The view from those windows takes in five mountain ranges.
PREVIOUS RIGHT: Apparently the game played by WPA men laying up Land's End House was who can find the neatest fit for the craziest rock.

Roger and Bessie's idyllic summer ended in a ritual that impressed them for life.

"When we took the job they gave us a brand-new flag, with the instructions that it must be raised every morning and brought down and folded just so every evening before sundown.

"We had been warned: 'By the end of the season the winds will have whipped your flag to ragged edges, and the sun will have faded it. You must not throw it away, or keep it. It must be burned, completely burned.' "

So on that last evening of their honeymoon in the sky Roger and Bessie pulled down their flag and took it to Steamboat Rock where Roger built a little brush fire and Bessie laid the folded flag.

Hands clasped together, half sad, half glad, the young couple watched it burn. End of summer, beginning of the world. ❧

Sources

Personal interviews with old timers and their families including:

Edith Agnew, Charles Aldridge, Uhlan Austin, Hazel Baker Austin, Elmer Barnes, Chet Beal, Mort Beckley, Roy Bell, Dale Blumberg, Robert Bowie, Marian Boyden, A. Allen Brown, Henry Bruton, Ray Burritt, Marge Hanson Butler, Caleb Casebier, Laura Clock, W.C. (Buster) Daily, Clarence Drexel, Charles Fairlamb, Anna Butler, Irene Hanson Butler, Edna Cranor, John Davis, J.D. Dillard, Howard Ensley, Clara Gilbert, Royden Girling, Jo Gore, Ferris Green, William Hager, Marge (Mrs. Ed) Hanson, Genevieve Hartig, Annie Hobson Grey, Harold Hammond, Morgan Hendrickson, Minnie Hoch, Gordon Hodgins, Guy Howard, Nelson Huffington, George Hunten, Ed January, Dr. Jim Jensen, Vivian Jones, John Kettle, Alfred Lanning, Roy Long, Lola Loss, Goldie Lyons, Lloyd Mathers, Helen Morgan, Hartel Morris, Jim Mowbray, Eda Baker Musser, Dudley Nixon, George Norris, Evaline Nutter, Floyd Pottorff, Letitia Hillman Obert, H.W. Oosterhous, Ethel Frost O'Rourke, Charles Parker, Cora Phoenix, William Pryor, Wilson Rockwell, Red Ruble, John Rozman, Grace Shock, Velma Shreeves, Elmer Skinner, Cecil Smith, Minnie Womack Smith, Delphine Spaulding, Charles States, Welland States, Nellie Stephen, Esther Watts Stephens, W.W. Stevens, Mabel Todd Stoneburner, Earle Stucker, Oscar Swanson, Andy Thliveris, Ray Toole, Ethel Smith (Tater Bill) Veers, Carol Wade, Alice Mannon Watkins, Dorcas Stockham Ween, John Wetterich, Will Weyrauch, Gay Williamson, Helen Hawxhurst Young.

Books

Athearn, Robert *The Denver and Rio Grande Western Railroad*
Archeology of the Eastern Ute, a Symposium, edited by Paul R. Nickens
Austin, Hazel *Memories of the School on the Hill* and *Surface Creek Country*
Boorstin, Daniel J. *The Americans, the National Experience.*
Cassells, E. Steve *Archeology of Colorado*
Chapman, Arthur *The Story of Colorado*
Chronic, Halka *Roadside Geology of Colorado*
Clock, Laura *Cabin and a Clothesline*
Cow Talk, Memoirs of George W. Menefee
Crumm, *Sally People of the Red Earth*
Cultural Resources Series No. 2, Historical Bureau of Land Management
Curtis, James *Riding Old Trails*
Daniels, Helen Sloan *The Ute Indians of Southwestern Colorado*
Dawson, Thomas F. and FJV Skiff *The Ute War*

Dunham, Dick and Vivian *Flaming Gorge Country*

Ellis, Arthur J. *The Divining Rod, a History of Water Witching*

Emmet, Robert *The Last War Trail*

Encyclopedia Britannica Fulsom points

Fairfield, Eula King *Pioneer Lawyer*

Farb, Peter, *Man's Rise to Civilization as Shown by the Indians of North America from Primeval Times to the Coming of the Industrial State*

Fay, Abott *Famous Coloradans*

Fennel, James, *A Guide to Hunting Rocky Mountain Mule Deer*

Ferrier, Mamie & George Sibley *Long Horns and Short Tales*

Foster, Robert J. *Geology, San Jose State College*

Francis, Theresa V. *Crystal River Saga*

Jefferson, James Robert W. Delaney, Gregory C. Thompson *The Southern Utes, a Tribal History*

Hodgins, J.E. and T. H. Haskett, *The Veterinary Science, 1895*

Huscher, Betty H. and Harold A. *The Hogan Builders of Colorado*

Jefferson, Delaney, Thompson *The Southern Utes, a Tribal History*

Jocknick, Sidney 1870-1888 *Early Days on the Western Slope*

Keener, James and Christine Bebbe *Grand Mesa, World's Largest Flattop Mountain*

Lathrope, Marguerite *Don't Fence Me In*

Lee, Willis T., *Coal Fields of Grand Mesa and the West Elk Mountains, Colorado*

Life of the Marlows, As Related by Themselves

Luchetti, Cathy *Women of the West*

Marsh, Charles W. *People of the Shining Mountains*

Monroe, Arthur W. *San Juan Silver*

Mutel, Cornelia Fleischer and John C. Emerick *Glacier to Grassland*

Nykamp, Rober H. "Distribution of Known Ute Sites in Colorado" *Archeology of Colorado*

Orawood, Harley *The North Form Hermit, Reuben Dove's Devious Trail*

Panati, Charles *Browser's Book of Beginnings*

Peterson, Ellen Z. *The Spell of the Tabeguache*

Petit, Jan *Utes, the Mountain People*

Powell, John Wesley, *Exploration of the Colorado River*

Plog, Fred *Physical Anthropology and Archeology*

Prairie, Peak, and Plateau Colorado Geological Survey

Rarey, J.S. *Taming Wild Horses*

Roeber, Clinton W. *West Elk Tales*

Rockwell, Wilson *The Utes, a Forgotten People, Uncompahgre Country*

Roe, Frank Gilbert *The Indian and the Horse*

Rose, Ernie *Utahs of the Rocky Mountains*

Savinelli, Alfred *Plants of Power*

Sharp, J. Ed and Thomas B Underwood - *American Indian Cooking & Herb Lore*

Shoemaker, Leonard *Saga of a Forest Ranger*

Sinnock, Scott, *Geomorphology of the Uncompahgre Plateau and the Grand Valley*

Smith, Ann M. *Ethnography of the Northern Utes and Ute Tales*

Smith, P. David *Ouray, Chief of the Utes*

Sprague, Marshall *Massacre, Money Mountain*

Ute Dictionary Ute Press

Ute Traditional Narratives, Ute Press. Edited by T. Givon

Ute Reference Grammar, First edition, Ute Press

Vandenbusche *The Gunnison Country*

Veers, Lawrence and Winona *Bits and Pieces of Olathe History*

Wood and Bache *United States Dispensatory 1833*

Trager, James. *The People's Chronology*

Williamson, Iain A. *Coal Mining Geology*

With the Colors Delta County WWI Memorial

Wormington, H. M. *Prehistoric Indians of the Southwest*

Young, Helen Hawxhurst *Skin and Bones of Plateau Valley History*

Young, Robert and Joann, *Geology and Wildflowers of Grand Mesa Colorado*

Journals, Collections, and Manuscripts

Burritt, Reed, The Burritt Family Recollections

Cameron, Mary. Collection of Forest Service material

Crum, Sally. Collection of Forest Service material

Delta Forest Service office Collection

Friars Dominguez-Escalante, journal

Huffington, Oscar, journal

January, Ed written memories

Montrose BLM office collection

Mamie Ferrier collection

Rockwell, Wilson *Delta County the Formative years*, manuscript

Womack, Eliza memoirs.

144 U.S. Geological Survey maps of Grand Mesa.

Delta Chief
Grand Junction Daily Sentinel
Surface Creek Champion
Journal of the Western Slope Volumes 1 through 5, Mesa State College
Karger, Maud, 1957 series of articles in the *Delta County Independent*
States, Dr. G.W. 1937 series of articles *Delta County Independent States*
Perry, Erin "Whatever Happened to..." column in Grand Junction
    Daily Sentinel
Cook, Alice Spencer, "Fishing Feud Lasts 50 Years," *Western Sportsman*
Gallacher, Walter, "The President Bags a Bear!" *Colorado Life*,
    May-June 1984
"Heliographs: A Flash from the Past" *New Mexico Magazine*
Hawxhurst, Alex "Early History of Plateau Valley"
Johnson, Stephen B. Jr. "Reminiscences of an Inveterate Colorado
    Skier" Journal of the *Western Slope* Mesa State College.
Newsweek Magazine, "Glaciers,"
"The Plateau Valley Story" by daughters of pioneers: Mrs. Aaron McKee,
    Miss Donna Helen Young, Mrs. John Hall, Mrs. Edwin Gunderson,
    Mrs. Dean Walck, and Mrs. Jack Long.

A

Adams, Carl 29, 31, 154
ADYC daisy 100
Alexander Lake 46, 189, 213, 214, 216, 222, 234, 246
Alexander Lake Lodge 246
Alexander, William
     homesteads lake 212-221;
     fish hatchery 214;
     disappears 219;
Alfalfa Run 202
Antelope Hill 112
Arkansas settlers 78, 161
arrowheads, 49, 56, 135
aspens, 73, 97, 98, 104, 115, 141, 143, 186, 196, 266
     cabin logs 38,
     carving on, 32-33
        sap uses 69
atomic bomb at Roulison 134
Austin 40, 53, 78,
Austin flood 202-204
Austin, Corky 204
Austin, Hazel 53
Austin, Uhlan 122

B

Bar I Ranch 107, 109, 122, 156
Barnes fiddlers 165
Barnes, Joshua 162
Baron Lake 17, 213, 216, 248
basalt 17, 138, 141, 147
bats, 90
Battle Park 141, 144
Battlement Mesa 2, 8, 17, 180, 182, 184, 237
Beaman, Judge D.C. 217, 222, 227, 228
bear 48, 74, 75, , 85, 100,
     Bear Dance 70-71;
     bounty on 86
     digs potatoes 38
     nature of 84

𝒲

Printed in the United States
50806LVS00005B/910-933